'Both valuable and readable, a lucid and elegantly flowing description of a people' John Lloyd, *Financial Times*

'An engaging guide to the land of *la dolce vita* . . . peels apart our easy definitions of a country beloved of many' Rebecca K. Morrison, *Independent*

'Italy remains the most fascinating of countries, often perplexing and yet always engaging. Hooper does it justice. People who don't know Italy will find this book a splendid introduction. Those who know and love the country will find much that is new as well as familiar, much that will have them nodding in agreement, some observations that will meet with the response, "not to my mind". It deserves to sit happily on the bookshelf beside Barzini; and that is high praise' Allan Massie, *Scotsman*

'Enjoyable and eye-opening . . . a deft and enjoyable treatment of an endlessly fascinating topic' John Gallagher, *Guardian*

'So readable . . . John Hooper gets to the heart of Italy in his cliché-free account of the country's character . . . Mixing the amusing titbit with the big picture, he provides context for the question that perplexes the occasional visitor: how come a country that has produced Berlusconi, "bunga bunga" parties, the mafia and an extraordinary bureaucracy is still so attractive?' John Kampfner, *Observer*

'An amusing and engrossing account of a thoroughly irresponsible nation' Brian Sewell, *Independent on Sunday*

'Thanks to his great curiosity, his splendid comparative and analytical perspective, and a fine eye for telling details, John Hooper gets under the skin of a fascinating people in a remarkable and compelling way' Bill Emmott

'This portrait of a nation is required reading for anyone heading to a Tuscan villa or Puglian beach this summer' Tom Robbins, *Financial Times*

'What's not to love? A thoroughly researched, well-written, ageless narrative of a fascinating people' *Kirkus Reviews*

ABOUT THE AUTHOR

John Hooper is Italy correspondent of the *Economist* and Contributing Editor of the *Guardian* and *Observer*. *The Italians* is the fruit of more than fifteen years based in Italy.

The Italians

JOHN HOOPER

PENGUIN BOOKS

PENGUIN BOOKS

UK | USA | Canada | Ireland | Australia
India | New Zealand | South Africa

Penguin Books is part of the Penguin Random House group of companies
whose addresses can be found at global.penguinrandomhouse.com.

First published by Allen Lane 2015
Published in Penguin Books 2016
001

Set in 10.56/13.15 pt Dante MT Std
Typeset by Jouve (UK) Milton Keynes
Printed in Great Britain by Clays Ltd, St Ives plc

A CIP catalogue record for this book is available from the British Library

ISBN: 978-0-241-95762-2

For Lucy

Contents

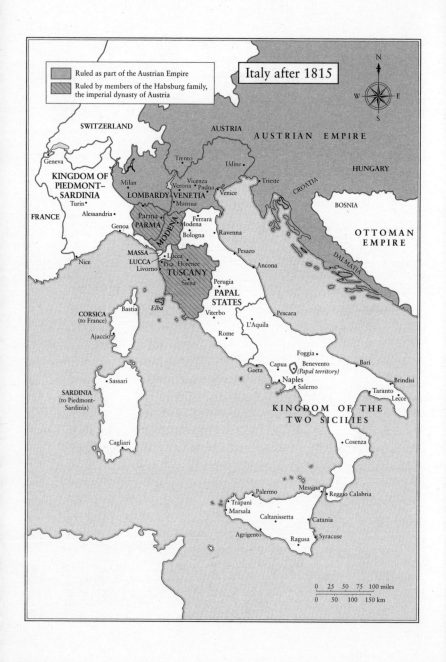

Modern Italy – the regions

Acknowledgements

A book like this is built on a myriad of observations and impressions, rather as limestone is formed out of an infinitesimal number of tiny shells. So my first and most important thanks go to all the Italians I have met over the years that I have spent in their country – friends, neighbours and casual acquaintances – because it is their descriptions of themselves and their explanations of their society, their recommendations and advice, their hints and silences that have done more than anything to give substance to this work.

I first lived and worked in Italy, briefly, at the age of eighteen and might never have returned except for the odd holiday had it not been for Paul Webster, who, in 1994, while foreign editor of the *Guardian*, suggested that I rejoin the staff of the paper as its southern Europe correspondent based in Rome. When I left Italy again, five years later, I had no plans to come back and would probably not have embarked on the writing of this book had Xan Smiley, the then Europe editor of *The Economist*, and Bill Emmott, its then editor, not arranged for me to become their correspondent in Italy. Warm thanks also to Alan Rusbridger, then as now the editor of the *Guardian*, who proposed that I be shared between the two papers and later agreed to my taking a period of unpaid leave to begin the writing of this book. John Micklethwait, the current editor of *The Economist*, also agreed to that, and later generously offered me a spell of paid leave so I could finish what I had started. John Peet, who has been the Europe editor of *The Economist* for most of the time I have worked for the paper in Italy, has been unstintingly tolerant of my periodic retreats into book writing.

In each of my spells as a correspondent in Italy I have benefited from the hospitality of national newspapers: first, *La Stampa* and, more recently, *Corriere della Sera*. It has given me access to a wealth of information about Italy and the Italians. I am very grateful to those who edited the two papers during the periods in which I worked on their premises: Ezio Mauro, Carlo Rossella, Stefano Folli, Paolo Mieli and Ferruccio de Bortoli; as well as to the Rome bureau chiefs and Rome supplement editors who were my immediate hosts: Marcello Sorgi, Ugo Magri, Antonio Macaluso, Marco Cianca, Andrea Garibaldi and Goffredo Buccini.

I would also like to take this opportunity to thank the reporters, specialist writers and regional correspondents of both papers. Italian journalists are unsparing in the help and advice they offer to their foreign colleagues, and over the years I have acquired a huge debt of gratitude to those of *La Stampa* and *Corriere della Sera* for their insights and their readiness to share their knowledge with an outsider. Those who made direct contributions to the contents of this book include Massimo Franco, Lorenzo Fuccaro, Daria Gorodisky, Stefano Lepri, Dino Martirano and Ilaria Sacchettoni.

Thanks also to Eliza Apperly, Elizabeth Bailey, Lara Bryan, Simon Chambers, Bianca Cuomo, Giulia Di Michele, Bea Downing, Katharine Forster, Will Harman, Sophie Inge, Yerrie Kim of EF Education First, Tom Kington, Flavia Manini, Maria Luisa Manini, Hannah Murphy, Laura Nasso, Marie Obileye, Lorien Pilling of GBGC, Hannah Sims, Helen Tatlow, Katherine Travers, Ed Vulliamy, Tom Wachtel and Sean Wyer.

Paddy Agnew, Antonio Manca Graziadei and Isabella Clough Marinaro generously agreed to bring their specialist knowledge to bear on chapters 14, 18 and 19 respectively. Francesca Andrews and Maria Bencivenni read through large sections of the book. Their observations and suggestions, which could have come only from a rich experience of the cultures and societies of both Italy and Britain, were invaluable. It goes without saying that the errors that remain are mine alone.

I could not have wanted for a more involved, enthusiastic or charmingly persistent agent than Lucy Luck. And I have had the immense good fortune to have as my editor Simon Winder, who is not only a successful writer himself but the author of books in a similar vein to my own. This one is all the better for his perceptive comments. Melanie Tortoroli at Penguin Group USA has been every bit as supportive (and patient).

My wife, Lucinda Evans, read the entire manuscript with the keen eye of a former national newspaper sub-editor. It has benefited greatly from her good judgement and feeling for words. But her main contribution has been a subtler one: she has been with me throughout my Italian adventure, and the insights and reflections she has shared with me along the way can be found in almost every chapter of the book that follows.

The Beautiful Country

'Il bel paese
ch'Appennin parte, 'l mar circonda e l'Alpe.'
'The beautiful country that the Apennines divide, and Alps and
sea surround.'

– Petrarch, *Canzoniere*, CXLVI, ll. 13–14, 1373 *

No one would choose to start a book at Porta Pia.

It is in one of the least attractive corners of central Rome, a place
where architectural styles from different periods sit uncomfortably
together like mutually suspicious in-laws. The biggest building in
the vicinity is the British Embassy, which dates from the 1970s. Its
architect, Sir Basil Spence, was at pains to ensure it blended in with
its surroundings. Not everyone is convinced he succeeded. The
embassy looks rather like a colossal, concrete semiconductor, torn
from the motherboard of a gargantuan computer.

The gate – the *porta* itself – takes its name from Pius IV, Michelangelo's last patron and the pope who brought the Council of Trent
to a successful conclusion, thereby launching the Counter-
Reformation. Michelangelo's friend and biographer Giorgio Vasari
wrote that the artist offered Pius three designs, and that the pope
chose the least expensive.† Nowadays, the gate he built forms one
side of a bigger structure – the side that faces towards the centre of

---

* All translations of epigraphs are by the author, unless otherwise stated.
† Michelangelo may have taken subtle revenge. In the middle of the tower, above
the gate and to either side of the entrance, there is an odd motif that looks

Rome. How much of Michelangelo's design has survived is open to question. A coin minted in 1561 when work began on the gate and an engraving made three years after its completion each depict a substantially different structure.

In the nineteenth century, another Pius – Pope Pius IX – had a courtyard put behind Michelangelo's gate (if it was any longer Michelangelo's gate) and added a new façade in the neoclassical style that looks away from the centre of the city. Around the courtyard between the two façades, Pius IX erected some buildings for use as customs offices. Rome was still then the capital of the Papal State, a sizeable territory that had been governed by the popes since the eighth century and whose latest ruler had indignantly refused to let it be incorporated into the new state of Italy.

Either side of Porta Pia stretch the Aurelian Walls. These were begun in the third century AD for the protection of ancient Rome. Lofty and sturdy, they continued to defend the city, with greater or lesser success, for the next fifteen centuries and it was only by blasting a hole through them at a point about 50 metres west of Porta Pia that Italian troops were able to force their way into Rome, complete the unification of the peninsula and put an end to the temporal power of the popes. Many of the soldiers who poured through the breach on that September morning in 1870 belonged to an elite corps of Italy's new army known as the Bersaglieri ('Marksmen'). The customs offices inside Porta Pia were later turned into a museum for the Bersaglieri.

The area around the gate, then, is an eclectic muddle. But it brings together within a few hundred square metres tangible allusions to the bits of their history of which Italians are proudest: the Roman Empire, the Renaissance and the Risorgimento.* Some,

---

suspiciously like a basin draped with a towel. It has been taken by some as a reference to Pius's origins. He was said to be descended from a line of Milanese barbers.

* The Resurgence: the movement that led to the ejection of Italy's foreign rulers and the unification of the country in the nineteenth century.

though not all, would add to that list the papacy and the Counter-Reformation, which brought with it the splendours of Rome's baroque churches.

What other people of comparable numbers can lay claim to such an extraordinary catalogue of achievements? One nation – even if it did not consider itself a nation until quite recently – produced the only empire to have united Europe and the greatest cultural transformation in the history of the West, one that shaped our entire modern view of life. Along the way, the Italian peninsula emerged as the pre-eminent seat of Christendom.

No other nation can boast such a catalogue of great painters and sculptors: Leonardo, Michelangelo and Raphael, of course. But also Donatello and Bernini, Piero della Francesca, Botticelli, Titian and Caravaggio. And there are others, like Mantegna, who are nowhere close to the top of the list but who would be hailed as national cultural icons in most other European countries. Then there are the architects – Brunelleschi, Bramante, Palladio; and the writers – Dante, Petrarch, Boccaccio; and the composers. Italy has given the world Vivaldi and the Scarlattis, Verdi and Puccini.

St Benedict, St Francis and St Catherine of Siena were all Italians. So, too, were Galileo, Christopher Columbus and Maria Montessori. Among other things, we owe to their country the Gregorian calendar, the language of music, time zones and double-entry bookkeeping. Italians invented the telegraph, the seismograph and the electric battery.

They gave us opera and Venice; the basilicas of St Peter's and St Mark's; the duomos of Milan and Florence; the leaning Tower of Pisa and the Trevi Fountain. Even if they have not actually visited them, most people know the names of historic cities such as Bologna, Perugia and Naples. But there are others scattered across Italy that few foreigners have heard of – places such as Trani and Macerata, Vercelli and Cosenza – that house more cultural treasures than are to be found in entire US states.

It is a mind-spinning legacy and one that understandably mesmerizes anyone who goes to Italy. But the picture that visitors take away in their mind's eye when they catch the flight home is, if not misleading, then certainly unrepresentative of Italy's post-classical history; unrepresentative of the lives of most of the people who have lived in what is now Italy since the fall of the Roman Empire. More illustrative of their experience is the heavily fortified medieval tower that stands just a few hundred metres west of Porta Pia. It was put there in the ninth century and reconstructed between the twelfth and fourteenth centuries. It is one of many that were built into the Aurelian Walls and which punctuate them at intervals as they stretch into the distance either side of Porta Pia.

For nearly a millennium and a half, the majority of the people we now call Italians lived in territories that were either ruled by foreigners or so tiny or so weak they were perpetually at risk of being overrun by outsiders. Why? For Luigi Barzini, the author of perhaps the best-known portrait of his people,[1] this was 'the crux of the Italian problem, of *all* Italian problems': 'Why did Italy, a land notoriously teeming with vigorous, wide-awake and intelligent people, always behave so feebly? Why was she invaded, ravaged, sacked, humiliated in every century, and yet failed to do the simple things necessary to defend herself?'

Part of the answer is to be found in Italy's divisive geography. For a start, almost one in every ten Italians lives on an island, physically detached from the rest of the nation. Sicily, the biggest island in the Mediterranean and with a population the size of Norway's, is quite big enough to be a state by itself. The landscape of the island is as varied as that of many larger territories. Sandy beaches and rocky shorelines, precipitous citrus groves and undulating wheatfields are all in their different ways typically Sicilian. There is an extensive plain outside Catania in the east and several mountain ranges, one of which has a peak rising to almost 2,000 metres. Even that, though, is dwarfed by Mount Etna, Europe's biggest active volcano, which is more than half as high again. Plans to link Sicily to the rest of Italy by means of a bridge or tunnel go back to classical times. But even though the island is only three kilometres from the mainland at the closest point, none of the plans has ever been realized – not least, in recent years, because of a fear that such a massive construction project could hand a bonanza to Sicily's Cosa Nostra and the 'Ndrangheta of Calabria, the region on the other side of the Straits of Messina.

Sardinia, the second-biggest Mediterranean island, is a five-hour ferry ride from the mainland port of Civitavecchia north of Rome and a ten-hour journey from Genoa. The Costa Smeralda in the north-east of the island has become a playground for Hollywood stars, European socialites, Arab royals and Russian oligarchs. But parts of the rest of Sardinia are desolate, and its uplands wild. The remote and hilly Barbagia district, once famed for brigandage, nurtures blood feuds the origins of which, in some cases, go back decades.

In winter, communities in the Aeolian and Aegadian islands off Sicily, the Pontine Islands in the Tyrrhenian Sea between Rome and Naples, the Tuscan archipelago, and even on islands such as Capri in the Bay of Naples, can be cut off for days on end by bad weather. The inhabitants of Lampedusa, 112 kilometres off the coast of North Africa, live further from their fellow Italians in the Alps than do New Yorkers from the people of Atlanta, Georgia.

Mainland Italians, too, are separated from one another, but by rock more than water. Though seldom described as such, Italy is one of Europe's most mountainous countries. The Alps stretch in a broad arc over the north so that on clear winter days their snow-capped peaks are as dramatically visible from Venice in the east as they are from Turin in the west. South of the valley of the River Po, which runs almost the width of the country at its broadest point, more mountains rear up. The Apennine range extends the length of the peninsula, stuttering out into isolated massifs as it veers into Calabria, the 'toe' of the Italian 'boot'. The reason Italians are not thought of as a mountain people, however, is that the vast majority live in the lowlands that account for less than a quarter of the country's surface and which essentially consist of the Po Valley and the coastal strip that fringes the peninsula.

The southern mainland, though often considered a single,

homogeneous region, is in fact extremely varied. The coastal areas of Calabria are typical enough of the Mediterranean shoreline. But inland lie two large expanses of rugged upland terrain: Sila in the north and Aspromonte in the south. In contrast, Puglia – the 'heel' of the 'boot' – is for the most part as flat as rolled-out pizza dough. Its endless sandy beaches have made it an increasingly popular tourist destination in recent years.

Between Calabria and Puglia lies Basilicata, one of the most beautiful and least-known corners of Italy. Much of it is mountainous, and most of what is not is hilly. Though still one of Italy's poorest regions, Basilicata stands to benefit from the discovery there of a large petroleum deposit, the Tempa Rossa field. Organized crime, which flourishes in Calabria, and to a lesser extent in Puglia, has made limited inroads here.

The same can be said of Molise and Abruzzo further north, both of which are also mountainous. The people of Abruzzo, or at least those who live in the interior (the region takes in a broad coastal strip as well), are identified with the qualities associated with highlanders the world over, including physical and mental toughness. The regional capital, L'Aquila, has the only rugby team of importance in the Mezzogiorno.* L'Aquila is in a breathtaking location, on a broad plain bounded by mountains to the north and south. But while its inhabitants are encircled by reminders of nature's grandeur, they also live with an uneasy awareness of its ferocity. Abruzzo is intensely seismic and in 2009 L'Aquila was hit for the fourth time in its history by a major earthquake. More than three hundred people lost their lives.

Campania, the region around Naples, offers a more easily recognizable image of southern Italy. South of Naples lies the justly famed Amalfi coast. Beyond that, south of Salerno, is another enchantingly beautiful but much less celebrated area, Cilento. Naples itself has a setting at least as dramatic as that of L'Aquila.

---

* The southern one third or so of mainland Italy, though often taken to include Sicily and Sardinia as well.

The broad sweep of its bay, overlooked by a brooding, smoking Mount Vesuvius, features on any number of old prints. When they were first made, Naples was regarded as a kind of earthly paradise. Goethe, who visited the city in 1787 and seems to have seen nothing of the poverty that has always been endemic to Naples, described it as a place where 'everyone lives in a state of intoxicated self-forgetfulness'. One wonders what he would make of the city and its surrounding region today. Campania is Italy's poorest region and in many respects its saddest. The holidaymakers who come to the region generally see only Capri or resorts such as Sorrento and Positano, but most of the people of Campania live in the immense hinterlands of Naples and Salerno, often in perilously sited or poorly built housing blocks – the visible manifestations of corruption and the capillary presence of the local mafia, the Camorra.

Lazio, north of Campania, is the land of the Latins, the ancient Latium. Much of it is flat, especially around Latina, which – despite its classical-sounding name – came into existence only under Mussolini in the 1930s when the surrounding marshes were drained. But Lazio also takes in the hills known as the Colli Romani, where the pope has his summer residence in a palace on the edge of an extinct volcano. Even a section of the Apennines falls within the region. Visitors to Rome in the winter who venture on to the Janicular Hill for a panoramic view of the city are astounded to see, seemingly immediately behind it, a range of snowy peaks. They are not quite as close as they look, but you can nevertheless ski at a resort less than a two-hour drive from Rome.

Beyond the capital, the countryside gradually becomes more characteristic of Umbria or Tuscany. Even before leaving Lazio on the Autosole, Italy's main north–south highway, you begin to see a distinctive terrain in which towering blocks of straight-sided, flat-topped rock jut out of the surrounding countryside. Some of these buttes are inhabited, as is the case with Orvieto, one of the many central Italian hill towns that have been places of refuge since ancient times.

Though it is the only landlocked region on the peninsula, Umbria is not mountainous, except in the south-east. For the most part, it is a region of high green hills abundantly watered in the winter months (and sometimes in the summer ones, too). The rain that falls on Umbria also replenishes the shallow waters of Lake Trasimeno, a rare example of an endorheic lake: one that has no rivers flowing out of it.

Most people's images of Tuscany are of the peerless, undulating landscape of the Chianti, between Siena and Florence. But in this region, too, there are ample variations within relatively short distances. South of Siena are the *crete senesi* (literally, 'Sienese clays'), which when parched in summer take on a lunar aspect. North of Florence is an extensive industrial belt. And then there are the ubiquitous mountains. The most celebrated are in the north-west of Tuscany. It is here that the quarries of Carrara are to be found, which have been providing sculptors with marble since classical times. Michelangelo's *David* and *Pietà* were both carved from blocks torn from the mountainsides near Carrara. A lesser range of the Apennines acts as a barrier to the Marche and its broad coastal plain.

Going north, as the Apennines bend westwards, the plain broadens out until it becomes part of the Po Valley in the region of Emilia-Romagna. As its name suggests, Emilia-Romagna is a composite of two regions: Romagna in the south, with its highly developed tourist resorts, which include Rimini, and Emilia, which extends as far as the Po and provides some of the best agricultural produce and most succulent cuisine to be found in Italy. Parma, home of both the eponymous ham and Parmesan cheese, is in Emilia.

The Po Valley regions par excellence are Veneto and Lombardy. What divides Veneto is not so much geography (though it extends into the Alps above Venice), but a sharp division between the inhabitants of the flat Venetian hinterland and those of the city of Venice, who have traditionally looked down on the mainlanders as uncouth peasants. Although the hinterland has a number of historic cities, including Padua, Verona and Vicenza, it was until comparatively recently one of Italy's poorest areas. In the period leading up to the

First World War, it was the biggest source of emigration outside the Mezzogiorno. And not even the years of Italy's 'economic miracle' (from the early 1950s to the early 1960s) had much of an impact on the region's backwardness. It was only in the 1970s that Veneto began to grow rapidly – so fast indeed that it is now Italy's third-richest region after Lombardy and Lazio. Evidence of its thriving, export-driven industries can be seen in the small factories and warehouses that break the horizons of Veneto's bleak landscapes.

Topographically, Lombardy is not dissimilar: from the plains in the south, either side of the Po, you climb through hills into mountains. But what sets the region apart are its sublimely beautiful lakes. Maggiore, which stretches into Switzerland, Como and Garda are the largest. Lombardy also includes Italy's financial capital, Milan, and a tradition of enterprise and prosperity that, in contrast to Veneto, stretches back to the Middle Ages. Today, Milan stands roughly halfway along a vast industrial corridor with at one end Mestre on the Venice lagoon and at the other Turin, the capital of Piedmont.

Once joined politically to Savoy on the other side of the Alps in modern-day France, Piedmont is the gateway through which many ideas from France and beyond have filtered into the Italian consciousness. It was the region whose leaders played the most active part in Italy's Unification and the one that provided the newly unified state with much of its constitutional, administrative and legal framework. Turin, home of the Fiat motor company, was to an even greater extent than Milan the hub of the Italian economic miracle. Nor is Piedmont's importance solely political or economic: south of Turin is an area of steep, undulating hills known as the Langhe. If Emilia is by common consent Italy's centre of gastronomic excellence, then few would dispute that the Langhe is its most outstanding wine-growing district: the home of Barolo and other less well-known but highly prized wines such as Barbaresco. The misty Langhe also yields most of Italy's white truffles and many of the hazelnuts that go into making Nutella.

Further south is rocky Liguria. Pincered between the Apennines as they curve westwards towards the French border and the Mediterranean, Liguria is small but densely populated. Its coastline, the Italian Riviera, was among the first spots to be discovered by foreign holidaymakers in the twentieth century, along with the Amalfi coast, which it to some extent resembles. Genoa, the capital of Liguria and its main port, was for centuries the seat of a maritime republic that rivalled – and sometimes bested – that of Venice. Christopher Columbus was one of the many seagoing sons of the Genoese Republic.

Between the northern salients of Lombardy and Veneto is the composite region of Trentino-Alto Adige, which has a predominantly German-speaking north and a mainly Italian-speaking south. This Alpine territory was once part of the Austro-Hungarian Empire. It was given to Italy as a reward for switching to the Allied side in the First World War. Since 1972, Alto Adige (which its German-speaking inhabitants prefer to call Südtirol; in English, South Tyrol) and Trentino have governed themselves more or less separately as autonomous provinces.

The region as a whole is one of five with a special constitutional status. The others are Sicily, Sardinia, and two more in the north. One, Alpine Valle d'Aosta, has strong links with France. The other, Friuli-Venezia Giulia, which borders Slovenia, divides roughly half and half into a mountainous north and a flatter south. Over the centuries, the rivers that flow from the Alps across the lowlands have provided useful boundaries for the division of the region, parts of which have gone back and forth more than once between the Venetian Republic, the Habsburg Empire, the Kingdom of Italy, Austria-Hungary and the former Yugoslavia.

The tortured history of Friuli-Venezia Giulia makes an important point about the Italians. Physical division helps to explain many of the differences between them. The mountains, seas and lakes that have kept them apart – and which were once vastly greater barriers than they are in the age of autostrade, jet aircraft and high-speed trains – have contributed greatly to Italy's linguistic, cultural and gastronomic diversity. What is true of Sicily is unlikely to be true of

Trieste. But then, what is true of the Umbrian town of Spoleto, say, may not even be true of Norcia, which is also in Umbria and less than 30 kilometres away, but reachable even today only by a circuitous route through the hills that takes forty-five minutes to drive.

If physical barriers had been the most significant obstacles to interaction over the centuries, however, you would expect that the most important single distinction would be between easterners and westerners, because far and away the biggest hindrance to communication is the Apennine mountain range. In fact, differences between east and west count for little. The key contrast in contemporary Italy is between north and south. Why? The answer to that question, and to the 'question of questions' posed by Barzini, can be found only in those passages of Italy's history that its people would rather forget – and of which most foreigners are barely aware.

2.

A Violent Past

'In Italy, for thirty years under the Borgias, they had warfare, terror, murder and bloodshed, but they produced Michelangelo, Leonardo da Vinci and the Renaissance. In Switzerland, they had brotherly love, they had five hundred years of democracy and peace – and what did that produce? The cuckoo clock.'

– Harry Lime in *The Third Man*, 1949 (dir. Carol Reed)

It was Christmas Day in the year 800. The King of the Franks, Charles I, who would come to be known as Charles the Great or Charlemagne, was attending Mass in the old basilica of St Peter's. Some years earlier, the then pope had appealed for the protection of the Franks, a Germanic people who had carved out a kingdom that stretched from today's Germany across most of modern-day France to the Pyrenees. Charlemagne's father, Pepin, had come to the aid of the papacy and his son regarded himself as its guardian. He was making what was to prove his last journey to Rome. His biographer Einhard wrote that he had gone to restore order in the city after Pope Leo III had been set upon by Romans who 'tore out his eyes and blinded him'.[1]

A later chronicler wrote that 'when the king . . . rose up from prayer, Pope Leo placed on his head a crown; and he was acclaimed by the whole populace of Rome'.[2] Historians have since raised sceptical eyebrows at the implication that the pope simply caught Charlemagne unawares. But the king's biographer, Einhard, insisted that Charlemagne 'at first had such an aversion [to the title of Emperor] that he declared that he would not have set foot in the church . . . if he could have foreseen the design of the Pope'.[3]

Whatever the truth of the matter, Leo's initiative and the events that surrounded it were to have momentous consequences for Europe, and Italy in particular. Very little of the subsequent history of the peninsula is comprehensible without some understanding of their effects, some of which can be felt even today.

Until he crowned Charlemagne, the history of Italy had followed a pattern not unlike that of the rest of Western Europe. The disintegration of the western half of the Roman Empire had laid open broad swathes of the continent to invasion by the wandering, mostly Germanic tribes that had gained military ascendancy over the Roman legions. The Italian peninsula, the heart of the original empire and the place where Roman culture and affluence reached its height, was particularly tempting.

By the end of the fifth century, most of modern-day Italy was being ruled more or less peacefully by Theodoric, the able leader of the Ostrogoths, the eastern branch of the Gothic nation. Had his state endured, it might have left behind a greater sense of Italy as a natural political unit. But the Ostrogoths were to rule Italy for only sixty years. One of the few reminders of their passing is Theodoric's magnificent white marble mausoleum, which can be seen to this day outside Ravenna, the city he made his capital.

Although independent in effect, Theodoric was a viceroy. He had been sent to claim the peninsula as an agent of what, until the collapse of the western half of the Roman Empire, had been its eastern half: the state with its capital at Constantinople (modern-day Istanbul) which later historians would call the Byzantine Empire.* As the Italians were about to find out in the most violent fashion, the Byzantine emperor had not forgotten that Italy was still part of his domain.

In 535 he dispatched an army to take back Italy from Theodoric's successors. It was the start of one of the goriest wars in history. The

---

* After Byzantium, the name of the ancient Greek settlement on the same site.

Gothic War lasted almost twenty years and, according to most estimates, it reduced the population by more than half. The Byzantine
forces eventually emerged victorious. But Italy, drained of its human
and other resources, was in no position to resist a new wave of Germanic invaders: the Lombards.

Their arrival ushered in another thirty-odd years of intermittent
warfare as the newcomers embarked on the bloody task of trying to
drive out the Byzantines. They never fully succeeded. By the early
years of the seventh century, Sicily, Sardinia and much of the south
were all still held by Constantinople. So, at least nominally, was a
broad stretch of territory that ran across the peninsula from
Ravenna in the north-east, where the Byzantine governor had his
seat, to south of Rome, where, amid the turmoil, the papacy had
begun to play an increasingly prominent role in the administration
of the city and its surrounding areas.*

When in 751 Ravenna fell to the Lombards, there was every
chance that Rome, which was theoretically under Byzantine protection, would follow in due course. Which is why Leo's predecessor
sought the help of the Franks. They did exactly what was expected
of them. And more. After overcoming the Lombards, Charlemagne's father, Pepin, handed to the papacy the right to govern not
only Rome and its environs but the entire band of territory in northern central Italy that was nominally part of the Byzantine Empire.
In doing so, he created the Papal State, a theocracy at the heart of
Europe that was to remain in existence for well over a thousand
years.

Leo's coronation of Charlemagne, an already crowned monarch,
was more than just an expression of gratitude for the Franks' military intervention. The pope was declaring him to be the emperor of
a reborn Western Roman Empire. Although the title conferred on

---

* The most important monument to survive from Rome's Byzantine period is the
half-ruined church of Santa Maria Antiqua on the edge of the Forum. Long
closed to the public to allow for the restoration of its frescoes, it was reopened for
a brief period in 2014.

Charlemagne lapsed for a while under his successors, it was revived in the middle of the tenth century and never subsequently relinquished. The territory that the emperors ruled eventually came to be known as the *Holy* Roman Empire – a reflection of their claim to a legitimacy that derived from the papacy, and through the papacy from God. Like the Papal State, the Holy Roman Empire would survive into the nineteenth century. At its greatest extent, it covered much of northern Italy, Sardinia, parts of eastern France, Switzerland, the Low Countries, Germany, some of western Poland, the modern-day Czech Republic and most of today's Slovenia.

The interaction between the papacy and the Frankish kings may have been momentous, but it was also richly ironic. Pepin had little enough right to hand Byzantine territory to the popes. But Leo had no right whatever to confer on Pepin's son the title of Roman Emperor. The claim of later popes to be the true heirs of Augustus and his successors was based on a document known as the 'Donation of Constantine'. This purported to show that, before making Byzantium his capital in 330, Constantine the Great, the first Roman emperor to convert to Christianity, had entrusted the western part of his domains to the then-reigning pope. But the 'Donation of Constantine' was a forgery; a lie. It had been concocted in the papal chancellery at some point in the eighth century.

By crowning Charlemagne, Pope Leo III may have felt he was asserting the right of the papacy to decide who should be emperor in the West. But he was also creating a rival heir to the legacy of ancient Rome. The competing pretensions of the papacy on the one hand and of Charlemagne's successors on the other would again and again bring death and destruction to medieval Italy. After 962, the emperors were Germans, and every time the emperor of the day felt the need to reassert his power or replenish his coffers an army would come marching through the Alps. Cities would be sacked, the surrounding countryside ravaged. There would be slaughter, rape and looting.

Yet the creation of this new empire did not just bring about conflict. It also led, in Italy as in Germany, to an abnormal degree of political fragmentation. Though a few of the Holy Roman Emperors opted to rule from Rome, most spent their lives on the other side of the Alps. The popes, for their part, were often more concerned with ecclesiastical and theological matters than with the mundane details of civil administration. And in any case their military resources were limited: they relied for the protection of the Papal State to a large extent on moral authority and mercenary troops.

The result was a power vacuum in the northern half of Italy in which many towns and cities, particularly those that had once enjoyed a degree of autonomy under the original Roman Empire, started to govern themselves. Successive popes, keen to curb the power of the Holy Roman emperors, encouraged the spread of these miniature semi-democratic republics, known as communes. When the communes began to be replaced by more personal and autocratic forms of government in the fourteenth century, Italy north of the Papal State became a patchwork of semi-independent principalities, duchies, marquisates, counties and tiny lordships dotted with the odd surviving republic. Wars between them were common.

The inhabitants of northern and north-central Italy in the late Middle Ages may have been divided and vulnerable. But for as long as the communes survived their citizens enjoyed a degree of control over their own affairs that was unthinkable in most of the rest of Europe. They were also increasingly prosperous: a surge in economic growth began towards the end of the eleventh century that was to last on and off until the start of the fourteenth, laying the material foundations for the Renaissance.

The most powerful of the republics in the north was Venice. But it was also the least typical. Venice's lagoon-dwelling inhabitants – originally refugees from the German tribal invasions – had never been even nominally subject to the Holy Roman Empire. They had elected their first duke, or doge, back in the eighth century after cutting themselves loose from the Byzantine Empire. Enriched by trade with the East, especially after the start of the Crusades, the

Venetian republic, or Serenissima,* grew to be an important naval power. By the start of the thirteenth century, the doges had an empire of their own that would eventually stretch as far as Cyprus.

By casting a protective mantle over the rest of northern and central Italy, the emperors not only encouraged the region to fracture internally but cut it off from the south. In the thousand years that followed Charlemagne's coronation, alliances were sometimes forged that involved this or that southern state. From time to time, an emperor would lead his army into the Mezzogiorno. And, for a while, the two halves of Italy were reunited as part of the empire. But, for the rest, the affairs of the north and the south were separate, and they developed as quite different societies.

Sicily was gradually conquered by Muslim forces in the ninth century and remained an Islamic emirate until the end of the eleventh. The 'foot' and 'heel' of the Italian 'boot' still came under direct Byzantine rule. But Muslim raiders established another, relatively short-lived emirate around Bari in the ninth century. A Lombard principality centred on Benevento survived for almost three hundred years after the Frankish invasion (it was divided after the middle of the ninth century). And, when the Muslim occupation of Sicily isolated the emperors in Constantinople from their remaining possessions further west, several territories nominally belonging to the Byzantine Empire became independent in practice.

Sardinia was one. Provincial governors who were also judges took over the administration of the so-called Giudicati into which the island was split. The Giudicati soon became hereditary kingdoms, one of which survived as an independent state into the fifteenth century. On the western seaboard of the Italian mainland, a number of the ports, together with their hinterlands – first Naples, then Gaeta, Amalfi and, briefly, Sorrento – became self-governing. Amalfi in particular enjoyed a golden age of wealth and influence in

---

* From its official title, *La Serenissima Repubblica di Venezia* (The Most Serene Republic of Venice). No one who has looked across the lagoon on a windless day can fail to understand how appropriate it was.

the tenth and eleventh centuries based on trade with the Byzantine Empire and a good deal of diplomatic opportunism (like the rulers of the other southern maritime states, the dukes of Amalfi had no qualms about forging alliances with Muslim potentates, or even pirates).

Sicily prospered, too, and for longer. Under the emirate, Palermo was probably the biggest city in Europe after Constantinople. Muslim rule there was snuffed out in the same way as Byzantine control of the mainland – by Norman mercenaries who had come to take part in the incessant conflicts that raged among the petty states of southern Italy, and between them and the Byzantine forces stationed there. By 1071 Byzantine rule in Italy had ended, and twenty years later a Norman was master of Sicily.

Fanatically Christian descendants of the Vikings, the Normans proved to be unexpectedly tolerant and intelligent rulers. On Sicily, they allowed a fusion of Arab, Jewish, Byzantine and Norman elements creating a dazzlingly eclectic culture. And it was a Norman who in the twelfth century brought Sicily and the mainland together as part of a unified kingdom. The south was to remain territorially united for most of the next seven hundred years, even though, for much of that period, Sicily and the mainland were governed as separate entities under the same crown.

In 1194 the emperor Henry VI conquered the Kingdom of Sicily, as the united state was misleadingly called, and for the following seventy years the whole of present-day Italy, with the exception of Sardinia, was brought within the Holy Roman Empire. For thirty of those years, under Frederick II, it was the rest of the empire stretching to the Baltic that was ruled from the Kingdom of Sicily and, specifically, from Palermo, where the emperor had grown up. Frederick's reign saw perhaps the most determined effort before the nineteenth century to bring all of Italy under the direct control of a single authority. But his efforts were resisted by the communes and resulted in almost thirty years of warfare. Vigorously opposed by the papacy, Frederick failed, and within a few years of his death a French dynasty had wrested the Kingdom of Sicily from the grip of the empire.

The island of Sicily was subsequently lost to the Crown of Aragon, the state in north-eastern Spain that included modern-day Catalonia. But in the fifteenth century a king of Aragon, Alfonso V, reunited the island (and Sardinia) with the mainland. After the Crown of Aragon merged with the Crown of Castile, southern Italy became a dominion of the new Kingdom of Spain, the realm that would soon be ascendant in the Mediterranean and far beyond.

The unity of the south under a succession of foreign rulers contrasted sharply with the fragmentation of the north. After a series of catastrophes in the fourteenth century, notably the Black Death, economic activity there recovered and gradually reacquired momentum. It is during this period, too, that the first great Renaissance works of art and literature make their appearance in Siena and Florence.

As Harry Lime rightly observed, Italians produced some of their greatest cultural achievements in precisely those periods in which they were in greatest peril.* The prosperity and emerging cultural brilliance of the states that replaced or absorbed the communes masked the acute danger they were in. By the middle of the fifteenth century, at the height of the Renaissance, northern Italy was split into more than a dozen states. Further south, the pope's temporal authority was severely circumscribed by the power of local nobles.

For as long as the Holy Roman Empire had held a cloak of protection over northern and central Italy, its inhabitants were safe from all but each other and the odd, irate emperor. To all intents and purposes, however, the cloak had been cast off by about 1300 and, just as the Italy of the fifth and sixth centuries had been a tempting prize for the Ostrogoths and Lombards, so the Italy of the fifteenth century – the land of the Renaissance and the richest territory in Europe – became an irresistible lure for the new nation states that were starting to challenge the Holy Roman Empire for dominance of the continent.

---

* He was wrong about the cuckoo clocks, though. They were invented, not in Switzerland, but in southern Germany.

It is often said that the Germans have never recovered from the Thirty Years War in the seventeenth century; that the brutality of that momentous clash between Protestant and Catholic armies hard-wired into their national character a sense of insecurity they have never been able to shake off. Something not so very different could be said of the Italian Wars that began in 1494 when a French army marched on to the peninsula. For almost sixty years, French, Spanish, German and Swiss armies criss-crossed Italy against a background of dizzyingly complex diplomacy that involved popes, foreign monarchs, the Ottoman sultan Suleiman the Magnificent and the rulers of Italy's tragically divided and competing states.

In 1527 the violence peaked in an attack on Rome that shocked all Europe. Some twenty thousand mainly German (and Lutheran) troops poured through the walls of the city at the start of an eight-day orgy of destruction that has come to be known as the Sack of Rome. Churches were pillaged. Nuns were raped. Priests were murdered. Noble houses were torched. Priceless classical treasures were smashed or looted. Romans thought to be wealthy were tortured so they would hand over their riches and, if they proved to have none, were often butchered anyway. Nearly a quarter of the population was killed.

The Italian Wars were scarcely the first to be waged on the peninsula in order to settle foreign scores. Nor were they necessarily more destructive than those that preceded them. But they were uniquely humiliating. They revealed in the most savage way the Italians' inability to sink their differences and work together for their common good. They put a ruinous and bloody end to the most culturally illustrious era of Italy's history. And they ushered in another, in which much of the north would join the south under foreign yokes. In the end, it was not the French but the Spanish – already masters of the South – who emerged as the dominant power. Under the treaty that put an end to the fighting, the extensive territories of the Duchy of Milan were given to Spain. Venice retained its independence, as did the other Italian duchies and republics. But in the new era of big, centralized nation states hungry for empire, their freedom of manoeuvre was severely limited.

Though it was far from obvious at the time, the sixteenth century also marked the start of Italy's economic decline relative to other parts of Western Europe. There was more than one cause, but probably the most important were the changes that were taking place in the pattern of world trade. The routes across the Atlantic had already begun to carry far more traffic and generate far greater wealth than those in the Mediterranean, while the Far East would soon replace the Near East as a source of imports for the increasingly wealthy nations of Western Europe.

The new political order imposed at the end of the Italian Wars was to remain in place for another one hundred and fifty years. But that did not mean the intervening period was peaceful. In the first half of the seventeenth century, Italy was the scene of several more wars, most involving the increasingly self-assertive kingdom of Savoy. The conflicts that would determine its fate in the next century, on the other hand, were fought outside the peninsula. But that only drove home the point that the Italian states had become pieces in a chess game in which the important moves were made on other parts of the European board. Austria now supplanted Spain as the main arbiter of the peninsula's destiny, though it subsequently lost the south to the Spanish branch of the Bourbon dynasty.

Thereafter, Italy's political geography remained substantially unchanged until 1796, when Napoleon Bonaparte, whose ancestry was more Italian than French, became the latest of many generals to lead his troops over the Alps. If only for a few years, the French were the masters of Italy. Napoleon redrew the boundaries of the various little states and gave them names borrowed from the classical past (so Tuscany, for example, became the Kingdom of Etruria).

Once the revolutionary wave had passed, the old order – as in most of the rest of Europe – was restored. The Spanish Bourbons, by now thoroughly Italianized, were given back the southern mainland and Sicily. Fiercely conservative, authoritarian and pro-monarchical, the leaders of early-nineteenth-century Europe wanted no truck with republics. Two were snuffed out in the settlement that followed the Napoleonic Wars. Genoa went to the House of Savoy, whose realm included Sardinia, Piedmont on the eastern side of the Alps and Savoy on the western side. Venice, proudly free for more than a thousand years, was handed to Austria, together with its extensive hinterland and what remained of its empire. The Austrians also got back the lands of the old Duchy of Milan. They thus gained control of most of northern Italy until the Risorgimento.

Almost fourteen centuries elapsed between the deposing of the last Roman emperor in the West and the Unification that followed the breaching of the Aurelian Wall near Porta Pia in 1870: sixty generations, more or less, of disunity, vulnerability to the whim of foreign rulers and the might of foreign armies.* Such things leave their mark on a people.

---

* Even Russian troops have fought on Italian soil: in 1799–1800, against the invading French Revolutionary Army.

3.

Echoes and Reverberations

'Noi siamo prodotto del passato e viviamo immersi nel passato.'
'We are produced by the past and we live immersed in the past.'
– Benedetto Croce, *La storia come pensiero e come azione*, 1938

I had been based in Italy as a foreign correspondent for only a short time when I received a letter from a reader, forwarded to me from the newspaper in London. It was quite unusual in those days to get any sort of feedback. Email was still a novelty in the mid-1990s. If you wanted to register your objections (or, more rarely, pay a compliment) to a journalist, you had to go to the trouble of writing a letter with typewriter or pen, putting it in an envelope and taking it to a post box. Few readers bothered. Those who did so were usually either mentally disturbed, utterly delighted or furiously angry. This one was furiously angry.

Some weeks earlier, in what had been more of a literary flourish than a serious assessment, I had referred to Italy as being 'charming but corrupt and chaotic'. It was that last word that had infuriated my British reader. How on earth could I claim it was chaotic? he asked. He had come to live in Italy a few months before and found that, on the contrary, life in Italy was infinitely better organized than in Britain. Having just returned to Rome from a trip to Naples, I found this more than a little baffling. But then I looked at the address at the top of the letter. The writer was living in Bologna. His Italy and my Italy were worlds apart.

He had based himself in a city that, in the Cold War years, the Italian Communist Party (PCI) had turned into a showcase for socialist government. As I was soon to discover when I visited Bologna myself, it was a place where not only did the buses run on time but the passengers knew when they were going to arrive because of electronic displays at the bus stops. These had been installed in Bologna years before they made their appearance in other European cities (twenty years later, they are only just getting to Rome). I, by contrast, lived and worked for most of the time in the southern half of Italy – it has usually produced more news than the rest – and in a very different and more disorderly society. There, the buses were dilapidated and the drivers thought nothing of roaring over pedestrian crossings at which people were waiting on either side to cross the road.

Nor were the Communists' ambitions for Bologna the only reason why it was – and is – different from cities further south. As you move north from Rome, *civismo*, which translates as 'public spirit' or 'social responsibility',* or just 'consideration for others', increasingly becomes a reality. The public spaces in towns and the common parts of buildings become cleaner and tidier. There is more evidence of a sense of community.

Conventionally, Italy is divided into three parts: north, south and central. The centre is usually taken to encompass the territories of the old Papal State, with the addition of Tuscany. It is a convenient division for, say, meteorologists. But it is of little help in understanding the nature of the country. Bologna is in Emilia-Romagna. Rome is in Lazio. They are both in central Italy. Yet it is clear to anyone who spends more than a few hours in both cities that they exist on quite different planes.

An alternative division of the country emerged in the pages of a seminal book published in the 1990s by an American political

---

* It is noteworthy, I think, that the English terms evoke respect for a much wider community – 'the public' or 'society' – whereas *civismo* derives from *civis* and *civitas*, the Latin words for 'citizen', 'citizenship' and the inhabitants of a city-state. Arguably, the only unit bigger than a family for which Italians feel an effortless and instinctive respect is the town or city they regard as home.

scientist.[1] Robert Putnam and his collaborators wanted to find out why some democratic governments succeed while others fail. So they looked at the records of Italy's regional administrations and concluded that their performances correlated to a large extent with the degree to which individuals and institutions in each region had developed traditions of mutual cooperation and trust, and that those traditions were strongest in areas whose populations in the Middle Ages had experienced self-rule, often as communes. Putnam's analysis implies a line that divides Italy into just two areas: north and south. Cities such as Bologna on the periphery of the old Papal State, which were in practice independent of direct rule from Rome for much of their history, would come within the north. His thesis may not account for everything. Matera in Basilicata, for example, is a city that exhibits a fair amount of *civismo*. But his book does highlight an important way in which Italy's history has contributed to its diversity. There are others.

Government by foreigners has given a different flavour to different regions. In ancient times, Greek settlers established themselves on Sicily and in parts of the southern mainland, leaving an indelible mark on the local culture. Among other things, the name of the Calabrian mafia, the 'Ndrangheta, is thought to be of Greek origin. In Sicily, the Greek bedrock was overlaid with layers of Arab and Berber influence, which also touched parts of Puglia. The presence of Muslims over a period of centuries is often cited as an explanation for the traditionally low status of women in Sicily, and for the prevalence of so many dark-eyed, dark-haired beauties among the women of Puglia. Some Italians will tell you that, paradoxically, you are more likely to encounter a blond-haired or redheaded person on Sicily than on the mainland, and that this has to do with more than a century of Norman rule. What is certainly true is that the Spanish left their mark on the Mezzogiorno and are often blamed for having infused the southern upper classes with a contempt for work and an aversion to investment in anything but land. Precisely the opposite values have long held good in the north, which was repeatedly invaded by people of Germanic stock. The Goths and – probably to a much greater extent – the Lombards changed the ethnic composition of northern Italy and parts of the south as well. Austrian rule in the north in the eighteenth and nineteenth centuries is clearly visible in the *mitteleuropäische* look of the architecture of Milan and cities further east. St Mark's Cathedral in Venice bears witness to the influence of the Orthodox Christian East with which the Venetians traded profitably for hundreds of years.

History – and specifically the endlessly shifting boundaries of the states in what is now Italy – helps explain why the country even today is such a linguist's playground. Several completely foreign languages are spoken within its frontiers. More than three quarters of the population of the Valle d'Aosta can speak either French or a Franco-Provençal patois. In the western districts of Piedmont there are some 100,000 Occitan speakers. And in the Alto Adige/Südtirol, in addition to German, which is spoken by about 70 per cent of the population – almost 350,000 people – there is Ladin, a language that is the mother tongue of some 20,000 Italians. Ladin is related to Friulian, which is spoken by far more people, around 300,000. Among the other languages to be found in Friuli-Venezia Giulia are Slovene, an archaic variant of Slovene known as Resian (considered by some experts to be a separate language) and various dialects of German.

Croatian has a toehold in Molise. And there are some fifty Albanian-speaking communities scattered across the southern mainland and Sicily. The Arbëreshë, as they are known, are descendants of refugees who fled from Ottoman rule, beginning in the fifteenth century. Integration has whittled down their numbers over the years,* but estimates of the number of Albanian speakers in Italy range up to 100,000. Another 20,000 or so Italians are reckoned

---

* Francesco Crispi, one of the heroes of the Risorgimento and one of Italy's earliest prime ministers, was of Albanian descent. The academic and politician Stefano Rodotà, who became the first head of Italy's data protection authority, is from an Arbëreshë village in Calabria. His daughter, Maria Laura Rodotà, is a well-known *Corriere della Sera* columnist and sketchwriter.

to speak a dialect of Greek called, appropriately enough, Griko. It lives on in a handful of villages in Puglia and Calabria, and even among some of the city-dwellers of Reggio Calabria. Catalan is still spoken in and around the town of Alghero in north-western Sardinia, where about 10,000 people regard it as their mother tongue.

Other countries also have substantial minorities who speak a foreign language, but what really sets Italy apart are the vast numbers of Italians who speak a dialect. Exactly where a dialect begins and a language ends is a matter for fine, and inevitably controversial, judgement. Sardinian, or Sardu, is generally regarded as a discrete language – its dissimilarity a product of the island's separateness from the rest of Italy for much of its history. In fact, Italian has fewer words in common with Sardinian than it does with French. And the two languages look very different when written down. For example, the Italian proverb, *'Il sangue non è acqua'* (the equivalent of 'Blood is thicker than water'), in Sardu becomes *'Su sambene no est abba.'* The overwhelming majority of Sards – about a million people – speak Sardu, which has three dialects of its own.

Piedmontese and Sicilian, spoken by 1.6 and 4.7 million Italians respectively, are also sufficiently distinct to be considered languages. Others would add Venetian, Lombard and Neapolitan. But then there is an almost infinite variation in the way that Italians speak among themselves at home and with others from the same city or region. The dialect term for an object, creature or activity in one place can be utterly different from the word used to mean the same thing just a few kilometres away. A coat hanger, for example, is known to some Italians as an *ometto*, to others as a *stampella* and to yet others as an *angioletto*. But it can also be a *gruccia, attacca-panni, appendiabiti, cruccia, stanfella, crocetta, crociera, appendino* or *croce*.[2]

While eager to stress the reasons why their city or region is unique, Italians tend to be less aware of their similarities. But the fact is that, while generating diversity, their history has also given them things in common. The knowledge that their forebears conquered the Roman Empire and gave the world the Renaissance engenders in Italians an inner self-confidence that is soon noticeable to anyone who lives among them and which can sometimes show up in a readiness – almost wholly lacking among their Spanish 'cousins' – to be individualistic. The sociologist Giuseppe De Rita has argued that their past has endowed Italians, like many Greeks, with something rather more than just self-confidence: an innate belief in their superiority.

'I've never thought Italians were racist in the classical sense of the term,' he once told an interviewer. 'They are, on the other hand, convinced of being superior because of a super-ego linked to the history they have behind them. At all events, they feel themselves to be more intelligent, brighter and better.'[3]

I can imagine there are many Italians who would scoff at some of that. If you live in some benighted village in the wilds of Basilicata, or on a housing estate in one of the industrial waste lands of the Po Valley, I don't suppose you think of yourself as heir to the traditions of Augustus and Leonardo. But the sense of pride that De Rita describes can certainly be detected among the Tuscans, the Venetians, the Romans and many others. What he said about Italians believing themselves to be smarter – more *sveglio* (awake or aware), more *in gamba* (bright) – than others is unquestionably true.

At the same time, there is a consciousness that Italians have repeatedly been the victims of invasion and oppression and, what is worse, by their fellow Europeans. It accounts for a feeling of mixed resentment and vulnerability that co-exists in the national psyche with pride. Take the Italian national anthem, '*Il Canto degli Italiani*', better known as '*L'Inno di Mameli*' after the writer of the lyrics.* National anthems are mostly about boasting and threatening; about telling the rest of the world of the beauty and other supposed merits of your country and taking advantage of the opportunity to let other states know that yours is powerful and not to be trifled with.

---

* Not the least remarkable thing about the Italian national anthem is that Goffredo Mameli was a mere twenty years old when he wrote it.

Americans proclaim theirs to be 'the land of the free and the home of the brave'. Britons call on God to save their queen:

> Scatter her enemies,
> And make them fall:
> Confound their politics,
> Frustrate their knavish tricks.

So what do Italians do? Well, in the second verse, they proclaim to the world:

> *Noi fummo da secoli*
> *Calpesti, derisi,*
> *Perché non siam popolo,*
> *Perché siam divisi.*

> We were for centuries
> Downtrodden [and] derided,
> Because we are not [a] people,
> Because we are divided.

Now, it can be objected that '*L'Inno di Mameli*' is a creature of its time; that between 1847, when it was written, and the day in 1870 on which the Bersaglieri burst through the Aurelian Walls, twenty-three years were to elapse, and that throughout that period Italians were still divided and downtrodden (though certainly not derided: the bravery of Italy's nationalists, and that of Giuseppe Garibaldi in particular, was widely admired and praised in the rest of Europe). It is also the case that the words quoted above are rarely heard. In military parades and at international football matches it is customary to sing only the first verse and the chorus.

But it is still remarkable, I think, that any nation should retain as part of its anthem a verse that is so searingly candid about its own past humiliations, let alone one that declares that 'we *are* not [a] people, because we *are* divided'. All the more so since '*L'Inno di*

Mameli' was not adopted immediately after Unification. Italy was at first a monarchy and for as long as it remained one the national anthem was the House of Savoy's *marcia reale* ('royal march'). It was not until 1946 that the Italian Republic chose *'L'Inno di Mameli'* and not until 2005, in fact, that its status as the national anthem was confirmed in law.

A people with a history like that of the Italians cannot but have a somewhat ambiguous view of foreigners. Whereas the British, the Spanish and the Turks have invariably come into contact with strangers in the role of conquerors and, later, governors, the reverse has been true of the Italians since the age of the Barbarian Invasions. It helps, I think, to explain the instinctive protectionism that you encounter in Italy but also the fatalistic acceptance of the idea that it is quite normal for crucial decisions on the future of the country to be taken by foreigners.

There is even a term – perhaps 'euphemism' is a better word – for the non-Italian considerations that need to be taken into account when framing government or party policy. They are referred to generically as the *vincolo esterno*, or 'external constraint'. For Italy's Christian Democrat-dominated governments during the Cold War, it was the view of any particular issue taken by the US administration and particularly the CIA. For their opponents in the Italian Communist Party it was the latest doctrine adopted by the Kremlin. Since the fall of the Berlin Wall, the principal *vincolo esterno* for Italian policy-makers has been represented by the European Commission in Brussels and, since the adoption of the euro, by the European Central Bank in Frankfurt. It is a nuisance, but it can also be a boon: Italian politicians, hemmed in on all sides by domestic pressures, often find that the only way they can impose necessary but unpopular measures is by justifying them to the electorate in terms of the *vincolo esterno*.

The ambiguity towards foreigners is particularly acute in the case of German speakers, who, as has been seen, have been the most persistent interferers in the affairs of the peninsula. It is only very recently that Italians have begun to pose the sort of questions that have been asked in Britain for years about whether the European Union in general, and the euro in particular, hold the potential for establishing German hegemony over the rest of the continent. Yet the suspicion and resentment of Germany and Germans is there, and it can burst to the surface at unexpected moments (as when Silvio Berlusconi, who was then Italy's prime minister, was addressing the European Parliament in 2003 and told a German socialist who was provoking him that he reminded him of a Nazi concentration camp guard).

Italy's fractured, violent history also helps, I think, to explain a more generalized fatalism among the Italians, and a horror of war. Other nations, too, abhor war and, usually, the more recent their experience of conflict, the greater their abhorrence. But in some societies war is also associated with more positive concepts: heroism, adventure, glory, and so on. In Britain, for example, bloodshed went hand-in-hand with imperial conquest and, though the idea of empire may no longer be exalted, Britons still look back with pride at the likes of Clive, Nelson and Gordon. In Serbia and other Balkan nations, fighting is linked to a past of courageous resistance to the Ottomans.

But in Italy, except among professional soldiers, such attitudes are largely confined to the neo-fascist fringe. Belonging to the armed forces does not carry with it anything like the same cachet that it does in Britain or the US.

I know from personal experience of having spent time in war zones that, on returning, people are often keen to hear about your experiences – not because of any morbid interest in death and violence but because armed conflicts generate extraordinary situations, bizarre anecdotes and, undeniably, a great deal of excitement. I soon realized, however, that in this respect Italians were an exception. As soon as I or someone else brought up the fact that I had been reporting a war or some other kind of conflict, they would as often as not deftly terminate the conversation or equally deftly turn it to another, more socially acceptable subject. For the vast majority of Italians, war is simply *brutta* (ugly, nasty) and discussion of it is to be avoided in polite company.

Of course, there is plenty of violent behaviour in Italian life – Mafia killings, football hooliganism and a high level of domestic violence. But physical aggression is often replaced by verbal abuse, and verbal insults seldom lead on to physical aggression. Knowing this, Italians will often say to each other things that, in other societies, would cause punches to be thrown or knives to be drawn. I know from working in Italian offices that tempestuous rows break out quite often and that, initially, you think that those involved are one snapped nerve away from coming to blows. But they often end as abruptly as they broke out, and the next day you see the participants holding a perfectly civilized exchange.

Politics echoes this. The violence of the language used routinely by Italian politicians is astounding. Take, for example, this, from Clemente Mastella, who was the justice minister in Romano Prodi's second government from 2006 to 2008: 'He is not a hero. He is merely moral dead wood.' Now, that sort of insult might be shouted across the House of Commons or hurled by a presidential candidate at his opponent. But the point about what Mastella said is that he was referring to one of his fellow Cabinet members, the then infrastructure minister, Antonio Di Pietro. So you can imagine the kind of things that are said between political adversaries.

Historically, the use of brute force has seldom offered a solution to Italians. The legates, governors and viceroys who ruled so many of them for so much of their history were always capable of summoning up far more military might than ever the Italians could, and the same was true of the foreign states that meddled repeatedly in Italy's affairs. It perhaps explains why Italians came to place so much faith in intelligence, diplomacy and guile, for these were the qualities that consoled them; those which allowed them, however fleetingly, to even the score with the foreigners who were, in effect, their colonial masters.

There is probably no scene in an Italian movie better known to

Italians than the one from *Totò Truffa 62* in which the comedian Antonio De Curtis ('Totò')* sells the Trevi Fountain to an American. Many of the characters Totò played would qualify for that most Italian of adjectives, *furbo*. It covers a range of meanings that in English go from 'smart' to 'cunning' and from 'crafty' to 'sly'. *Fare il furbo* means to jump a queue. The command *non fare il furbo* would translate roughly as 'Don't try to get clever with me'. *Furbo* is certainly not a compliment. But the connotations attached to *furbizia* are quite often positive ones. If an Italian tells you that you have just been *furbo* or *furba* in some way then, more often than not, he or she will say so in a tone of mixed surprise and complicit approval.

It would be unfair, though, to run away with the idea that *furbizia* is a national characteristic. As the journalist and wit Giuseppe Prezzolini first remarked back in the 1920s, the *furbo* coexists with – and preys on – another kind of Italian he dubbed the *fesso*. That is by no means a compliment either. It means 'idiot'. Prezzolini explained that you are a *fesso* 'if you pay the full-price rail ticket, don't get into the theatre free, don't have an uncle who is a *commendatore* or a friend of the wife who is influential in the judiciary or education; if you are neither a Freemason nor a Jesuit; tell the taxman your real income [or] keep your word even at the cost of losing thereby'.

The distinction between the two tribes had little to do with intelligence, Prezzolini argued. It was just that the *'fessi* have principles', whereas the *'furbi* only have aims'. The division he captured has held good to this day. Indeed, an entire history of modern Italy might be written in terms of the never-ending struggle between its *fessi* and its *furbi*. As you might expect, the *furbi* usually come out on top, except for brief periods such as the one that lasted from the end of 2011 to the beginning of 2013, when Mario Monti, an arch-*fesso*

* Little known outside Italy, Totò remains one of the country's best-loved comedians, along with Alberto Sordi and Roberto Benigni. Like Chaplin, he specialized in playing the 'little man', but he was in fact an aristocrat – the illegitimate son of a marquis, who adopted him. De Curtis's titles included those of 'Imperial Highness', 'Palatine Count', 'Knight of the Holy Roman Empire' and 'Exarch of Ravenna'.

(though no fool), governed the country with a Cabinet made up largely of *fessi*.

That does not mean the *furbi* are necessarily more numerous. In fact, the only systematic attempt to gauge their numbers of which I know reached the opposite conclusion. For a book on queuing,[4] a journalist interviewed a hundred of his fellow Italians. One of the questions was whether they ever tried to *fare il furbo* and get ahead in queues. Fifty-four said 'never'. Thirty-five answered 'sometimes'. And eleven said they 'always' tried to jump the queue.

If *furbizia* has deep roots in Italy's post-classical history, then so does a complex of entwined assumptions and attitudes for which, so far as I am aware, there is no particular word. Long experience of power changing hands in ways they were unable to influence has made Italians intensely wary of nailing their colours to any one mast. Historically, principles, ideals and commitment have proved dangerous. Those who survived were those who took care not to show their hand, those who adroitly shifted position in time to be on the right side when the outcome of the latest power struggle became clear.

Some years ago, I was invited to dinner by an Italian nobleman after attending a commemorative event to do with the Second World War. As the evening progressed, I asked the count what memories, if any, he had of the conflict. His role turned out to have been a dramatic one. As a boy, he had been sent by his father to intercept the advancing Allied troops and warn them that they were heading into a trap – an ambush laid by the Germans in a narrow pass.

'You see, my father was the commander of the local partisans,' he said.

Now, this was pretty unusual. Titled landowners did not normally take leading roles in the Resistance, which was dominated by communists. And I said as much.

'Yes, well, my father had quite a lot of ground to make up in 1944, you see,' he replied. 'He had been part of Mussolini's innermost circle.'

The nobleman's father was by no means the only one to hedge his bets. Many of Italy's leading northern industrialists played a deft hand, appearing to collaborate with the Germans who occupied northern Italy after the fall of Mussolini while at the same time secretly providing information to the Allies and even, in some cases, cash to the partisans.

By overthrowing Mussolini and withdrawing from the Axis, the Italians emerged from the war purged of fascism and on the side of the Allies. As a result, Italy benefited from post-war US aid – unlike Spain and Portugal, which continued to be governed by their respective fascist dictators. The sense of betrayal felt by the Germans when the Italians changed sides in 1943 was compounded by the memory of their having also switched allegiances in the First World War. Though Italy formed part of the Triple Alliance with Germany and Austria-Hungary, its government held back when war broke out in 1914. This was by no means unwarranted: Austria-Hungary was the first to violate the ground rules of the Triple Alliance, by failing to consult Italy before it declared war on Serbia and pitched the world into its first global conflict. The Italian government felt, understandably enough, that it was no longer under an obligation to the other members of the alliance. It joined the conflict the following year on the other side after Britain and France secretly promised the Rome government additional territory in the event of victory.

Alliances among the various states that now compose Italy were often subject to abrupt revision, and yet the history of the peninsula has been noticeably short on decisive turning points. There have been very few revolutions or coups* – and virtually no successful

---

* In modern times, there have been at least two attempts by neo-fascists to seize power. In 1961, the then head of the military police, Giovanni De Lorenzo, hatched a plot known by the name of *Piano Solo*. The other, planned for 7 or 8 December 1970, was led by Prince Junio Valerio Borghese. However, doubts have been expressed about the seriousness of both these attempts to seize power, especially *Piano Solo*.

ones. The Risorgimento and the installation of Mussolini's dictatorship stand out as exceptions – moments when Italians were pushed into a radical break with the past, in part at least by the force of idealism.

The much longer periods of democracy before and after the Fascist era were more characteristic of the rest of Italy's history, even if the men who featured prominently in them are less well remembered than Garibaldi or Mussolini. Who outside Italy, for example, has ever heard of Agostino Depretis? Or inside, for that matter. You will search the country in vain for a monument to Depretis or a piazza named in his honour. Outside his native province of Pavia, there are only a handful of streets dedicated to his memory: one, for some reason, in the southern town of Andria.

Yet Depretis was one of the few politicians who could be said to have dominated the Italy of his day. He was prime minister nine times, more than any other politician since Unification. Some of his Cabinets were, admittedly, pretty short-lived. One lasted eighty-eight days (a reminder that endless changes of government have always been characteristic of Italian democracy and were not, as is often claimed, a product of the abnormal conditions of the Cold War).* Nevertheless, Depretis stamped his personality on the period from 1876 until his death in 1887 as emphatically as Silvio Berlusconi did on the first decade of this century.†

So why has Depretis been wiped so comprehensively from the folk memory of the country he governed? Perhaps because he is associated with two things Italians would rather forget. It was while he was prime minister that Italy made its debut as a colonial power by occupying the Red Sea port of Massawa, and today not even the

---

* Italy's constitutional arrangements exaggerate the extent of the instability. Prime ministers cannot reshuffle their Cabinet without forming a new government. By the reckoning of most other democracies, Depretis was prime minister three times.

† Depretis was out of office for thirty-one months in eleven years; Berlusconi for twenty-four months in ten and a half years.

right seeks to glorify Italy's ill-starred imperial adventures. But – to the extent that people today even know of his existence – Depretis is also linked to the emergence, just a few years after Unification, of a phenomenon known as *trasformismo*. This is a word that has been taken from biology into the rich vocabulary of Italian politics. It means the building of parliamentary majorities by means of encouraging defection. Lawmakers can be persuaded to leave the party for which they were elected by offers of preferment (or something more tangible), or just by a fear of being caught on the losing side. Depretis's cynical promotion of *trasformismo* shocked those of his contemporaries who had hoped a united and independent Italy would live up to the highest ideals of the Risorgimento. The journalist Ferdinando Petruccelli della Gattina described him as being 'born a political malefactor in the way others are born poets or thieves'.[5] But it can be argued that even today modern Italian politics owe as much to the spirit of Depretis as they do to that of Garibaldi.

Most democratic constitutions offer scope for lawmakers to switch their allegiances once they are elected. But few, if any, developed countries see quite as many politicians do so as in Italy. In the whole of the British parliament from 2005 to 2010, for example, only one MP 'crossed the floor of the House' in the sense of leaving one party to join another. Ten more 'resigned the whip' to become independents, mostly to pre-empt expulsion from their party after becoming involved in some kind of scandal. But by the end of Italy's 2008–12 legislature, well over a hundred of the 630 deputies were in a parliamentary group different from the one to which they had belonged at the outset. About half were independents. The rest had joined other parties.

Ideological ambiguity has been a hallmark of Italian politics since the foundation of the Republic in 1946. The Vatican-backed Christian Democrat Party (DC), which dominated politics for much of the Cold War period, was almost impossible to categorize as right- or left-wing. It is often described as having straddled the centre, but even that is not really correct. In line with Catholic doctrine, it was, socially, extremely conservative – as reactionary, in many respects, as Spain's Francoists or the followers of Salazar in Portugal. Yet there was a Christian Democrat trade union federation and in the early days of the DC some members of the party, men such as Giuseppe Dossetti, were genuine radicals.

If the distinguishing characteristic of the Christian Democrats was their ideological ambivalence, then that of Italy's Communists was their moderation. Their greatest theoretician, Antonio Gramsci, argued as early as the 1930s for a protracted 'war of position', a painstaking erosion of the cultural hegemony of the bourgeoisie, which may have been conceived as a prelude to revolution, but which gradually turned into a substitute for it. After the Second World War, Gramsci's successor, Palmiro Togliatti, backed a policy of co-operating with the Christian Democrats and trying to recruit a broad range of people from all levels of society, particularly small businesspeople. After Khrushchev denounced Stalin in 1956, Togliatti was the first of the Western communist leaders to distance himself from Moscow, introducing the concept of 'polycentrism', according to which communism had many points of reference, not just the Kremlin.

By 1969 the PCI was openly at loggerheads with the Soviet Union. Four years later, its new secretary, a Sardinian aristocrat, Enrico Berlinguer, proposed a three-way alliance or 'historic compromise' between the Communists, Socialists and Christian Democrats as a bulwark against the kind of far-right backlash that had just toppled Salvador Allende in Chile. Berlinguer was also a leading proponent of democratic and implicitly non-revolutionary 'Eurocommunism', which drew on Gramsci's writings for much of its theoretical framework.

Ambiguity and moderation may be of the essence in Italian politics, but the opposite usually seems to be true. Party leaders and government ministers hurl abuse at one another, deliver ultimatums and issue threats, so that for much of the time the country appears to be on the verge of crisis, if not collapse. But, beneath the turbulent surface, there is usually space for an accommodation to be reached and good sense to prevail. Issues remain arguable, and thus negotiable. The same is true of Italian life in general. Imprecision is, on the whole, highly prized. Definition and categorization are, by contrast, suspect. For things to remain flexible, they need to be complicated or vague, and preferably both. Which is why the need was felt for one of the strangest job titles ever conferred on a politician.

4.

A Hall of Mirrors

Little girl on beach: 'What's the time?'
Man in deckchair: 'Who knows? The true truth will never be known.'

— Altan cartoon published in *L'Espresso*, 15 July 2004

Roberto Calderoli is one of the more outrageous figures to have strutted across the Italian political stage in recent decades. He once said that he had kept a tiger in his house, but had to get rid of it after it ate a dog. A senior member of the Northern League, he is noted, among other things, for having walked a pig across land designated for the construction of a mosque and having described the losing French team in the 2006 soccer World Cup final as made up of 'Negroes,* Muslims and Communists'. Earlier that same year, Calderoli lost his job as a minister in Silvio Berlusconi's government. It was at a time of violent protests in the Muslim world over the publication in a Danish newspaper of cartoons of the prophet Mohammed. During a television interview, Calderoli unbuttoned his shirt to show that he had one of the caricatures printed on a T-shirt underneath. Three days later and with great reluctance, Calderoli resigned from the Cabinet.

He was back as a member of Berlusconi's next government, occupying a post that, as far as I am aware, has never existed in any

---

* The word he used was *negri*, which, unlike *neri* ('blacks'), nowadays has clearly pejorative overtones.

other administration anywhere else in the world. Calderoli was made Minister for Simplification. The Cabinet post he occupied disappeared in the next Cabinet, led by Mario Monti, but the simplification portfolio remained and was entrusted to a junior minister. It should be made clear that the simplification in question was legislative in the case of Calderoli and bureaucratic in the case of his successor. But their appointments underlined an important point about Italy, which is that all sorts of things are immensely complicated.

'The Italian legislative corpus,' remarked the authors of a recent study,[1] 'has long represented a labyrinth even for the shrewdest legal practitioner because of its complexity and its sheer volume.' No one knows for certain how many laws there are. In a typical act of showmanship, Calderoli arranged in 2010 for a bonfire on which he claimed to burn 375,000 laws and other regulations that had been nullified by his department. The oldest was from 1864. Estimates of the number of statute laws in force at the time of Calderoli's appointment varied widely, from around 13,000 up to 160,000, excluding those passed by regional and provincial legislatures. The government declared that, as a result of his ministry's work, the tally had been reduced to around ten thousand. But that was still almost twice as high as in Germany and three times as high as in Britain.

If the law in Italy is complex, then the way in which it is enforced and implemented is, if anything, even more so. For a start, there are five national police forces. Apart from the Polizia di Stato, there are the semi-militarized Carabinieri and Guardia di Finanza (a revenue guard charged with curbing tax evasion, detecting money laundering and patrolling Italy's territorial waters). Then there is the Polizia Penitenziaria, whose officers guard the prisons and transport prisoners, and finally the Corpo Forestale dello Stato, responsible for patrolling Italy's forests and national parks. In addition, there is a myriad of provincial and municipal police forces. Altogether, Italy has more law-enforcement officers than any other country in the

European Union.* The scope for overlap, rivalry and confusion is considerable.

The same is true, and to a far greater extent, of the bureaucracy. According to a study made by the farmers' union, the Confederazione Italiana Agricoltori, paperwork and time-costly formalities rob the average Italian of about twenty days a year. It used to be the case, for example, that Italians had to renew their passports annually. Even now, they have to buy a stamp once a year to ensure the document remains valid.

Excessive bureaucracy is often a response to corruption, the idea being that it inhibits bribery and the trading of favours. That has long been given as a reason for India's legendary red tape, and is doubtless one of the explanations for Italy's. But whatever the original intent, the effect is often to facilitate corruption rather than limit it: faced with administrative obstruction, the exasperated victim reaches into his or her pocket in an attempt to persuade the official in question to take a short cut. Officials, of course, know that full well, and will sometimes deliberately make things more difficult in the hope of extracting a sweetener.

Basilicata's Tempa Rossa oilfield was discovered in 1989. But it was not until twenty-three years later that the then government gave the thumbs-up for petroleum to be extracted, by which time the consortium involved had been required to assemble around four hundred official authorizations. Since there are four layers of government in Italy – national, regional, provincial and municipal – any relatively large project will almost certainly require approval at more than one level and, in many cases, at all four. And since it is highly unlikely that the town council, the provincial authority, the

---

* The comparison is somewhat unfair, however, since many of Italy's law-enforcement officers fulfil duties which elsewhere fall outside the scope of police work. This is certainly true of the Carabinieri, which is a branch of the armed forces and takes part in overseas peacekeeping missions; the members of the Guardia di Finanza, who act as tax inspectors, customs officers and border guards; and the Polizia Penitenziaria.

regional executive and the central government will all be of the same political orientation, an investment that is welcomed at one level may well run into hostility at another. Sometimes, it proves impossible to reach the necessary consensus even when the enterprise has the full backing of the government in Rome. In 2012 the multinational gas producer BG gave up on plans to build a giant liquefied natural gas terminal near the port of Brindisi after eleven years of wrestling with the various layers of authority. By then, it had spent some €250 million.

The diffusion of power in Italy has deep historical roots. Many of the territories that are regions today were once nations in their own right. And, in many towns and cities, particularly in the centre and north of the country, there is a folk memory of the days when the citizens were absolute masters of their affairs. Their elected representatives are usually fiercely resistant to any kind of interference by a higher authority. As the saying has it, *Ogni paese è una repubblica* ('Every village is a republic'). But the complexity of Italy's administrative and governmental arrangements often seems to reflect something else – a downright mistrust of simplicity.

Tourists who come to Rome are often struck by the fact that many of the capital's pedestrian crossings have been left without repainting for so long that it is hard to know whether they are still in existence, legally or otherwise. For a long time I thought it was because of a lack of sufficient funds. But then my wife and I went to live in a flat overlooking just such an ill-defined semi-crossing. Because it was so difficult for motorists to see, especially when it grew dark, it was notorious for accidents. After an entire family was mown down there one night, action was finally taken. A team of workmen arrived and painted blindingly white stripes at intervals across the road. From being the merest hint of a pedestrian crossing, it suddenly became the clearest in that part of Rome. But, it would seem, it was just too strident – too adamant – for someone in authority. A few weeks later, another team of workmen turned up and painted a thin layer of some murky substance over the stripes so that they became a comfortingly dim off-white.

A crossing that stated incontrovertibly – in black and white, no less – that pedestrians had an unconditional right to go, at that point, from one side of the road to the other would have come perilously close to affirming an objective truth, and the notion of objective truth is something that in Italy often causes unease.

Perhaps Roman Catholic doctrine has something to do with it. All Christians are taught that the truth is something only God knows, and indeed embodies.[2] But the concept is particularly borne in on Catholics by the sacrament of confession. Contrary to what many non-Catholics – and even some Catholics – believe, the priest in the confessional does not forgive sins. What he gives is a sort of provisional absolution on the basis of the penitent's apparent repentance. But whether the sins have really been wiped from the celestial slate depends on the sincerity of the repentance, which only God can know. That said, subjective truth is hardly Catholic doctrine. Indeed, Pope Benedict XVI singled out 'moral relativism' – the idea that there are no ethical absolutes or certainties – as a philosophical aberration that represented a grave threat to Christianity.

Whatever the reason, a lack of belief in ascertainable truth, and even in incontrovertible facts, can be detected in many aspects of Italian society from the media to the legal system and from politics to macro-economics. In all sorts of areas, issues remain stubbornly disputable, no matter how much hard fact is thrown at them.

Take, for example, Project MOSE,* the plan for constructing movable barriers at the mouth of the Venice lagoon so as to protect it from flooding. The plan was first mooted in the 1970s. Faced with interminable wrangling between supporters and opponents of the scheme, the non-governmental organization Venice in Peril finally decided to establish the balance of scientific opinion. In 2003 it organized a conference in Cambridge that brought together more

---

* Ostensibly, this is an acronym: MOdulo Sperimentale Elettromeccanico. But *Mosè* is the Italian version of Moses and the name of the project also alludes to the parting of the Red Sea.

than 130 of the world's most distinguished experts on civil engineering, marine ecology and lagoon hydrology. Their conclusion was clear: a barrier would not, of itself, solve Venice's problems, but it would make a valuable contribution in the short term while longer-term solutions were found.

If the good souls behind Venice in Peril thought their conference would put an end to debate in Italy itself, they were greatly mistaken. For the opponents of the scheme, which was eventually begun that year, it was as if the engineers, scientists and environmental experts who gathered in Cambridge had never written or delivered their papers. After work began on the MOSE Project, I found myself travelling in from Venice airport one day on a water taxi with a very senior Italian official. The subject of the barriers came up and I remarked that the start of work was good for the city. A shadow passed over the face of my travelling companion. He was clearly distressed by such professed certainty.

'Well,' he began, shifting uncomfortably, 'my friends in Venice are not so sure . . .'

The official was – I happen to know – fully aware of the conclusions of the Cambridge conference. Yet here he was giving equal weight to the opinions of the world's leading experts on the one hand and his friends in Venice on the other.

Scepticism about ever being able to reach firm conclusions is both reflected in, and encouraged by, the Italian language. The word *verità* means 'truth'. But it also means 'version'. If a dispute arises, there will be my *verità*, your *verità* and doubtless the various *verità* of others. Italian newspapers are full of headlines such as 'The Portofino Slaying – The Countess and The Latest Truth'.

The implicit – if not explicit – acknowledgement of more than one truth gives rise to some of the distinctive characteristics of Italian journalism. Let me say straightaway that, like most correspondents in Italy, I have developed great respect for the acumen of my Italian counterparts: their energy, persistence and ability to identify in a trice the essence of a story are all admirable. But the conventions under which they operate do not make for the kind of clarity to which the media normally aspire. In the newspapers and on the websites of many countries, for example, good practice consists of beginning a news story with a crisp summary of the facts: 'The trial arising from last year's disaster at the Acme Italia plant heard the foreman had been left by his wife on the night before.' Some Italian newspapers, and news websites, notably the financial newspaper *Il Sole-24 Ore*, do begin their stories that way. But most of the national dailies still tend to use what, in the trade, is known as a 'dropped intro'.

An Italian report of the same court hearing might begin, for example, with the fly that buzzed persistently around the head of the presiding judge – a metaphor for the nagging doubts surrounding the case that will then be wound skilfully through the rest of the story. Or it might open with a reconstruction of events that owes at least as much to the assumptions of the reporter as to established fact: 'As he stepped from the bus outside the Acme Italia plant on that fateful Wednesday, Luigi Rossini's mind was not on the problems that had dogged his production line for months, but on a woman. And a very special woman. His wife.' The impression left with the reader is that he or she has been told a story. Usually, it is a well-written and gripping or entertaining story, but a story all the same.

Much the same approach can be discerned in reluctance to provide readers with the facts they need to make a judgement on what is said by public figures. Italian politicians, like politicians the world over, often talk self-interested nonsense. In many other places, it is seen as part of the reporter's job to check what politicians confidently declare against published records and statistics. If, as happened in Italy not long ago, the prime minister says that his country's schools are the best funded in Europe, it is expected that the journalist reporting those words will make a check and perhaps insert a paragraph to the effect that, according to the European Union's statistics, school funding in Italy is only slightly better than average. Some Italian reporters do exactly that. But it is not the norm. It would be considered a bit disrespectful. The prime minister, like everybody else, should be allowed his *verità*. That is not to say that his political opponents will not contest his assertions, and that their *verità* will not then be conscientiously reported in the media. But it is left to the reader to decide which side is right.

It could be argued that, in this respect, Italian journalists have been years ahead of the revolution in media practice brought about by the Internet. Italian newspaper journalists have not assumed the role of information arbiters – 'gatekeepers', in the jargon – to the same extent as their counterparts in much of the rest of the world. But the problem with this approach is that it allows politicians and others – particularly vested-interest groups – to get away with the unchallenged propagation of falsehoods, both blatant and subtle.

A good example of the latter arose in the 1990s with the 'expulsion' of clandestine immigrants. As Africans, Asians and Latin Americans began streaming into southern Europe, successive Italian governments reacted to public unease with statistics to show that in the last month – or year, or whatever – so many thousand irregular immigrants had been caught and expelled. As the years went past, and the number of black and brown faces on the buses and in the Metro increased almost by the day, people began to suspect they were not being told the whole story. Yet it was only towards the end of the decade that it was explained to the public through the media what precisely had been meant by 'expelled'. Once identified, unauthorized immigrants were served with an expulsion order. Then they were let go. It meant that, if they were caught again, they could face jail. But otherwise they could either wait around for an immigration amnesty of the sort that has been granted several times in Italy, or move on to another EU country, where their status would be more ambiguous.

The underlying reality was that Italian politicians, like their peers in the rest of Europe, realized their country needed immigrants. Privately, they would admit it. Because of Italy's ultra-low birth rate,* it had to take in people from outside if its economy was to grow and its welfare state – and, in particular, its pension

* See below, page 152.

system – was to remain sustainable. But Italian politicians also knew that immigration, and particularly clandestine immigration, was a sensitive issue with the electorate. Paper 'expulsions' offered a delightful way out. As Romano Prodi once said, with only a touch of exaggeration, 'In the Italian political debate, it is hard to distinguish the real problem, which is never talked about, from the fictitious problem, which is fought over ferociously.'*

In 2011, as Italy drifted towards near-catastrophe in the eurozone debt crisis of that year, the former editor of *The Economist*, Bill Emmott, wrote an article for *La Stampa* marvelling at the number of myths circulating in discussions about the economy: an area where, as he said, you might have thought it was easy to check how things really were. It was not just politicians who were propagating these myths – most of them comforting – but prominent financiers, business representatives and government officials. It was said with confidence, for example, that Italy was the EU's second-biggest exporter (when, in fact, it had dropped to fifth place); that the Italians were still Europe's biggest savers (when, in fact, they had fallen behind the Germans and the French) and – most perniciously – that negative growth in the south was cancelling out positive growth in the rest of the country. The reality was that the Mezzogiorno's overall performance in the previous ten years had been better than that of the centre and the north.

An even more dangerous fairy tale that went unchallenged at this time was that Italy's huge debts, which were already heading for 120 per cent of its GDP, were of no one's concern but the Italians'. This was supposedly because nationals held all but a very small proportion of its sovereign bonds, its government's IOUs. This was just not true. In fact, about half of Italy's public debt at that time was owed to foreigners. The potential for its shaky public finances to cause a Europe-wide, if not worldwide, economic crisis was considerable. Yet Italians were rarely told that.

* It should be noted that Prodi's own government did no more than others to clear up the confusion over supposed expulsions.

Anyone who has sat through a trial in Italy will know that the same principle of polite non-contradiction can hold good in court, too. One of the most sensational cases in Italy's legal history was the one in which an American student, Amanda Knox, and her Italian boyfriend, Raffaele Sollecito, were accused of murdering Knox's British flatmate, Meredith Kercher. Both were given hefty prison sentences at a trial in which the prosecution claimed that the victim had been killed in a bizarre sex game that turned brutally and tragically violent. But between the trial and the appeal, court-appointed experts poured scorn on the forensic evidence submitted by the prosecution so, by the time the case returned to court, not only were the two young appellants on trial but also Italy's methods of investigating and prosecuting serious crime.

Such was the publicity given to the case that, when counsel were finally ready to sum up, it was no exaggeration to say that the eyes of the world were on the frescoed underground courtroom in Perugia where the appeal was being heard. So it was all the more surprising that, as he listened to their final pleas, the judge made no move to interrupt counsel, who repeated as fact claims that had been utterly discredited in earlier hearings. Each of the lawyers had his or her *verità*. It was only fair that they should be allowed to air it. How on earth the lay judges who sat alongside the professional judges were expected to get at the truth is anybody's guess. But then, when the case was over, the presiding judge gave an interview in which he appeared to say that the task was, anyhow, impossible.

'Our acquittal is the result of the truth that was created in the trial,' he said. 'The real truth will remain unresolved, and may even be different.' Lewis Carroll could not have put it better.*

---

* In March 2013 the Court of Cassation, Italy's supreme court, upheld an appeal by the prosecution, quashed the acquittals of both defendants and ordered their appeals to be reheard in Florence. In January 2014 Knox and Sollecito were again found guilty of murdering Kercher. Sollecito's 25-year sentence was reinstated. Knox's sentence, of twenty-six years, was increased to twenty-eight years and six

I have sometimes reflected that the last part of that comment – 'The real truth will remain unresolved, and may even be different' – deserves to be carved in marble on a suitable monument that could then be erected in the centre of Rome. Time and again, important turning points in Italy's modern history have been wrapped in a dense fog of discrepancy and contradiction as the various players aired their particular *verità*. You might start with the fate of its Fascist dictator, Benito Mussolini.

On the morning of 27 April 1945, at Dongo on the banks of Lake Como, a partisan commissar, Urbano Lazzaro, was checking lorries carrying German troops out of Italy when he discovered Mussolini in the back of one of them. The dictator was wearing glasses, wrapped in a greatcoat and had a helmet pulled down over his face. Two days later, as dawn broke over Milan, early-morning strollers were confronted with a gruesome sight in Piazzale Loreto. Hanging upside down from meat hooks attached to the roof of a petrol station were the bodies of the dictator, his mistress, Clara Petacci, and three senior Fascist officials. But what exactly happened in the intervening forty-eight hours will probably never be known.

The official version is that the decision to execute Mussolini was taken at a meeting of partisan leaders and that the job of killing him was given to Walter Audisio, a communist commander whose *nom de guerre* was Colonnello Valerio. But, in a book he wrote in 1962, Lazzaro said the man he saw and who was identified as Colonnello Valerio was not Audisio but Luigi Longo, a very senior Communist official who, two years later, would become the leader of the Italian Communist Party. The implication was that Longo's involvement had been hushed up so as to wipe the blood from the hands of a man destined for the top. Meanwhile, Audisio, who originally said Lazzaro had been present at the execution, named a different person in his memoirs, published thirty years later.

Officially, Mussolini and Petacci died at the gates of a villa

---

months. Lawyers for both defendants said they would lodge a fresh appeal with the Court of Cassation.

overlooking Lake Como on the afternoon of the day after they were caught. But in 1995 Lazzaro complicated matters further by saying they had been killed earlier, after Petacci tried to grab a gun from one of the partisans who was escorting them to Milan for what was intended to be a public execution.

At about the same time, yet another version began to emerge. It came from a retired Fiat executive, Bruno Lonati, who had been a communist partisan. Lonati said *he* had killed Mussolini on the orders of a British secret agent and that the execution took place even earlier in the day, at 11 a.m. In 2005 the state-owned RAI television network broadcast a documentary containing new evidence in support of Lonati's version. According to this, the British agent's mission was to ensure Mussolini was killed and recover compromising letters written to him by Winston Churchill. The wartime British prime minister was claimed to have secretly considered with Mussolini the possibility of a separate peace – a clear breach of his agreement with the US President, Franklin Roosevelt, that they would not cease hostilities until they secured the unconditional surrender of each of the Axis powers.

As the bodies of Italy's dictator and his lover were being stoned by the mob in Piazzale Loreto, the first moves were being made in what would later come to be known as the Cold War. A few days earlier, Russian troops had fought their way into Berlin and on 2 May raised the red flag over the Reichstag. The division of Europe that followed was to provide fertile ground in Italy for the nurturing of mysteries. And this was particularly true of the years following the student revolts of 1968, when the spirit of revolution swept through Europe and fears grew in Washington and elsewhere that Italy risked falling into the hands of Marxists.

On 12 December 1969 a bomb went off in Milan a few hundred metres from the Duomo, in Piazza Fontana. Sixteen people were killed. To this day, nobody can say for certain who planted it, or why. The police originally blamed the attack on anarchists, but the case against them soon fell apart and suspicion fell on neo-fascists, one of whom had close links with an officer in the Italian secret service who was also a convinced far-right-winger. The suspects were tried but cleared on appeal. Every year, to this day, friends and relatives of the victims gather on the anniversary of the bombing to call in vain for answers and justice.

The Piazza Fontana bombing was the first in a succession of unexplained terrorist attacks over the next fifteen years. Bombs exploded on trains, at an anti-fascist rally and – most lethally – in the railway station at Bologna in 1980. Altogether, more than 150 people died in what is thought to have been a campaign by neo-fascists and rogue members of the intelligence services. The supposed aim was to create an atmosphere of constant trepidation in which people would be more apt to back conservative, or perhaps even authoritarian, responses.

Bombs, though, were not the only causes of mysteries that have proved insoluble to police and judges alike. In 1974 a young magistrate uncovered evidence of an organization called the Rosa dei Venti ('the Weather Vane'). It was suspected of planning terrorist attacks and of having links to an organization set up by NATO. After a warrant was issued for the arrest of the head of Italy's secret service, the investigation was transferred to Rome, where it rapidly lost momentum.* The Rosa dei Venti has since been all but forgotten. What exactly it was and what exactly it did will probably never be known. Equally impenetrable mysteries were to develop out of the crash of an Italian airliner off the island of Ustica in 1980 and the attempted assassination of Pope John Paul II the following year.

For true connoisseurs of the unexplained, however, nothing is perhaps quite as tantalizingly baffling as the story of Pier Paolo Pasolini's last, unfinished book, *Petrolio*. After the poet, novelist and

---

* In the 1980s the Rome prosecutors' office, which oversees investigations in the capital, won the nickname of *il porto delle nebbie* ('the misty port') because of the way so many sensitive inquiries disappeared into a dense judicial fog, never to be heard of again. The phrase comes from the title of the Italian translation of Georges Simenon's 1932 novel *Le port des brumes* (in English, 'Death of a Harbour Master').

film director was murdered in 1975 – and the reasons for his death are themselves a mystery – it was found that Pasolini had left a manuscript running to more than five hundred pages. It was divided into numbered sections the author called *Appunti* ('Notes'). The central figure in *Petrolio* is a man (who turns into a woman halfway through) working for the state-owned oil and gas company, ENI. The book was not published until seventeen years after Pasolini's death, by which time one of the *Appunti* – number 21 – had disappeared. Pasolini's family has always denied it was stolen. But there has long been speculation that *Appunto 21* was made to vanish by someone because it contained embarrassing revelations about ENI and/or its executives. One theory is that the missing section contains the key to the death in 1962 of the corporation's swashbuckling boss, Enrico Mattei, who was killed in a plane crash. Another hypothesis is that the disappearance of *Appunto 21* has something to do with the fact that Pasolini owned one of the very few copies of a pamphlet that claimed to reveal secrets about a later ENI president, Eugenio Cefis. The pamphlet disappeared from circulation immediately following its publication in 1972.

In 2010, thirty-five years after Pasolini's death and eighteen years after the publication of his strange, unfinished work, another hugely controversial – and inscrutable – figure, Marcello Dell'Utri, dropped a bombshell at a press conference ahead of the opening of that year's antiquarian book fair in Rome. Dell'Utri, a bibliophile, advertising executive, politician and close associate of the former prime minister Silvio Berlusconi, said he had been offered part of the manuscript of *Petrolio*, prompting excited speculation that the typewritten sheets he had seen included the missing *Appunto 21*. Dell'Utri said he would put the pages on display during the book fair. But he never did. The only explanation he gave was that 'The person who promised them to me disappeared.'

That person – whoever he or she may have been – would have fitted nicely into the cast of a play by Luigi Pirandello. And the same could unquestionably be said of Marcello Dell'Utri, a Sicilian like

Pirandello, who in 1997 was put on trial accused of colluding with Cosa Nostra.*

Pirandello is a quintessentially Italian writer – perhaps *the* quintessentially Italian writer – forever gnawing away at the boundaries between reality and fiction, madness and sanity, past and present. The audience at a Pirandello play is repeatedly disconcerted and misled. Apparent certainties are undermined. Ostensible facts prove illusory. It is, in short, very much like the experience of living in Italy.

His *Sei personaggi in cerca d'autore* (*Six Characters in Search of an Author*) is probably Pirandello's best-known work. But another of his plays is even more relevant in this context: *Così è (se vi pare)*, variously translated into English as 'Right You Are (If You Think So)' and 'It *Is* So (If You Think So)'. It is a flat-out assault on the notion of objective truth. The play centres on the attempts, by a group of middle-class men and women in a provincial town, to find out about the newly arrived Ponza family, and particularly the elusive Signora Ponza.

They are presented with two accounts: Signor Ponza's mother-in-law, Signora Frola, claims that Signora Ponza is her daughter and that the possessive Signor Ponza is cruelly keeping her shut up at home. Signor Ponza, on the other hand, says his mother-in-law is mad. He says her daughter was his first wife, who died, and that Signora Frola continues to delude herself into thinking that she is the mother of his current, second wife. Signora Frola insists that, on the contrary, it is her son-in-law who is crazy. He then appears to confirm that view, but afterwards explains that he did so in order not to interfere with her fantasies. Finally, Signora Ponza is brought into the proceedings and declares that she is both Signora Frola's daughter *and* Signor Ponza's second wife.

But, she says, 'I am she whom you believe me to be.'

---

* The case dragged through the courts for seventeen years. In 2014 Dell'Utri was arrested in Lebanon ahead of a definitive ruling by the supreme court on his appeal against a seven-year jail sentence. His appeal was subsequently thrown out and a request was made by the Italian authorities for his extradition.

5.

Fantasia

Michele Misseri:* It was me. It was me. I killed Sarah with these hands. I ask God: why didn't he have me struck by lightning at that moment? Why did he let me kill that child?

Interviewer: Mr Misseri, how can you be believed?

MM: I have always told the truth. Right from the start, when they questioned me, I said it was me.

Interviewer: You have given seven versions in eight months.

– From a report in *La Repubblica*, 1 June 2011

It must have been such a powerful image – Italy's man of destiny, Benito Mussolini, riding at the head of a column of 300,000 armed Fascists, marching on Rome to enforce an ultimatum to the king. After he came to power, schoolchildren were taught that three thousand 'Fascist martyrs' had died in the insurrection and that, on their way to the capital, Mussolini and his Blackshirts crossed the River Rubicon, just like Julius Caesar when he, too, marched on Rome to seize power in 49BC.

But it was all nonsense. Only about thirty thousand men were involved. Many were unarmed. And the overwhelming majority arrived in Rome by train after their leader had been appointed prime minister within the terms of the constitution.

Mussolini was nothing if not an audacious illusionist. When Hitler visited him in 1938, he decided the Rome the Führer saw on his way in from the airport should be at least as impressive as the Berlin

---

* Uncle of murder victim Sarah Scazzi, who disappeared on 29 August 2010.

he himself had seen the year before. So houses along the route were spruced up and, in some cases, pulled down. That of itself was not particularly exceptional perhaps. But Mussolini went further – much further. He ordered artificial trees to be planted along the route and cardboard façades depicting lavish villas to be erected at intervals. The barrels of some of the artillery that Hitler was shown – at a suitable distance – were made of wood.

It is scarcely unusual for totalitarian regimes to deploy myth and falsehood. More surprising is the use in Italy of similar techniques by the democratic regime that followed the downfall of Mussolini's dictatorship. The official version, which held sway until the 1990s, was that the Republic was born of the resistance to German occupation and the Nazis' Fascist Italian allies. Every year on Liberation Day, 25 April, and on every other convenient occasion in fact, the Christian Democrats and their allies, who soon came to monopolize power in post-war Italy, paid homage to the Resistance and the heroic exploits of the partisans.

Heroic is by no means too lavish an adjective in this context. Historians reckon that of the 100,000 Italians who joined the Resistance 35,000 lost their lives – a shockingly high casualty rate, proportionally well in excess of that in most of the Allied units that took part in the Italian Campaign. The death rate among the partisans is a useful corrective to the view that Italians were reluctant to die for their country in the Second World War.

But the fact is that most of the partisans – about 70 per cent – were Communists. And the central aim of the Christian Democrats and the four parties with which they allied in various combinations for more than forty years was to ensure that the Communists never got into government. Some of the partisans, it is true, had been Christian Democrats, but most of them joined the Resistance only after Mussolini's fall from power.

The Cold War that followed the Second World War supplied plenty of opportunities for the exercise of what in Italian is called *fantasia* – a word whose meaning lies somewhere on the permeable frontier between 'imagination' and 'creativity'. But perhaps the most remarkable example was the Terzo Corpo designato d'Armata. This was an army unit, 300,000-strong, deployed in the 1950s on the flat Venetian hinterland as a bulwark against invasion by the Soviet Union and its allies. Except it never existed.

It was a giant bluff thought up by the Italian army as a substitute for having to recruit, train and arm hundreds of thousands of actual soldiers. A real lieutenant general was appointed to command it. He had genuine headquarters in Padua and a tiny staff whose job was to generate mountains of paperwork which, leaked to the appropriate intelligence services, sent a message to the Soviet Bloc countries that if they tried to fight their way into Western Europe through north-eastern Italy they would face stiff resistance. Troops – most of them imaginary – were recruited, promoted and eventually discharged from Terzo Corpo designato d'Armata. Fuel was stored and ammunition distributed. But mostly on paper.

The existence – or rather non-existence – of the Terzo Corpo designato d'Armata came to light only after the end of the Cold War, in 2009, when a newspaper reported on the problems it was still creating for the army. It had been disbanded in 1972, but the tons of paper it had generated could not be destroyed. In Italy, officially secret documents can be pulped only once they have been declassified – and they can be declassified only by the department or unit that created them. In this case, the unit no longer existed. And, in effect, never had.

Historically, *fantasia* has been the Italians' most valuable resource. It enabled them to outwit foreign occupiers, invaders and other meddlers. It helped them create their unrivalled cultural heritage, and that in turn sometimes made the soldiers who used Italy as a battleground more reluctant than they might otherwise have been to shell and bomb Italian cities.* *Fantasia* has been a source of creativity from engineering to fashion. And it can be glimpsed in other,

---

* Most recently, in the Second World War, the retreating German army renounced military action to defend first Rome and then Florence. Orvieto was saved by a pact between the local British and German commanders.

more trivial aspects of Italian life. Elsewhere, for example, politicians give their parties descriptive but dull titles such as the New Right or the Socialist Workers' Party. But in Italy *fantasia* has been brought to bear. Berlusconi began the trend by using a football chant, '*Forza Italia!*', as the name of the movement with which he launched himself into parliament in 1994. Then his rival Romano Prodi hit back by founding an alliance he dubbed the Ulivo ('Olive Tree'), one of the components of which was the Margherita (or Daisy) Party. Since then, we have seen the emergence of a Five Star Movement. In much the same way, crass non-Italians give current affairs shows on television names such as *Focus* or *Panorama* or *The World Today*. On Italian channels at the time of writing there is *Porta a Porta* (*Door to Door*), *Ballarò*, which is the name of a Palermo street market, and *Le invasioni barbariche* (*The Barbarian Invasions*).

But *fantasia* is a two-edged sword. It can be used positively or negatively. And it is also at the root of a lot of the deception that bedevils Italian life. It is no coincidence that this should be the central theme of the best-loved book in the Italian language. *Pinocchio* was written in 1883 as a tale for children, warning of the perils of lying. The puppet whose nose grew whenever he told a fib was swiftly recognized as a character of universal significance. And nowhere does he resonate more than in his native Italy. Just as Don Quixote, with his preposterous idealism and touchy pride, immediately struck a chord with the Spanish, so Pinocchio speaks to Italians in a very special way as a caricature of many of their national virtues and vices. He is bright (he learns to walk almost instantly), easily distracted and fundamentally kind-hearted. But he also combines, and to an exaggerated extent, the characteristics of both the *furbo* and the *fesso*. He is simultaneously mendacious and gullible. Whenever he is in a fix, he resorts to a convenient lie. But he is not quite as clever as he thinks. And his eagerness to believe that he can become rich without effort makes him easy prey for the Fox and the Cat, genuine professionals in the business of deception.

Carlo Collodi,* the author of *Pinocchio*, would no doubt be delighted to know how popular his character remains well over a century after he first appeared in print. But he might be dismayed to know that the spirit of Pinocchio is still very much alive in his native Italy. Cheating in school and university exams, for example, does not attract anything like the same degree of condemnation that it does in most other societies. It is euphemistically described as *copiare*, which also means 'to copy'. To cheat in other contexts is *barare*, *truffare* or *imbrogliare*.

Luca Cordero di Montezemolo is a respected industrialist. He has been chairman of Fiat and Ferrari. For a time he was the president of the bosses' federation, Confindustria. Yet he proudly revealed during an encounter with students at the business-oriented Luiss University that 'At school, I was the world champion at *copiatura*.'[1] Silvio Berlusconi made his earliest profits by writing essays for other students to hand in as their work.

You do not need to look far in the Italian press to find articles excusing – or even praising – cheating in exams. This, for example, from a columnist in *Il Giornale*: 'Trying to cheat means trying to deceive, and it is obvious that it is reproachable. But frankly I do not see in it the malicious intent to perpetrate a serious deception. It has always been done. It is done. It will continue to be done. It is a sign of very human weakness: you are insecure; you happen to be unprepared; a little bit of help, and perhaps the difficulties can be resolved and the test passed.'

The devices used by Italian school and university students to give themselves what is, when all is said and done, an unfair advantage, constitute a testament to their ingenuity for which you cannot help but have a sneaking admiration. In lots of countries, you could find an equivalent of the *bigliettini*, tiny crib sheets that are hidden about the examinee's person. But in Italy there is an item of clothing specially made for carrying them. It is called a *cartucciera*: a cotton

* Collodi was a pen name. He was born Carlo Lorenzini.

garment resembling a cartridge belt (after which it is named), worn around the waist under normal clothing. Crib sheets on every subject likely to arise in the exam can be put in its pockets and discreetly extracted according to need.

With the arrival of the Internet, things have become even more sophisticated. Websites have been set up offering pens, watches and even sweatshirts with hidden compartments for *bigliettini*. Mobile telephones have also opened up new possibilities for the inventive and unscrupulous, as have smartphones. The educational authorities swiftly banned both, but the prohibition can be circumvented: the trick is to arrive with two and hand in one.

By far the biggest challenge to the validity of examinations created by digital technology comes from hacking. In the old days, the questions were sent to schools around Italy by post and kept by the head teacher until the day of the exam. In theory, they could be stolen, although they seldom were. Even if that happened, though, the information contained in the letter from the ministry in Rome was only of use to an individual student, or at most to his or her schoolmates. Once they began to be stored and transmitted electronically, however, they could be accessed by a determined teenage hacker and distributed nationally.

The most important exam in the life of Italian pupils is the dreaded *maturità*, which they take at the end of their school careers and which decides whether they can apply for university. For several years in a row, accurate reports of the subjects to be covered were put up on the Internet before the three-day written exam. By 2012 the education ministry in Rome was deploying counter-measures that the then minister himself compared to those of the CIA. The questions were drawn up in an underground bunker at the education ministry in Rome, protected by closed-circuit television and officers of the Carabinieri. Only eight people were given access. From there, the questions were sent to secondary schools around Italy in a so-called 'digital envelope' that could be opened only by means of a 25-character alphanumeric password divided into two sections. The first was sent out several days before the *maturità*, and the second half an hour before the start of each exam. Any school that found itself disconnected from the Internet could get the password from the first television channel of Italy's state broadcaster, RAI, which transmitted it as a subtitle to its programmes from 8.30 a.m. onwards. Failing that, the principal of a school where even the electricity had been cut off could call for a paper version. These were kept in a safe in the office of the prefect, the provincial representative of the interior ministry, who would order it to be rushed to the school in a high-powered Carabinieri patrol car.

According to a book on the subject, *Ragazzi, si copia* – and the fact that an author could find enough material on the subject to fill a book itself speaks volumes – a survey conducted among ten–thirteen-year-olds found that only 26 per cent claimed never to have cheated. The same book added a characteristic justification: 'cheating means reprocessing. I would add that, to cheat, you need to know'. What is striking about that comment, though, is that it came not from a student but from the headmaster of a school in Milan. Small wonder that when an examination was held a few years ago in Turin for aspiring school principals, 9 out of the 460 candidates were disqualified after it was discovered that they had brought in dictionaries stuffed with *bigliettini*.

In parts of Italy, there are people who, for a relatively modest consideration, will go into court to perjure themselves on your behalf. If, for example, you have caused an accident by straying on to the wrong side of the road, he or she can be counted on to swear blind that you were on the right side. In 2010 investigators discovered a veritable perjury exchange in Naples. It centred on the court of the Justices of the Peace and involved more than a hundred witnesses-for-hire whose word could be bought for between €25 and €100. In a separate investigation in Rome, police listened in on two private detectives who were bringing an expert fibber to the capital for €1,000 with all expenses paid.

Not that perjury is always committed for money. To a striking extent, trials in Italy – and particularly high-profile ones – can become a morass of conflicting evidence. The wife who originally told police she was in the kitchen when she heard screams now says she wasn't in the house at all, while a friend has come forward to say she saw her in the supermarket. Meanwhile, Uncle Rosario, who had testified that he was away in the regional capital that day, has been found never to have left his home town, and his wife, who heard the tell-tale footsteps on the gravel path, has changed her story and now says there was only one person running away from the scene of the crime, and not two.

'They take us for idiots,' said a judge in Aosta after just such a case had passed through his court. 'It's incredible how easily they lie in front of a judge . . . without the least attention paid to the plausibility of their stories.' He estimated that the number of witnesses brought before him who told the truth was between 20 and 30 per cent. 'Lying amuses and pleases,' he said. 'It does not bring social contempt.'

The problem of getting at the truth is also perhaps one reason for the prevalence of wiretapping in Italy. According to a study published by the Max Planck Institute in 2003, the number of warrants issued annually in Italy – 76 per 100,000 of the population – was higher than in any of the other countries surveyed. The corresponding figure was 15 per 100,000 in Germany, 5 in France, 6 in England and Wales and only 0.5 in the United States.[2]*

Among the few foreign firms to have successfully penetrated the Italian market is the UK-based mobile telephone operator Vodafone, which acquired a controlling stake in an Italian firm, Omnitel, in 2000. It has since taken a one third share of the market. There have been various reasons for its success. Its earliest advertising campaign, built around a distinctive-looking model and actor, the part-Maori, Australian-born Megan Gale, made a huge impact. Since then, Vodafone has deployed a string of catchy slogans,

---

* It could be argued, however, that the figures for Britain and the US are no longer an accurate reflection of the extent of official snooping. As the former National Security Agency contractor Edward Snowden has since revealed, Britons and Americans are under close surveillance through other means.

shrewdly aimed at Italian sensibilities, to keep itself in the public eye. But I suspect that some modest part of its success is due to its having offered a unique service. It is known as Alter Ego and enables customers to have two numbers on the same SIM card. As the company explains, 'you can pass from one to the other simply and quickly by using the menu [and] choosing to be contactable only on the active number or both'. Perfect for cheating husbands or wives, and mighty useful for anyone, in fact, who wants to make him- or herself temporarily unavailable. Vodafone confirmed that Alter Ego was available only in Italy. It was, said a spokesman, a 'local market initiative'.

It is tempting to speculate that the Italians' abiding fascination with illusion also helps to explain the unusually prominent role in their culture of masks. Noble families in ancient Rome kept death masks of their ancestors. Masks were an integral part of the Commedia dell'Arte, which emerged in Venice during the sixteenth century. And it was in Venice, too, that the masked ball developed at about the same time.

The masks used in a masked ball are used to withhold identity, by placing an assumed face in front of the true one. This is close to what Jung had in mind when he adopted as his term for the apparent self the Latin word for 'mask', *persona*. But masks can be used for more than one purpose. In the Commedia dell'Arte, they serve not to distract from reality but to heighten it by presenting the audience with a caricatured representation of the character of the wearer. In ancient Rome, they were intended to mirror reality: death masks were donned by professional mourners at the funerals of family members.

Illusion and falsehood can certainly be used to deceive. But they can also be used to communicate. Many of the events in Shakespeare's *Othello* never actually happened. Michelangelo's *David* is not a real man, any more than Botticelli's *Venus* is a real woman. But no one would think of calling Shakespeare a liar or accuse Michelangelo and Botticelli of deception. Their creations transcend the issue of authenticity because they serve to communicate ideas and represent ideals. And nowhere is this power of fabrication to send messages grasped more instinctively or used more widely than in Italy.

This is partly because Italians, like other southern Europeans, are naturally theatrical. There are exceptions, of course. I have known plenty of Italians who are less animated than the majority of Swedes. But you only have to spend time in Italy, and particularly in bars and restaurants, to see that people interact with one another using facial expressions and hand movements that are, in general, more animated and expressive – more dramatic, in a word – than is the case in the more temperate northern Europe.

This often complicates relations between Italians and foreigners in their country. One of the other foreign correspondents in Rome when I first worked there had spent much of his professional life in the Far East and was convinced that the relationship of Italians to northern Europeans and North Americans was a bit like that of Europeans and Americans to Asians.

'People in much of South-East and East Asia show their emotions in ways that are barely discernible to us, so we tend either to think that they lack feelings or dismiss the issue altogether by labelling them as "inscrutable",' he once said. 'I think a lot of Italians regard us in the same way. Our expressions of surprise or disappointment or annoyance or whatever are so much less evident than theirs we just go "under their radar".'

It is certainly more difficult to show Italians that you are angry. So you gradually develop an ability to lose your temper at will. As you turn up the volume and your physical gestures become increasingly expansive, you can sometimes see on the faces of the people you are dealing with an expression of dawning realization mingled with almost pleasurable surprise: all of a sudden, and in a way that has nothing to do with philology or semantics, you are speaking their language.

If Pirandello is the archetypal Italian writer, then opera – packed with searing emotion expressed without reserve – is the quintessential Italian art form. Its origins in the late sixteenth century are exclusively Italian. It grew out of the discussions and experiments of the Camerata, a group of Florentine writers, musicians and intellectuals whose main aim was to revive the blend of words and music that was known to have existed in classical Greek drama.* An Italian, Jacopo Peri, composed the earliest recorded opera, *Dafne*, which was first performed in 1598, and it was in an Italian city, Venice, that the first public opera house, the Teatro San Cassiano, was opened in 1637.

In the nineteenth century, moreover, opera became entangled with the concept of Italian nationhood (as it did, with rather more questionable effects, in Germany with Wagner). This was largely because of Giuseppe Verdi.† His *Nabucco* deals with the Jews' Babylonian captivity. It includes the stirring 'Chorus of the Hebrew Slaves', often known by its opening words as *Va Pensiero*, in which the exiles sing of their longing for their homeland 'so beautiful and lost'. In recent years scholars have questioned whether Verdi intended *Nabucco* to carry a political message. But there is no doubt that the composer was an ardent supporter of the nationalist cause or that *Va Pensiero* came to be seen in retrospect as a metaphor for the subjugation of the Italians by their foreign masters. The subject matter of some of his later operas, such as *La Battaglia di Legnano*, was overtly nationalist, and in 1861 Verdi became a member of Italy's first parliament.

It can often seem as if there is still a close link between Italian politics and opera, or at least operatics. You might expect, for example, that of all the parties in Italy the Northern League (which, by the way, has taken *Va Pensiero* as its own) should be the most

---

* One of the Camerata's most influential members was Galileo Galilei's father, Vincenzo Galilei, who proposed the decisive leap from polyphony to monody in the accompanying music.

† Verdi's own surname was coincidentally symbolic. It could be understood as a coded reference to the king under whom Italy would eventually unite: an acronym of Vittorio Emanuele, Re d'Italia. So when audiences joined in chanting '*Viva Verdi*' they could feel they were doing more than just praising the composer.

down-to-earth. Its founder, Umberto Bossi, claimed to speak for the hardy, less demonstrative folk of the Po Valley – the descendants not of florid Latins but supposedly of the Gauls, Goths and Lombards who settled in the north of Italy over the centuries. These are the people who like to think of themselves as living in *l'Italia che lavora* ('the Italy that works'). Bossi termed northern Italy Padania and at different times called for it to have autonomy or independence.

Back in the mid-1990s he decided he needed to realign his move-ment by making it more separatist in orientation. Anywhere but Italy, a party leader in the same situation would summon an extra-ordinary congress, make a rousing speech in favour of independence and then set up working groups and policy committees to recast the party's programme. Bossi opted instead for what one newspaper columnist at the time called 'the most colossal political farce ever seen in Europe'.

The play-acting began one Sunday in 1996 when the League leader went with his most senior officials to the spring that gives birth to the Po, over 2,000 metres up in the Alps. There, he ceremo-niously filled a glass phial with the 'sacred water of the Po'. Then, he and his supporters descended the river in a flotilla of boats, carry-ing the phial to Venice, where Bossi read out a declaration of independence that began with a quotation from Thomas Jefferson.

'We, the peoples of Padania, solemnly proclaim that Padania is a federal, independent and sovereign republic,' he intoned. An Italian flag was then lowered and the League's green and white standard raised in its place. A 'transitional constitution' distributed at the same time made it clear secession would not take place immedi-ately. It empowered a 'provisional government' that had already been formed by Bossi to open talks with the central government on an agreed separation, but set a deadline of September 1997. After that, failing agreement, the League's unilateral declaration of inde-pendence would take 'full effect'.

Wars have broken out over less.

But not in Italy. A former president of the constitutional court called in vain for Bossi to be arrested. Police clashed briefly with far-left- and far-right-wing demonstrators protesting at his initiative. But the overwhelming majority of Italians understood his descent of the Po for what it was: an elaborate symbolic gesture. They were right to do so. September 1997 came and went, and Padania – if it can be said to exist – stayed firmly within Italy. In fact, no one much noticed the deadline had expired. But everyone had been made aware that the League's orientation had changed – at least, until the next tactical switch.

Part of the fascination exerted by Italy's mafiosi is the way that they, too, communicate by means of signs. Less than a year after Bossi's melodramatic descent of the Po, I was at the other end of Italy, in Catania, at the foot of Mount Etna, being driven through crime-infested backstreets in a police car code-named 'The Shark'. At the time, Catania was Italy's most violent city – a battleground on which Cosa Nostra was fighting for territorial ascendancy with a variety of more or less organized criminal gangs. The underworld murder rate, in a city the size of Cincinnati or Hull, was running at two a week.

On the night I arrived, the latest victim was found. He had been shot in the face and throat. Either before or after, his skull had been battered in with a rock. The way he met his death was violent, but no more so than if he had been killed by rival hoodlums in Moscow or Macao. What made it stand out was that the circumstances of his death had apparently been arranged in such a way as to send a message. An Uzi sub-machine pistol of the sort favoured by Cosa Nostra had been laid across the corpse at a point just above the knees.

The policemen with whom I spent the morning were certain this would have a precise significance; that it would be immediately comprehensible to at least one other mobster; and that if they could only decode the message it would help advance the investigation into the gang war raging in their city. For much of the patrol they debated why the gun had been put at that specific point on the body, whether it really belonged to a member of Cosa Nostra, whether any significance could be attached to the position of the safety catch and whether there was a meaning to be read into the way the victim's limbs had been arranged.

The patrolmen were behaving in a way Italians do instinctively when faced with something new, or dramatic or out of the ordinary. Nothing – but nothing – is ascribed to chance. This is maybe the biggest single difference between the world views of northern Europeans on the one hand and those of southern Europeans, and especially Italians, on the other. The former tend to view the latter, condescendingly, as besotted with conspiracy theories. But the fact is that southern Europeans, and particularly Italians, *are* conspiratorial. What is more, they often talk in metaphors and communicate with symbols. And since so much is therefore deceptive or illusory, given a choice between a simple explanation and a tortuous one, you are just as likely to be right if you plump for the second.

This is also the rationale behind what is known as *dietrologia* (literally, 'behind-ism') – the peculiarly Italian art of divining the true motive for, or cause of, an event. If a minister successfully campaigns for, say, greater resources for the physically handicapped, the *dietrologo* will not believe for one second that it is because he or she has their best interests at heart. He will note that the minister's brother-in-law's wife is on the board of a company that makes, among other things, prosthetics. And if a newspaper mounts a campaign against, say, a firm for secretly selling eavesdropping equipment to an unsavoury foreign dictatorship, the *dietrologo* will note that the paper's shareholders include a company that operates in the same sector as the one whose wrongdoing has been uncovered. The essence of *dietrologia* is that it dismisses the notion that anyone could act purely for reasons of moral conviction.

But then in Italy what you get is seldom what you see – or hear. I was once having coffee with a fellow journalist and the conversation turned to an incident that had made news that week. It was election time, and Silvio Berlusconi was bringing his campaign to an end in Rome. The pollsters all agreed that the capital was critical to the outcome of the vote, but Rome had never been particularly easy terrain for Berlusconi, who comes from Milan. So it was not difficult to understand how his campaign aides had reacted when the AS Roma captain, Francesco Totti, said he would be voting against Berlusconi's candidate in the mayoral election that was being held at the same time. The engaging Totti had the status of a demigod among AS Roma fans and, in a city where, for many, soccer is more of a cult than a sport, his remark could have swung the vote. The night before, at his closing rally, Berlusconi had made things worse for himself by saying Totti was 'out of his mind'.

But that morning, he had abruptly changed his tune. In a radio interview he praised the Roma captain as 'a great lad and great footballer'. He went on: 'I've always been fond of him. And anyway his wife works for a TV channel in my group.'

Returning to the newspaper office where we both worked, I must have said something like: 'So, Berlusconi has buried the hatchet,' because my Italian colleague stopped dead in the street and looked at me with utter astonishment.

'You really haven't understood, have you?' she asked.

'What?'

'That wasn't a burying of the hatchet. For me, that was a *warning*. He was saying: "Watch it, Totti. Remember that your wife works for my company. One more remark like that before election day and she could be looking for work elsewhere." That's the way any Italian would have understood it.'

The use of symbols and metaphors; the endless interplay between illusion and reality; the difficulty of getting at a commonly accepted truth: these are all things that make Italy both frustrating and endlessly intriguing – not least because they raise the tantalizing question of why a people who spend so much of their time peering behind masks and façades should nevertheless be so concerned with appearances; with what they see on the surface.

6.

Face Values

'*L'unico metodo infallibile per conoscere il prossimo è giudicarlo dalle apparenze.*'

'The only infallible way to know another person is to judge him by his appearance.'

– Antonio Amurri, *Qui lo dico e qui lo nego*, 1990

The hero of Sandro Veronesi's novel *La forza del passato*[1] never got along with his father. For one thing, his late father was – or, at least, seemed to be – a diehard right-winger. At one point, Veronesi's hero-narrator remembers an evening in the 1970s when they were watching a press conference given by the then leader of the neo-fascist Italian Social Movement (MSI), Giorgio Almirante. His mother was in the kitchen, baking a cake:

He and I were alone, without mediators, an ideal situation for degeneration. Almirante was speaking, and I kept quiet in order to let my father make the first move, the better to decide on which attack to unleash; but strangely, rather than his usual opening provocation (something like 'he's certainly not wrong there'), this time he kept quiet, too. By then Almirante had gotten to the fourth answer and neither of us had yet said a word, when, finally, my father spoke. 'Never trust men who wear short-sleeved shirts under a jacket,' he said.

Astonished, the narrator looks more closely at Almirante. The sun-tanned MSI leader seems perfectly dressed, 'but his naked arms peeped out from beneath the sleeves of his impeccable blue jacket, and once you noticed it, that detail made him look vaguely obscene'.

A lot of people – Americans in particular – like their politicians to look good. But Italians not only want their politicians to dress immaculately; they and their media are endlessly scrutinizing what they call – using the English word – their *look*, the way in which they dress, in a search for clues to their true personalities. I remember a comparison that covered an entire page of one of the national dailies between *il look* favoured by Silvio Berlusconi and that projected by his then rival for the prime ministership, Romano Prodi. It began with their ties (Berlusconi stuck rigidly to a white, bird's-eye pattern on dark blue, while Prodi favoured regimental-style diagonal stripes in various colours), and progressed by stages to their choice of underpants. Prodi apparently wore roomy boxer shorts, while Berlusconi favoured clingy briefs. The source of this information about their underwear was not disclosed.

Whenever a new president is elected, he, too, will be given the head-to-toe treatment. Giorgio Napolitano, Italy's first ex-Communist head of state, presented quite a problem because his fashion sense was, well, rather what you would expect of a man who was then in his early eighties. But that did not stop the style analysts from dissecting his 'southern, cultured middle-class' *look*, starting with his Borsalino and ending at his lace-up shoes. Readers were solemnly informed that the incoming president 'favours those in black or brown, and always made of leather'.

This same narrowed sartorial gaze is trained on foreign politicians, too. When the Italian-American Nancy Pelosi was chosen as Speaker of the House of Representatives, newspapers back in her 'old country' inevitably reported the event with pride. But the focus was not perhaps what she might have expected. 'Nancy D'Alesandro Pelosi, aged 66', ran a caption beneath a large photograph of the lady who had just become the highest-ranking woman politician in US history. 'Born in Baltimore. Moved to California. Likes to dress in Armani.'

Some years later, when the British went to the polls, I was sitting at my desk in *Corriere della Sera*'s Rome office when the telephone rang. At the other end of the line was a colleague on the political staff of the *Guardian*.

'John, I've just had the most *extraordinary* call from someone who claimed to be working for *Corriere*,' she began.

'No, she's entirely genuine,' I said. 'I gave her your number.'

'Oh, well, that's a relief,' said my colleague. 'You see, all she wanted to know about the candidates was how their wives were dressing. It was *quite* bizarre.'

I have the resulting article on the desk in front of me as I type. 'STYLES COMPARED' is the headline. In a graphic spanning the width of a page, each of the main party leaders is shown next to his wife. There is a general description of their tastes in fashion. But in addition there are little inset circles with magnified photographs of the telling details: Sarah Brown, the wife of the Labour leader, 'red wedges with opaque blue tights (€63)'; Miriam González Durántez, the Spanish spouse of Nick Clegg, the Liberal Democrat contender, 'bag made by hand in Brazil from the ring-pulls of 1,000 tin cans (€52)'; Samantha Cameron, wife of the Conservative candidate, 'Jig-saw belt (€33)'.

The paper's readers were told that Cameron chose inexpensive accessories 'to seem chic, but not privileged', and that although Brown had been criticized for her ill-matching clothes 'some people think she does it on purpose as a contrast to the too-perfect Samantha'.

It is inconceivable that any British paper would analyse in such intricate detail the dress sense of the contenders in an Italian election, let alone that of their wives. But then, in Italy, what can be seen on the surface is constantly being scrutinized for clues as to what might lie below. It goes some way towards explaining the paradox mentioned at the end of the last chapter: one reason why Italians place such emphasis on what is visible is because they assume it is a representation of something that it is not. And that is only to be expected in a society where so much is communicated by means of symbols and gestures.

No people on earth express themselves as visually as the Italians. Hand gestures – it is true – exist in every part of the world, and some are international: we all know what someone means if he rubs together his thumb and index finger. But only the Italians can draw on such a vast range of hand signs, each linked to a precise meaning. Sometimes, if you cannot hear a conversation, you can get the overall gist just by watching.

There are gestures for hunger, agreement, dissent, wedlock, *furbizia*, insistence, negation, voluptuousness and complicity. There are different movements for communicating the drinking of water and the drinking of wine. Hand signs can be used in place of entire sentences such as 'See you later' or 'Get to the point.' I once did an inventory of gestures and had no difficulty reaching a count of ninety-seven.

The 'gesticulation quotient' varies considerably from person to person and situation to situation. By and large, the more intense the conversation, the more likely the participants are to use their hands. And, in general, the use of physical gestures diminishes as you go up the socio-economic scale.

You are unlikely, for example, to see your lawyer raise his chin and jab his index finger at his open mouth rather than tell you he thinks someone is being greedy. But it is quite possible that, if a beautiful and elegantly dressed woman of his acquaintance walks into the room, he might well be tempted to open his arms with the palms of his hands facing upwards in the movement that says 'You look fantastic.'

That is another reason for the importance of what is visible – the sheer enthusiasm for beauty that infuses life in Italy. Unless they go back to classical times, Italians cannot take pride in a glorious imperial past. Even the Venetian Empire was pretty small beer when compared to the empires of Spain and Portugal or, more recently, those of Britain and France. There were moments when the states of central and northern Italy were richer than any in Europe. And from Galileo Galilei to Enrico Fermi, Italians have more than held their own in the area of scientific discovery. But their truly outstanding contributions to mankind have been in the arts, and particularly the visual arts. Historically, Italians have stood out in anything that has had to do with what is visible, be it the art of the Renaissance or modern car design. The areas in which they have excelled include painting, architecture, sculpture, cinema, and of course opera, which gives visual expression to music. As for fashion, they have been setting international trends since Shakespeare had York in *Richard II* cite:

> Report of fashions in proud Italy,
> Whose manners still our tardy-apish nation
> Limps after in base imitation.

Frequently, appearance in Italy comes before more practical concerns. Elsewhere, for example, advertisements for computers and other technological gadgets concentrate mainly on specifications and performance: the gigabytes of RAM, the density of pixels on the display, the number of ports, and so on. But advertisements intended to woo Italian consumers often have none of that. One, for laptops produced by the Taiwanese firm Asus in 2010, showed the company's latest slimline 'notebook' next to an array of filled champagne glasses. Alongside was the slogan – 'Tech in Style' – with the word 'style' printed in a font so big it filled much of the page.

In many other countries, female police officers are made to cut their hair short because of the risk that long hair might be grabbed by an assailant. In Italy, that is thought unacceptable. It is quite normal to see lush tresses cascading out from beneath uniform caps. In the semi-militarized Carabinieri, there is a rule that the hair must be gathered, but it does not stop female members of the force from looking a million dollars. There was one at a station near my office in Rome who had her jet-black locks in a pony-tail that fell from under the back of her cap to between her shoulder blades.

Some years ago, in the middle of winter, one of the papers ran an article on how to cope with the fashion dilemmas posed by illness.

The headline was: 'FEVER? I'M DRESSING SEXILY. FROM LINGERIE TO SCARVES: HOW TO SURVIVE INFLUENZA WITH GLAMOUR'. It presented a range of suggestions on how to prevent 'self-respect vanishing at the first sneeze'. Along with pretty pyjamas and brightly coloured thick socks (in place of 'distinctly unseductive slippers'), a hot-water bottle was 'considered a "must"'. But – readers were earnestly advised – it would be 'better to choose one with a designer label'. The article was illustrated by a photograph of a model with only slightly unkempt hair clutching a mug that presumably held something hot and comforting. But her pyjamas, which were open right down to below her navel, were gossamer-thin. If she really had had the 'flu, it would soon have turned into pneumonia.

The time and care expended by shop assistants in Italy on the wrapping of gifts can be astonishing. The cost of the purchase is irrelevant. The same care will be taken in wrapping a discounted paperback book as a pair of diamond earrings. Blithely indifferent to the queue building up behind you, the assistant will patiently fold over corners to form perfect isosceles triangles; use different-coloured (but always exquisitely contrasting) wrapping paper to create diagonal stripes across the package and then tie it with a length of ribbon that is made to end in delicate spirals. The finished package will then be handed to you with aplomb.

It is entirely consistent with the emphasis that Italians place on the visual that their longest-serving modern leader should have been a TV mogul. Silvio Berlusconi did not, in fact, start in the media business. He began his career as a property developer. While still in his early thirties, he embarked on the construction of a huge residential complex outside his home city known as Milano Due, or Milan Two. His first involvement with television came about as the result of his setting up a cable TV service for the residents. It was only later that he conceived the idea of breaking the state-owned RAI's monopoly of national television by putting together networks of local stations that would each show the same programmes at the same time. With the help of the Socialist leader and prime minister Bettino Craxi, Berlusconi became the owner of three of Italy's seven channels – a position of media influence unparalleled in any other democracy.

He turned to politics after Craxi became mired in scandal and fled the country. In 1994 he announced he would be running in that year's general election. The way he did so was to set the tone for the rest of his career in public life. Another contender might have issued a press statement or announced his intentions at some high-profile gathering. Not Berlusconi. He sent a slickly produced video recording to all the main television channels to be broadcast on their news bulletins. He was filmed sitting behind his desk in the way that prime ministers and presidents do when they make televised addresses to the nation. The none-too-subliminal message was that Berlusconi was already in charge. The impression of lofty condescension was reinforced by his choice of language: he had decided not to do anything so banal as to enter politics, become a candidate or throw his hat into the ring; no, he had decided, he said, to *scendere in campo*, a sporting term that translates into English as 'take to the field' but which in Italian uses the word for 'descend'. In a nine and a half minute message, he went on to portray himself as a champion of personal freedom, economic liberalism and political innovation.

The last of those claims was unquestionably true. His party, Forza Italia, was unlike any political movement that had come before. It had been put together in less than a year, largely by Marcello Dell'Utri, the head of the advertising arm of Berlusconi's media empire.* For the most part, Forza Italia's earliest officials were Dell'Utri's executives. Few people gave Berlusconi much of a chance when he launched his campaign, not least because his main allies were the maverick Northern League and a party of neo-fascists, the ideological heirs of Mussolini. But when the vote was held just two months later, their ramshackle alliance won a decisive victory.

* See above, pages 53–4.

Berlusconi's first government did not last long. The Northern League, which had yet to evolve into a party of the far right, was constantly at odds with the neo-fascists (notwithstanding their claims to have become 'post-fascists') and often with Berlusconi himself. After a mere eight months the League's leader, Umberto Bossi, ordered his followers in parliament to defect to the opposition, sealing the government's fate. For Berlusconi, it was the beginning of a long spell in the political wilderness. But, in 2001, after luring Bossi into a new alliance, he won a landslide victory and remained in power for the next five years.

Narrowly defeated in the 2006 general election, Berlusconi was back as prime minister two years later. His third government* made a promising start. But a year after his election victory its leader became entangled in the first of a string of scandals over his private life. After Berlusconi was found to have attended the birthday party of an aspiring showgirl, his wife issued an extraordinary statement describing her husband as a 'sick man' who 'consorts with minors'. Over the next two years Italy's prime minister was claimed to have hosted parties in his Rome palazzo at which women outnumbered men by four to one; a recording that purported to capture his intimate pillow talk with a prostitute was posted on the Internet, and he was accused of having intervened with the police on behalf of a Moroccan runaway, Karima el-Mahroug, who had attended so-called bunga bunga parties at his mansion near Milan while still only seventeen years old.†

But polls showed that what counted for more with the Italian

---

* Technically, his fourth, because of a reshuffle in 2005. See footnote on page 36, above.

† El-Mahroug, who also styled herself Ruby Rubacuori or Ruby the Heartstealer, was above the age of sexual consent in Italy when she attended the bunga bunga sessions but below the minimum age at which she could be paid for sexual services. Berlusconi was found guilty in 2013 of paying a juvenile prostitute and taking advantage of his official position to coerce the police. In 2014 he was acquitted of both charges on appeal. At the time of writing, it is unclear whether the prosecution intends to lodge a further appeal with the supreme court.

electorate was Berlusconi's response to the worldwide financial crisis that began in the US in 2007 with the collapse in the market for sub-prime loans and led into the turmoil that engulfed the eurozone in 2009. One of Berlusconi's guiding principles was always to remain unrelentingly optimistic. Long before he entered politics, he would tell his salespeople that he expected them to 'carry the sun in their pockets'.[2] Accordingly, his response to the gathering storm clouds was to deny that Italy would be affected. In one sense, he was right: Italian banks did not suffer the kind of disasters that befell financial institutions in the US, the UK and elsewhere. But the shock waves from the crisis shook the overall Italian economy more than that of almost any other country in Europe. In 2009, as Berlusconi continued to radiate good cheer, Italy's GDP was falling by 5.5 per cent. For a while, it worked.* But as unemployment grew and bankruptcies soared, growing numbers of Italians realized that the situation was not as rosy as their prime minister was insisting.

Investors were meanwhile becoming progressively more concerned about the possibility of Italy defaulting on its vast public debts. The government's borrowing costs started to climb, gradually at first but then with alarming speed. Yet Berlusconi seemed almost physically incapable of acknowledging the gravity of the situation and enacting the drastic but necessary measures needed to deal with it. Against a background of escalating panic on international markets, he stepped aside in late 2011 to make way for a non-party government headed by economist and former EU commissioner Mario Monti.

The relief was almost palpable. After tendering his resignation to the president, Berlusconi slipped out of a side door of the palace to avoid a mob outside that had every so often been breaking into renditions of Handel's 'Hallelujah' chorus. Seldom has a prime minister stepped down in such humiliating circumstances.

But though his many detractors may be loath to admit it, Silvio Berlusconi can fairly claim to be among the modern world's most successful politicians. Despite widespread predictions that his

---

* See below, page 82.

resignation signalled the end of his political career, and notwithstanding a conviction for tax fraud two years later, the TV magnate was still a leading figure in the public life of his country twenty years after entering politics. No Italian since Mussolini had impressed his personality on his country as decisively, nor had any European politician outside the former Communist Bloc succeeded in generating a cult of personality such as that which enveloped the diminutive media tycoon in his heyday.

Not even Charles de Gaulle arrived at political rallies to be met by a song such as the one sung by Berlusconi's followers, '*Menomale che Silvio c'è*' (roughly, 'Thank Goodness for Silvio'), which begins as follows:

> *C'è un grande sogno*
> *Che vive in noi,*
> *Siamo la gente della libertà*
> *Presidente siamo con te*
> *Menomale che Silvio c'è.*

> (There is a great dream
> Which lives in us,
> We are the people of freedom
> Prime minister, we are with you
> Thank goodness for Silvio!)[3]

Nor did Margaret Thatcher have a fan club with a website[4] offering devotees souvenir T-shirts, bags and aprons. The website also carried a quotation that hinted at the view of democracy held by many of his followers. The quotation, attributed to Aristotle, reminded visitors to the site that 'A state is better governed by a good man than by a good law.'*

---

* In fact, Aristotle never wrote anything of the sort. He put it as a question: 'Now the first thing which presents itself to our consideration is this, whether it is best to be governed by a good man, or by good laws?'

So how did he do it? How did he persuade Italians in their tens of millions that he was the 'good man' they needed? Why did they elect him as their leader, not once, nor even twice, but three times?

There are several answers to that question. His opponents, whose political roots were either in the old PCI or the left wing of the Christian Democrat Party, were ideologically heterogeneous and prone to squabbling. The same could be said of Forza Italia and its allies. But the parties of the left and centre-left were representatives of two failed creeds. Christian democracy may not have been discredited to the same extent as communism after the fall of the Berlin Wall, but in its Italian form it was profoundly compromised by its leading role in the increasingly corrupt system that was used to run the country until the early 1990s.

A further important reason for Berlusconi's success was his talent as a communicator. From the outset, he spoke to voters in a plain, unadorned Italian, drawing his metaphors from family life, eschewing the subjunctive and deploying a simple – and, on occasion, even crude – vocabulary that was instantly recognizable to the man or woman in the street. He also had the inestimable advantage for a politician of not seeming to be one. Right from the start, he portrayed himself to the electorate as an outsider and, in many respects, he remained one: as his aides often remarked, Berlusconi was at his most successful when he was being spontaneous, incautious, irreverent and humorous. His frequent gaffes served only to convince potential supporters that, ultimately, he was 'one of them'.

Berlusconi was born into a lower-middle-class family in Milan and, for many Italians of a similar background, particularly those who were self-employed, one of his greatest attractions was that he seemed to be tolerant of tax-dodging. He described himself as a liberal. But the freedom he was taken to be offering was the one after which many an Italian hankers – to do *'quello che gli pare'*, whatever he or she likes. Nowhere is this truer than in the field of taxation.

A prime minister cannot, of course, openly tell people that he is happy to turn a blind eye to tax-dodging. Nor did Berlusconi ever do so. But he set out his thinking on the subject in 2004 when, as prime minister, he attended a ceremony to mark the anniversary of the founding of the Guardia di Finanza, whose officers carry out many of the functions of tax inspectors. 'There is a rule of natural law that says that if the State asks you for a third of what you have earned with your hard work, it seems a fair request and you give it over in exchange for services,' he told his audience. 'If [the State] asks you for more, or a lot more, then you are being overwhelmed by the State and so you set about inventing systems of avoidance or even evasion that you feel are in accordance with your private sense of morality and which do not make you feel guilty.' Four years later, he declared that if 'taxes are between 50 per cent and 60 per cent it is too much and it is thus justified to practise avoidance or evasion'.[5] Ironically, though, his governments did not reduce taxes. In 2008 he fulfilled an election pledge to abolish a much-disliked house tax. But the overall tax burden grew.

All that said, Berlusconi entered politics with two exceptional advantages. In the first place, he was among the richest men on earth, the head of a business empire stretching far beyond the media into retailing, insurance, asset management and, of course, sport, in the form of AC Milan. According to Forbes, his wealth peaked at almost $13 billion in 2000.[6]

That sort of cash can come in handy in politics. It helped him to return to power at the general election the following year when, at a cost of 37 billion lire ($26.5 million), he distributed a copy of a hagiography of himself to every household in the land. His political opponents have repeatedly claimed that his almost unlimited resources helped him to survive crucial no-confidence votes that risked toppling his governments. In the run-up to one such, no fewer than ten members of the Chamber of Deputies shifted their allegiance in Berlusconi's favour. In 2013 a senator who had abandoned the centre-left seven years earlier alleged that Berlusconi paid him €3 million to do so. Berlusconi, who denied the claim, was put on trial, charged with bribery, the following year.

His other, immense advantage, of course, has been his hold over the media. He entered politics as the owner of a publishing house,

Mondadori; a weekly news magazine, *Panorama*; and, through his brother, he controlled a daily newspaper, *Il Giornale*. But it was Berlusconi's hold on television that counted more than anything.

Italians are unusually dependent on TV for their news and information. Even before the Internet began to make inroads into circulation, less than one Italian in ten bought a daily newspaper. And as recently as 2014, and despite the spread of the Internet, an unusually extensive poll of voters found that more than half took their news predominantly or solely from TV.[7]

While in opposition, Berlusconi was able to rely on the support of the three channels belonging to his Mediaset network. But when he was in government, he could also exert influence on the three belonging to RAI. The effect of this videocracy, as it has been termed, is impossible to demonstrate in any quantitative way. But it can be illustrated.

In 2010, for example, a poll was carried out to determine Italians' perceptions of the economy. One of the multiple-choice questions asked when, in recent years, unemployment had been at its highest. In fact, it had been rising ever since Berlusconi's government had come into office two years earlier. Yet the largest number of respondents gave as their answer 2007 – the year *before* he returned to power. There was a similar misconception about the overall health of the economy. On average, those who took part in the survey vastly underestimated how much it had shrunk. It was not until the following year that Italians began to realize how bad the situation was.

Ever since 1994 Berlusconi and his media flunkies have succeeded in changing not only perceptions, but the meaning of words. The head of Mediaset began his political adventure with a massive handicap. Casting around for support, the only people he could find, apart from the Northern League, were the neo-fascists, the pariahs of post-war Italian politics. When he first expressed support for them, most people were deeply shocked.

So, instead of acknowledging that he had put himself at the head of an alliance packed with far-right-wingers, Berlusconi began to refer to his followers and allies as 'moderates'. His coalition was of the 'centre-right'. At first, people took it for the nonsense it was. But Berlusconi and his television channels hammered at the terms relentlessly – '*moderati . . . centro destra*' – and gradually, over the years, they have become universally accepted.

Gianroberto Casaleggio, the Internet guru who co-founded Italy's anti-establishment Five Star Movement, once quipped that living in Berlusconi's Italy was rather like inhabiting the simulated reality of the 1999 sci-fi movie *The Matrix*.[8] Certainly, perceptions inside the country were markedly different from those outside. And it helps, I think, to explain one of the paradoxes of recent years: why a man widely regarded in the rest of Europe as a buffoon was able to garner such a high level of support from a society where people are almost obsessively concerned with the impression that they make on others.

A lot of non-Italians have heard of *bella figura*. Far fewer understand what it really means. In the case of English speakers, this is because neither of the words corresponds exactly with an English equivalent. In Britain and the US, beauty is thought of as something almost entirely separate from virtue. But in Italy the two concepts overlap. *Bello* (*bella*, in the feminine) translates as 'beautiful', 'pretty' or 'handsome'. But it also means nice, fine – and good.* A 'good deed' is *una bella azione*.

As for *figura*, it covers a range of meaning that extends from 'picture' to the impression made on others. Perhaps 'image' is the nearest English equivalent, except that *figura* has more to do with the way you appear to others than the effect you wish to project.

---

* This point can be overstressed. The same is true of the German *schön* and of other adjectives in other languages. But it is nevertheless striking how often *bello* and *bella* are deployed in Italian. It is not perhaps strange that *bella* should be used in the same way as 'love' or 'honey' in addressing a woman. But the use of *bello* is worthy of remark. Whereas, in addressing another man, a Briton might use 'mate', an American 'buddy' and a Spaniard '*tio*' or '*macho*', an Italian will use the equivalent of 'handsome'.

Fare una bella figura is to make a positive impression, though not necessarily in a visual way. The shop assistant who wrapped that present will probably have told you, for example, that by turning up with a large box of fruit jellies or a bottle of vintage malt whisky,* you will '*fare una bella figura*' (though it goes without saying that you will make an even better impression on your hosts if your gift has been exquisitely wrapped; in fact, you would *fare una brutta figura* were you to turn up at the door with your gift, however pricey, wrapped in nothing but a paper bag).

In several respects, *figura* is close to Far Eastern concepts of 'face'. And since Italians generally agree on the need to avoid losing face, they are prepared, in the same way as Chinese or Japanese, to go to great lengths to ensure that others do not do so. A chief executive who has utterly mishandled the running of a firm will not usually be openly berated at the annual general meeting and denounced in excoriating fashion in the financial media. It will be quietly agreed between all concerned that he is not up to the job, at which point he will be got rid of in the most discreet manner possible and in a way that allows him to keep his dignity and his reputation.

Dread of *facendo una brutta figura* is omnipresent in Italian society. It explains why there are so few laundrettes, and why the few that do exist are used mostly by poor immigrants and foreign students. It is why Italians put on suntan cream *before* they get to the beach or pool. It is why town and city councils arrange for their best-looking cops to direct the traffic in the main square. And why Italians above a certain social standing are reluctant to travel on public transport.

Bella figura is also why Italians of both sexes will endure remarkable discomfort in the interest of keeping up appearances.

---

* Italians first developed a taste for whisky in the Dolce Vita days of the early 1960s. Until the early 1990s they were among the world's most avid consumers of malts, notably Glen Grant, which was bought by the Campari group in 2005. By then, however, overall consumption had begun to fall. Italy remains the world's fifth-largest market for malts, but the most recent figures show that sales are a third of what they were at their peak.

Throughout the rest of the Mediterranean, from Spain to Israel, male office workers cope with the summer heat by changing into short-sleeved shirts sometime around June. But in Italy that would be to run the risk of being thought, like Almirante, 'vaguely obscene'. So, even as the temperatures climb towards 40°C in late July, the sort of Italians who wear a suit or jacket and trousers to work remain stubbornly – and willingly – imprisoned in shirts that allow them to shoot their cuffs. Look down and you will probably see that they are also wearing heavy leather shoes (because they keep their shape) and long socks (because one of the worst sartorial gaffes you can commit in Italy is to reveal an expanse of flesh between sock top and trouser hem). The women, meanwhile, will very likely be wearing clinging tops and figure-hugging skirts or trousers. Like the men, they cannot be comfortable. But they feel they are *facendo una bella figura*, and that matters more than mere comfort.

The same need for the approval of others would seem to lie behind the boom in demand for plastic surgery. The international statistics in this area are unusually patchy, but figures taken from a report compiled for the International Society of Aesthetic Plastic Surgeons (ISAPS) and based on statistics for 2010 indicate that Italians are exceptionally ready to submit themselves to cosmetic procedures of all kinds. In a cross section of twenty-five countries, Italy was second (behind Greece) for the number of plastic surgeons per 100,000 of the population and third, behind South Korea and Greece, for the number of procedures – surgical and non-surgical – relative to the population. The number of cosmetic procedures carried out in Italy in 2010 was, proportionately, more than 30 per cent higher than in the United States. France, Spain and Germany all lagged behind, while the figure for Britain was barely a quarter of that for Italy.

What makes these figures all the more striking is that they refer to a country widely regarded as having an unusually high proportion of good-looking men and women. I am struck, for example, by the number of Italian women who have had lip enhancement procedures. The evidence is all too painfully visible, many having apparently been done on the cheap and botched. This is doubly tragic because you suspect they were unnecessary in the first place: most Italian women have good, full mouths that need no attention.

It brings to mind the anorexic teenagers who look into the mirror as slim girls and see fat ones staring back. And, if the results of a survey for the US-based nutrition firm Herbalife are to believed, that is precisely the frame of mind of about one in seven Italians. In 2005 the pollsters it commissioned found that while 40 per cent of Italians thought they were overweight, only 26 per cent actually were.

For the most part, the preoccupation with *bella figura* is harmless enough. It can be argued that it makes the human landscape more decorative and life in Italy generally more attractive and enjoyable. There are elements in the *bella figura* mentality of a concern to fit in with the other members of society. In some respects, it counterbalances what Italians call *menefreghismo*:* not caring a damn about other people.

But the *bella figura* mentality also points to a deep-seated insecurity, oddly at variance with *menefreghismo*, that echoes the Italians' historic vulnerability and fragile sense of national identity. What is more, the corollary of all this reverence for whatever is *bello* is a tendency to despise, shun and hide whatever is *brutto* – or rather, anything judged to be so.

It sometimes takes months, or it may take years, but sooner or later you notice something odd: that handicapped people in Italy are almost as rare as redheads on the streets and in the bars and restaurants. There are disabled mendicants in the bigger cities, for sure. But they are almost always foreigners. And the same is true of the tourists you see being pushed around in wheelchairs.

So where are the Italians with evident physical deformities? Where are the blind and the paraplegic? And where, among all these beautiful people, are the Italians who suffer from Down's syndrome

---

* From *me ne frego* ('I don't give a damn').

or cerebral palsy? The sad truth is that large numbers are at home and out of sight – kept there, in many cases, by their relatives' feelings of shame, discomfort and embarrassment, and in others by the lack of facilities for the handicapped in a society that seems never really to have made provision for them.

The invisibility of Italy's disabled, like much else in society, may also owe something to the huge influence of the Roman Catholic Church. Ideas that developed in medieval times, though long since discredited, continue to exercise a subtle influence. One was that deformity was a punishment from God.

Handicapped Italians are not the only invisible ones. My personal experience, and that of friends, is that Italians are exceptionally reluctant to be seen when they are seriously or terminally ill. It is also noticeable how few women you see in Italy in the last months of pregnancy. This is paradoxical, since pregnancy in Italy is wrapped in a fair amount of encouraging rhetoric. Women who are expecting a child are referred to as being *in dolce attesa* ('in sweet expectation'): a phrase that is not just used by solicitous elderly relatives but in, for example, airport announcements telling them they can go to the head of the queue. In practice, as well as in theory, mothers-to-be are treated with reverence. But then they are carrying within them that most precious of all gifts – life.

Life as Art

'*L'unica gioia al mondo è cominciare. E' bello vivere perché vivere è cominciare, sempre, ad ogni istante.*'

'The world's only joy is beginning. It is wonderful to live, because living is beginning, always; at every instant.'

— Cesare Pavese, *Il mestiere di vivere*, 1952

Tyson was trouble on four legs.

A huge-jawed brute, his forebears had been bred to fight in the pits of old. Unfortunately, no one ever managed to get across to Tyson that those days were over. He was ready to take on any dog in the neighbourhood. His owners assured us he was perfectly friendly with human beings. But that *verità* wore thin on the day my wife tried to stroke him and only just managed to pull back her hand in time.

Others might have had difficulty in seeing Tyson's good qualities. But his owners adored him. And as he grew old and infirm they lavished progressively greater attention on him. It is hard to overstate their selfless devotion to their pet.

As time passed, it became equally hard to resist the thought that they might have been doing Tyson a favour if they put him out of his misery. Night after night, he was taken out and – barely able to stand, let alone walk – he was encouraged with infinite patience to drag himself, paw over shaky paw, into the street to relieve himself. In the end, even that became impossible and Tyson was finally put to rest.

His case was by no means exceptional. A foreign vet I knew said that Italian owners were noticeably more reluctant than, say, Britons or Americans, to have their pets euthanized. They extend to animals, in other words, a belief that has immense weight in Italy: that life is so precious it must be prolonged and protected in all circumstances and to the very last.

One way in which this shows up is in opposition to capital punishment. No matter how conservative in other aspects an Italian politician may be, he or she is likely to be as appalled as the most fervent radical by the sort of executions that are common occurrences in the United States. Occasionally, the case of some unfortunate American on death row is given publicity, perhaps in a magazine article or a television documentary, and it becomes a national scandal in Italy. Sometimes, the prisoner facing execution is an Italian-American. Often, there is a doubt over the condemned person's guilt. But not always. After the case is brought to light, a barrage of letters and emails is loosed off at a doubtless bemused state governor and, as the days and hours tick away towards the moment of execution, growing pressure is brought to bear on politicians in Italy and Italy's diplomats in Washington to lobby for a reprieve. When, as usually happens, the campaign proves to be in vain, there is a sense of national outrage. However disunited Italians may be in other respects, on this issue they think almost as one.

Why? The obvious answer is Roman Catholic teaching on the sanctity of life. But is it the right one? The Church's 'theology of life' is a comparatively recent evolution in its thinking, which has served to ensure that its attitude to capital punishment is consistent with its doctrine on such matters as artificial birth control, *in vitro* fertilization and stem cell research. But the fact is that executions were commonplace in the old Papal State, and the Vatican City State did not get around to abolishing the death penalty* until 1969 – 123 years after Michigan, the first US state to do so.

It could be argued that, since Italians have had such an

---

* It was never used, however, and was prescribed as the sentence only for the assassination, or attempted assassination, of a pope.

overwhelming influence on the Catholic Church, it is their reverence and enthusiasm for life that has shaped the Vatican's teaching and not the other way around. The first state in modern times to abolish the death penalty was an Italian one, the Grand Duchy of Tuscany, in 1786. The day on which the death penalty was dropped from its penal code, 30 November, was declared a public holiday in Tuscany in 2000. The ruler of Tuscany at the time was an Austrian, but he was inspired to enact his reform by an Italian, Cesare Beccaria, who has a claim to have been the world's first penologist. The short-lived Roman Republic was the next state to do away with executions, in 1849, and the Republic of San Marino was not far behind.

The view that life is infinitely precious goes hand in hand with Italians' determination to live it to the full. As much as possible is done to improve on mundane reality, minimize what is dull, maximize what is agreeable, and generally file off the rough edges of existence.

Flattery is all-pervasive. Imagine you have just got into a taxi in Rome and are going to a street that not everyone has heard of. You give the name of the street to the driver and he says something like 'I know it: it's the one that runs between Via Settembrini and Via Ferrari.' A Londoner in the same situation might answer 'Exactly.' A New Yorker might say 'Right.' But in Italy it would be positively curmudgeonly not to exclaim *'Bravo!'*, the term for 'Well done', which literally means 'Clever'. The driver has been flattered and it is now incumbent upon him to make the rest of the journey as pleasant an experience as possible. In the same way, all women are automatically *belle* and the genuinely pretty ones are *bellissime*.

This very Italian talent for dusting life with a thick layer of stardust is deployed liberally throughout the year. But perhaps it comes to the fore with greatest effect during Lent. In the Catholic tradition, this is meant to be the grimmest forty days in the calendar – a time of repentance and self-denial leading up to the commemoration of Jesus's trial and agonizingly painful death. But in Italy it never seems to be quite that bad.

First of all, as in many other countries, there is Carnival – a brief spell of self-indulgence before the long weeks of abstinence. This is when, in Italy, you see small children on the streets dressed up in a range of bizarre outfits: some as princesses, others as ghouls, super-heroes, pirates, and so on. Depending on the calendar, Carnival falls sometime in the period from early February to early March, and the children's costumes introduce a touch of colour to one of the more doleful phases of the year.

Carnivale, like every other festival in the Italian calendar, also brings with it a range of seasonal delicacies, such as *sfrappole* (thin strips of pastry that are fried and sugared) and *castagnole* or *frittelle* (little doughnuts sprinkled with sugar and filled with crème pâtis-sière). These hyper-calorific delights are meant to be swept from the shops once Lent begins, yet somehow they remain temptingly avail-able for weeks after Ash Wednesday, starting to disappear only once St Joseph's Day is firmly within sight.

The feast day of Mary's husband always falls in Lent and is marked by Catholics as a day of abstinence on which meat is kept from the table. But – at least in the south, from Rome downwards – the deprivation is alleviated more than a little by the appearance of *zeppole*: baked cream puffs, often topped with candied fruits. By the time the last *zeppole* have been consumed, the end of Lent is nigh.

Before it is reached, however, there is the bleakest day in the Christian calendar to be got through – Good Friday, when altars are stripped of their adornments, priests officiate in black and no bells are rung. This most sorrowful of festivals is a public holiday in many countries that Italians regard as semi-heathen, including Brit-ain, Denmark and Sweden. It is also a national festival in several others that do not even have majority Christian populations, includ-ing Indonesia. But in Italy, it is just another day. The shops are open, as are the banks and theatres. And you cannot help but wonder whether this it not because Good Friday is the day of the year Ital-ians consider most *brutto*.

At all events, once it has been got through, the nation is ready for Easter Sunday and the celebration of the Resurrection, the joys of chocolate eggs and a whole new range of seasonal delicacies, including the *colomba*, an Easter cake shaped like a dove, Neapolitan *pastiera* and *pizza pasquale*, a cheese-flavoured sponge enjoyed in Umbria and other parts of central Italy.

Life, in other words, is returning pleasantly to normal. And, in many respects, normal life in Italy – at least in the way it has evolved in recent decades – is decidedly pleasant. There is the beauty of the cities and the countryside; the elegance of the clothes; and, of course, the sunshine.

'*Più tosto che arricchir, voglio quiete,*' wrote the poet Ariosto: 'Rather than riches, I want tranquillity.' And for the most part his compatriots have taken the same view. Italians are certainly not lazy. A lot work extremely hard, particularly in family businesses. But it is rare for them to view work as anything but a necessary evil. A survey commissioned by the weekly news magazine *Panorama* in 2006 found that two thirds of Italians would give up their work if they could be guaranteed the relatively modest sum of €5,000 a month. In the same way, retirement is usually seen as entirely positive. There seems to be none of the fretting that goes on in Anglo-Saxon societies about how to cope with a loss of identity. I have known plenty of Italians who have gone into retirement and sometimes I have bumped into them in the street or when they have made a return visit to the offices where they used to work. Not once have I heard any of them express anything but unmitigated delight at no longer having a job.

I have been a guest in the offices of two separate Italian newspapers, and in neither was anything much done to make the experience of work more enjoyable. There seemed to be a generalized acceptance that this would be futile. Apart from maybe a round of drinks at Christmas, there were none of those events that in British and American offices are intended to boost corporate morale and forge team spirit. Nor, most strikingly, were there any rites of passage. When the time came for employees to retire, they simply disappeared. One day they were there at their desk; the next they were gone. There was no little party in the boss's office to say 'Thanks and all the best for the future'; no whip-round among the staff to pay for a farewell present; not even a note on the corkboard to record the fact that, after ten, twenty or maybe even thirty years with the company, Giulio or Giulia was leaving. He or she just went. Like Lewis Carroll's Snark, they 'softly and suddenly vanished away'.

It is all of a piece with the razor-sharp line which most Italians draw between work and leisure. I sometimes like to take a report or other document with me to lunch so I can read it at leisure over my food. But on more than one occasion, I have been approached by Italian workmates in a state of dismay mingled with disapproval.

'That's a very bad habit, you know,' said a senior newspaper executive when he saw me leafing through some papers over a bite to eat in a café-restaurant near the office. Lunches, like other meals, are sacred occasions on which those sitting at the table should be concentrating only on the food and wine set before them or enjoying the conversation.

But then, if leisure is prized by Italians, the everyday pleasure of eating is hallowed. 'I once overheard a conversation in an Italian train between two businessmen who were strangers to each other,' the British cookery writer Elizabeth Romer wrote. 'For the entire two-hour journey they discussed with passion their particular way of making *spaghetti alla carbonara* and other pasta sauces.' Anyone who has lived in Italy will have had a similar experience. At one level, cuisine for Italians is what the weather is for Britons – a suitable topic for conversation between strangers that avoids the risks associated with politics, religion and football. But not entirely. Sometimes you hear impassioned arguments which, as the disputants draw close enough to be understood, turn out to be about, say, the use of *pancetta dolce* (unsmoked bacon) as opposed to *pancetta affumicata* (the smoked variety). If the issue at stake is the use, in place of pancetta, of *guanciale*, which is made with pig's cheeks, then things can become really quite acerbic. In central Italy, there are those who, one feels, would rather lose a month's wages than admit that *bucatini all'amatriciana* can be made with anything other than pork jowl.

This is partly because of the identification between cuisine and family. Recipes are passed on from mother to daughter and become part of a family's sense of identity. Food also plays a crucial role in strengthening family bonds. Whatever their other commitments, children are expected to be at table for dinner. It is where the affairs of the day are discussed, problems addressed and complaints aired. When they grow up, those same children will be expected to be at their mother's lunch table on Sunday. In the cities, you can set your watch by the traffic jams that build on Sundays before lunch, as families return to the home of the previous generation, usually stopping along the way to buy a cake or tart for the last course.

The role of the table in Italian life is relentlessly emphasized in advertising of all kinds and even reflected in the grammar of the language. *Il tavolo* is the word for the physical object, whereas *la tavola*, the same word but in the feminine, is untranslatable into English. Its connotations encompass the meal and its preparation, quality and consumption, and – most importantly – the enjoyment of it. *Il tavolo* is a piece of furniture on which to rest plates and cutlery. *La tavola* signifies an experience in which china and glass, knives and forks, play only a very small and functional part. When, for example, Italians want to describe the joys of good eating and drinking, they talk of '*i piaceri della tavola*'.

It was not until quite recently, however, that Italian cooking came to be recognized as something other than a poor second to French, even by the Italians themselves. Giuseppe Prezzolini, the writer who first divided his compatriots into *furbi* and *fessi*, was well ahead of his time – at least as far as international opinion was concerned – when in 1954 he asked, 'What is the glory of Dante compared to spaghetti?' For at least fifteen years afterwards, the more accepted view was that Italian gastronomy meant no more than cheap, rough wine in straw-covered flasks and mounds of pasta, all plonked down on chequered tablecloths.

Several factors have played a part in changing perceptions since then. One has been a marked improvement in the quality of Italian wine. Another has been the spread of enthusiasm for the

Mediterranean diet. In previous centuries, foreign travellers had noted with regret and disdain the dearth of meat in the Italian diet. Animal fat and protein was what counted as prestige food, and it was thought to be anything but unhealthy. The man who did more than anyone to overturn that view was an American physiologist, Ancel Keys, who highlighted the link between saturated fats and heart disease. *How to Eat Well and Stay Well the Mediterranean Way*, which he and his wife, Margaret, published in 1975, offered an alternative yet still delicious diet rich in olive oil, vegetables, pulses and fish.* Perhaps most importantly of all, Italian food is quite simple to prepare – a factor that has weighed progressively more as people have come to expect good cuisine in the home as well as in restaurants and hotels.

But it is not as easy as it might seem to reproduce in Birmingham or Boston that tasty dish sampled on a memorable evening in Tuscany or overlooking the Bay of Naples. More than any other internationally renowned cuisine, Italy's depends for its impact not on complex sauces or obscure spices but on the quality of the ingredients. A perfectly ordinary dish of, say, rigatoni with basil and tomato sauce can be transformed into an exquisite gastronomic experience if the passata (the sieved tomato pulp) used to make it is of high quality. Even today, many city-dwelling families in Italy make and bottle their own passata from tomatoes grown on land that they or their relatives own.

This intimate link between the quality of the cuisine and the quality of the ingredients is central to the Slow Food movement, which came into being in 1986 in protest at the opening of a McDonald's near the Spanish Steps in Rome. The aim of Slow Food is to preserve regional cuisines and the use of locally grown vegetables and locally reared livestock. It is not specifically an organic food

---

* Dr Keys, who devised and gave the initial letter of his surname to the K-ration, the small but notorious food pack given to American soldiers in the Second World War, took his own advice. He lived for many years in southern Italy and died at the age of a hundred.

movement, but many of the restaurants that adhere to its principles use organic ingredients and wines. The movement claims more than 100,000 members in some 150 countries. In 2004 its founder, Carlo Petrini, a culinary journalist, founded a University of Gastronomic Sciences in his native town of Bra, near Turin. It is part of a complex that also includes a Michelin-starred restaurant and a hotel. Subjects include nutritional science, the chemistry of taste and the history, aesthetics and sociology of food.

By contrast, fast food has made only limited incursions into Italy. There are only about 450 branches of McDonald's,[1] compared with more than 1,200 in both France and Britain, which have populations of approximately the same size. As for Starbucks, it has never even ventured into Italy. It has branches in more than sixty countries outside the United States. There are Starbucks in countries such as Germany, France and Spain, where the local coffee is of high quality. But not a single one in Italy. Asked why, the company's CEO, Howard Schultz, once attributed the decision not to get involved to 'the political issues and the economic issues' in Italy.[2]

Some Italian foods and dishes have been around for centuries. Writing in 1570, Bartolomeo Scappi, the chef of Pope Pius V, declared that the best cheeses in Italy were Parmesan and Marzolino, both of which can be found today in any Italian grocery store. He also mentioned 'Casci Cavalli', an obvious reference to the cheese now known as Caciocavallo which is produced throughout the south.

Naples was also known at the time for a dish that consisted of a layer of dough 'no more than an inch thick without a top crust' which local people referred to as 'pizza'. But words can be deceptive, and in Italy they have often been used in the past to denote ingredients and dishes that carry quite different names today. When Boccaccio in *The Decameron* has the practical joker Maso del Saggio describe a mountain in the Basque country 'all of grated parmesan cheese [on which] dwell folk that do nought else but make macaroni and raviuoli', he is not alluding to what you would expect to find in a modern trattoria. His macaroni were most likely dumplings made of dried split beans, and the ravioli would have been rissoles. Boccaccio also had his character imagine 'a rivulet of Vernaccia', but whether it would have had much in common with the crisp, light wine served in Tuscany today is impossible to know. Orvieto, for example, is nowadays mostly dry but for centuries was honey-sweet.

Olive oil, of course, has been around for centuries, and doubtless millennia, in Italy. But until comparatively recently it was a costly luxury food in many regions. Lard was the cooking fat used by most Italians in the Middle Ages. Starting in the fifteenth century, butter became increasingly popular in southern as well as northern Italy.

In much the same way, pasta has long been a part of Italian cuisine but only quite recently acquired the dominant, pervasive role it plays now. The oldest form is thought to be lasagne, which is known to have been cooked in ancient Rome, though not quite in the way it is today. Dried pasta seems to have been invented quite separately, in North Africa, as expedition food for desert caravans. It was probably brought to Sicily by the island's Muslim conquerors. In a codex published in 1154, a Moroccan geographer and botanist known as al-Idrisi described a thriving pasta manufacturing industry near Palermo, which exported its products to Muslim and Christian countries alike. Among them was a string-like pasta then known by the name *itrija*. Dried pasta had the same advantages for seafarers as it did for camel drivers, so it is hardly surprising that it next appears in Genoa; it is mentioned in a document written in 1279. Production of vermicelli, which was to remain a Genoese speciality, had begun by the fourteenth century. The consumption of pasta continued nevertheless to be associated with Sicilians until, in the eighteenth century, the nickname *mangiamaccheroni* gradually came to be bestowed on the Neapolitans. By 1785 Naples had 280 pasta shops.

Grated cheese was used for flavouring from an early stage, but sugar and cinnamon were also thought to make tasty accompaniments. Pasta was often prepared in quite different ways, boiled in broth or milk rather than plain water. In their study of the history of Italian cuisine, Alberto Capatti and Massimo Montanari quote an early cookery writer who was adamant that 'macaroni must be boiled for a period of two hours'.[3]

Nor was tomato sauce added until comparatively recently. The tomato, which almost certainly reached Italy through Spain, had acquired its name – the *pomo d'oro*, or 'golden apple' – at least as early as 1568. But it was treated by Italians – as indeed by many other people, including Americans – with immense suspicion, and entered Italian cuisine only very slowly. The first mention of tomatoes in a written recipe comes at the end of the seventeenth century. Over the next hundred years, tomatoes seem to have won a firm place in Neapolitan cooking. But right up until the end of the nineteenth century it was more usual in central Italy to use *agresto*, a concoction made of sour grapes, to give 'bite' to a dish.

The New World food that caught on most rapidly was maize, which was soon being planted in the Veneto and used as the basis for an existing dish, polenta, which had previously been made exclusively with buckwheat.

As not a few foreigners have noted, Italian food is the ultimate comfort food, and that point has not been lost on Italians either. One of the characters in Ettore Scola's award-winning movie comedy *C'eravamo tanti amati*, called spaghetti 'the great consoler for all woes, more so than love'. And over the centuries, as explained at the start of this book, Italians have needed plenty of consoling.

War and civil strife, often resulting in deprivation, have made a huge contribution to the richness of Italy's gastronomic repertoire. The use of rocket (*eruca sativa*) in salads, a culinary fashion which spread to the Anglo-Saxon world only in the 1990s, originated in the grubbing for edible weeds by Italians during and after the Second World War. As Capatti and Montanari wrote:

The techniques devised in times of famine to render edible even the smallest, most basic resources of the land – the ability to make bread out of wild berries and grape seeds, recounted in so many medieval and modern chronicles, or to concoct a soup with roots from the underbrush and herbs from the ditches – all clearly testify to the difficulties of people whose daily lives were constantly threatened by the outbreak of catastrophe.

In view of the unceasing evolution of Italian cuisine, it is ironic that today's Italians should be so deeply suspicious of any kind of culinary innovation. Chefs in the luxury restaurants and five-star hotels of the bigger cities may improvise and experiment, but at home, in the corner bar and the neighbourhood trattoria or osteria what wins approval is doing things in exactly the same way as last week and the month before and the year before that.

I always find it striking that if you go into a sandwich bar run by Italian immigrants or their descendants in London or New York you will often encounter a dazzling array of inventive fillings. Yet back in Italy, with the exception of a few self-consciously trendy establishments, they are wholly predictable: ham and mozzarella, mozzarella and tomato, tomato and tuna, tuna and artichoke, and so on. They are all delicious. But they are always exactly the same.

Ethnic cuisines are still viewed by many Italians with deep mistrust, and to the extent that a lot of ethnic restaurants exist largely to cater to immigrants. Chinese food is thought acceptable in the sort of 'Where can we go that is cheap and informal?' way that many Britons still think of Indian food. But then Chinese cuisine bears some resemblance to the Italians' own: dumplings are very much like ravioli, just as noodles resemble fettuccine or linguine. Surprisingly, perhaps, the one kind of imported food that has become fashionable in Italy is the altogether more exotic sushi. Even so, a calculation based on the totals given at the time of writing by Trip Advisor shows that, in Rome, Japanese restaurants accounted for 1.25 per cent of the total and all ethnic restaurants for less than 6 per cent. In cosmopolitan Milan the overall figure was 17 per cent, and in Naples 7 per cent.

In the same way, the majority of shoppers remain deeply suspicious of imported foods, and their sensitivities are recognized by manufacturers who, whenever possible, stress that a product has been prepared or grown in Italy. The daughter of an Anglo-Italian marriage once told me how, when she was a girl, she was sent to spend the summer with her grandmother in Italy. Shortly after she arrived, her *nonna* discovered that she had brought with her a jar of peanut butter. Holding it up, she turned to her granddaughter with an expression of bottomless pity.

'*Figliola mia*,' she said. '*Ma come ti sei ridotta*': impossible to translate, but roughly, 'My darling girl, have you been reduced to this?'

Decades after the introduction of the EU's single market, Italian supermarkets remain virtually bereft of foreign produce. You will find some German beer, no doubt, and the odd packet of mass-produced French or Dutch cheese. But what else there is will have been confined to a tiny exotic foods section where foreigners can satisfy their outlandish tastes for things such as bamboo shoots and corned beef.

The lack of good foreign cheeses is particularly striking because this is one of the very few areas where Italy's contribution to gastronomy is modest. There are mozzarella and Parmesan, of course, but they are mainly for cooking with rather than eating on their own. Apart from Gorgonzola and a few others, such as Marzolino, Italian cheeses are pretty uninspiring. The same is true of Spain, even though the Spanish cheese-making industry has advanced by leaps and bounds in recent years. Both countries have a border with France, whose offering in this area is surely unrivalled. But whereas, if you go into a Spanish supermarket nowadays you will find a counter laden with cheeses from France and indeed many other European countries, in most Italian supermarkets you will be lucky to find a chunk of Edam and some packets of Brie and Camembert. Once, at the cheese and cold meats counter of a Tuscan supermarket, I asked for feta, which until then I had always thought of as being quintessentially Greek.

'Good stuff this,' said the assistant as he wrapped it up. 'Italian.'

I know several otherwise highly sophisticated Italians who flatly refuse to eat anything but Italian food. One who does eat foreign fare went on a touring holiday of France some years ago. He is what the French would call a *bon vivant*. I know for a fact he does not hold back on his spending when it comes to food and drink. When he returned, I asked him how it had gone.

'Fine,' he said. He had driven up to Normandy, down through Paris to Brittany, then across the country to Lyons, from where he had followed the Rhône down to Provence. 'Very enjoyable,' he added. 'You can't eat well, but . . .'

On another occasion my wife and I were invited to a dinner party given by a Frenchwoman living in Rome. The guests were all in their thirties or forties. Several of their friends came from the art world. They were apparently as sophisticated and cosmopolitan a group of people as you could assemble in the Italian capital. The woman next to me was the curator of a state-owned collection. When the first course arrived – a delicious concoction involving beans, tomatoes and onions – her jaw dropped.

'But where's the pasta?'

Our hostess explained that, in France, it was not customary to serve pasta, but that there would be plenty of carbohydrate available during the rest of the meal in the form of bread and potatoes. The curator was not reassured. She barely touched her first course, picked at the second and spent the rest of the evening looking miserable and, of course, rather hungry.

It is this sort of stubborn adherence to tradition that has helped to preserve the integrity and identity of Italian cuisine. But in many other areas of life its effects have been profoundly negative – and nowhere more so than in the economy.

8.

Gnocchi on Thursdays

E debbasi considerare come non è cosa più difficile a trattare, né più dubia a riuscire, né più pericolosa a maneggiare, che farsi capo ad introdurre nuovi ordini. Perché lo introduttore ha per nimici tutti quelli che delli ordini vecchi fanno bene, et ha tepidi defensori tutti quelli che delli ordini nuovi farebbono bene.

'And it ought to be remembered that there is nothing more difficult to take in hand, more perilous to conduct, or more uncertain in its success, than to take the lead in the introduction of a new order of things, because the innovator has for enemies all those who have done well under the old conditions, and lukewarm defenders in those who may do well under the new.'

– Niccolò Machiavelli, *Il principe*, 1513 (trans. W. K. Marriott)

Foreign correspondents sooner or later learn to distinguish between bomb explosions and backfiring exhausts; between gunfire and firecrackers. And what I'd heard on that morning in Rome was unquestionably the flat crack of pistol shots. But it was on one of those glorious spring days when it is hard to believe that anything evil could be happening in the world, much less at the end of the street where you live. For a few seconds, I refused to believe the evidence of my own ears. Then came the shouts and a confused hubbub.

Shortly after 8 a.m. on 20 May 1999 Massimo D'Antona, a professor who lectured on employment law at universities in Rome and Naples, was on his way to work when he was gunned down by members of the reborn Red Brigades. The killer fired at least nine bullets into the 51-year-old academic, including a *coup de grâce* to the heart. D'Antona's crime in the eyes of the New Red Brigades was to have drafted legislation for Italy's then centre-left government intended to introduce greater mobility into the Italian labour market by making it easier for employers to both hire and fire.

His place was later taken by another university teacher, Marco Biagi. In 2001 Biagi became an adviser to the incoming centre-right government of Silvio Berlusconi. The following year, he, too, was shot dead on a street by the New Red Brigades.

The assassinations of D'Antona and Biagi highlighted in the bloodiest way the dangers that face anyone – on the right or the left – who tries to bring about radical change in Italy. It can be argued that reforming employment legislation is a special case: that it directly affects the lives and livelihoods of millions of people; that it is a natural cause for far-left activists and the terrorists who from time to time lurk in the shadows beyond them. But labour markets have been liberalized in other countries without people losing their lives, and anyone who lives in Italy soon realizes that a fear of change and a craving for security form part of the warp and weft of Italian life.

Sooner or later, people who come to live in Rome notice that just about every establishment in the capital that serves food, from the costliest expense-account restaurant to the humblest self-service *tavola calda*, has gnocchi (dumplings, usually made of flour or potato, or both) on its menu on Thursdays. And, in most cases, they are not to be found there on any other day of the week. It is one of those reassuring little rituals that are so characteristic of life in Italy: every Thursday you go for lunch and the server tells you with a beaming smile that conveys both pride and satisfaction '*Oggi abbiamo gnocchi al ragù*' or '*al pesto*' or '*alla Sorrentina*', or however they have decided to cook them. If you then say that you don't really fancy gnocchi and that you'd rather have pasta or rice that day, the smile will often fade to be replaced by a look of puzzlement. You are being contrary. You are going against the universally accepted order of things.

What is remarkable about this tradition is that, firstly, it exists nowhere but in Rome and, secondly, that no Roman (or at least no

Roman I have ever met) knows why it exists. There is a Roman saying, '*Giovedì, gnocchi; Venerdì, pesce; Sabato, trippa*' (Thursday, gnocchi; Friday, fish; Saturday, tripe), which suggests that the ritual has its origins in the Roman Catholic dietary injunction against eating meat on Fridays. It would have made sense to eat something filling on the days before and after the one on which you were limited to fish and vegetables. But I doubt if today's Romans, many of whom in any case ignore the ban on meat, take that into consideration. Nevertheless, and almost to a man and woman, every Thursday they can be seen tucking into gnocchi. Because eating gnocchi on Thursdays is what you do.

Various explanations have been put forward to explain the Italians' love of the familiar and their mistrust of the new. It has been argued that the sense of trepidation that pervades life in Italy has something to do with the fact that the country is so prone to natural disasters. Volcanic eruptions, earthquakes, landslides, mudslides and floods are all relatively common occurrences. Malaria was endemic in many parts of the peninsula until the twentieth century. And the inhabitants of Naples and Catania live today, as they have always done, with the knowledge that their lives could suddenly be changed for ever (or even snuffed out) by an eruption of Vesuvius or Etna. Since the Second World War there has been a fatal earthquake in Italy on average every six or seven years. The most deadly, which struck the area between Campania and Basilicata in 1980, took the lives of 2,570 people. Landslides and mudslides are even more common and quite often they, too, are fatal. The worst in recent times took place at Sarno, south of Naples, in 1998: 161 people died as torrents of mud and rock swept through the town and surrounding villages following days of heavy rain.

Because of their peculiar geological characters, Rome, Naples and some other cities are also prone to so-called *voragini*: sinkholes that open up in the earth without warning. Local newspaper supplements quite often show photographs of cars, or even buses, balanced precariously on the edge of a *voragine*. Sometimes, the picture will be of a miserable-looking family next to a giant hole that has appeared overnight in their living room.

Life in Italy is certainly unpredictable. But, historically, it has been human intervention rather than 'acts of God' that has made it such a dangerous place in which to live. And I suspect that Italians' instinctive distaste for radical change stems in large part from their long experience of violence and oppression. Whether it came in the form of an invasion by a foreign army, a raid by Muslim pirates or slavers, or the overthrow of a local potentate, sudden breaks with the past have rarely been for the better.

Mussolini and his Blackshirts reinforced that lesson. For once in their history, Italians embraced and endorsed an abrupt change, and in the end it led them to disaster. Since the Second World War change has mostly taken place after careful orchestration or lengthy discussion, and in a way that is usually gradual – and often ineffective. As in Germany, the experience of dictatorship produced a backlash against decisiveness. Their country having been brought to its knees by the concentration of power in the hands of one man, Italians – like Germans – made a conscious decision that, in future, power would be spread as widely and evenly as possible.

The Germans opted for geographical diffusion, creating powerful regional governments and decentralizing the institutions of the state so that the ministries were in one city, the supreme court in another, and the police headquarters and the central bank in a third and fourth. The Italians, on the other hand, gradually adopted a system that came to be known as *lottizzazione*, a term also used for the division of land into plots. Areas of influence were divided up between the five parties that had access to a place in government, and later the system was extended to include even the Communists.

The dispersion of power in this way proved to be innately conservative because it created an almost infinite web of checks and balances that served to block drastic reform. At the same time, the long hegemony of the Christian Democrats, who perhaps inevitably became more reactionary in office, made for Conservatism with a big C as well as conservatism with a small one. The Christian Democrats, backed by the Roman Catholic Church, created a society that was inherently wary of change, political or otherwise.

Portugal and Spain had even more reactionary governments. But they were dictatorships that forced their attitudes on the rest of the population and prompted a progressive, popular backlash. Italy, on the other hand, never saw anything comparable to Portugal's Carnation Revolution or the transition from dictatorship to democracy that took place in Spain. Left-wing movements created and supported by young Italians undoubtedly posed a drastic – and sometimes violent – challenge to the established order after 1968. But they were outlived by the Christian Democrats, with the result that, when the post-war order eventually crumbled in the early 1990s, it was replaced not by left-wing reformers, let alone revolutionaries, but by a new right led by Silvio Berlusconi. Italy has experienced only two periods of left-wing government since the Second World War. One lasted from 1996 to 2001; the other from 2006 to 2008: a total of just seven years.

Berlusconi, who returned to office in 2001 and remained there for eight of the next ten years, bolstered the conservative alignment of society. But if the centre of gravity in Italian politics is to the right of that in many other European countries, it is to some extent because Italian society as a whole remains conservative. That does not, of course, mean there are not plenty of Italians with progressive or radical ideas. But opinion polls suggest that, on a wide range of issues, a high percentage of the population holds conservative attitudes. In the World Values Survey carried out between 2005 and 2008, for example, respondents were asked if homosexuality was justifiable on a scale from 1 (never) to 10 (always). In Italy, the proportion of 'never justifiable' responses was 51 per cent, far higher than in France (15 per cent) or Spain (10 per cent). In Britain the figure was 20 per cent, and in the US 33 per cent. When the same question was asked with respect to abortion, Italians proved to be less tolerant than the citizens of any other Western European country: 39 per cent thought it was never justifiable, compared with only 17 per cent in Spain and 14 per cent in France.

This conservatism is not restricted to politics or the issues that often feature in political debate. Though with significant exceptions, Italians tend to be wary of embracing new technology. For people with a hot summer climate, for example, they remain extraordinarily reluctant to use air conditioning. It has become relatively common in offices, but it is still remarkably little used in homes. When the temperatures soar into the thirties Celsius, as they do every July, you can bet that on any given day you will sooner or later meet someone who tells you that he or she did not sleep a wink the night before because of the heat. In Rome at least, a high proportion of the taxi drivers stoutly refuse to turn on air conditioning that is only a click of a switch away on their dashboards, and become progressively grumpier as the day wears on.

Then there is the Italians' reluctance to spend money on dishwashers. In 2005 white-goods manufacturers commissioned an international study which found that, whereas they were installed in 70 per cent of American homes and 40 per cent of British ones, the equivalent figure for Italy was just 31 per cent. Those figures are not especially surprising, perhaps, since average incomes are lower in Italy than in Britain, and much lower than in America. Altogether more remarkable are the answers given by those who did not have a dishwasher. Nearly a third said that they would accept one only if it were given as a gift. Almost one in five said they would send it back even if it were.

In both these cases, other factors than sheer conservatism may be at work. Many Italians explain their reluctance to use air conditioning on grounds of health: by moving from an unnaturally cold environment into a naturally hot one, they risk cramps or worse. As any physiotherapist will tell you, there is some truth in this. But the dangers can be mitigated by setting the thermostat to a temperature that is cool rather than icy. I suspect that another reason is the cost of the electricity needed to run air conditioning at home and that of the extra fuel needed to power air conditioning in cars. Italy has long had some of the highest electricity tariffs and fuel prices in Europe.

Financial considerations, though, do not help to explain other aspects of Italian technophobia. They were, for example, among the Europeans slowest to equip themselves with personal computers and take advantage of the Internet. By the mid-2000s, according to a survey by the government statistics office Istat, more than half of Italian homes were without a computer. And only about a third were connected to the Web.[1] The most common reason given was that computers were 'useless' or 'uninteresting'. A later survey found that the median amount of time spent online by Italian Internet users actually fell between 2007 and 2008.[2] By the latter date, Italy lagged behind not only Spain but Portugal in online access. It was even further behind France and Britain. Part of the explanation is that Italy has an elderly population. But what was true of households was also true of the government. Despite promises to the contrary by Silvio Berlusconi and his ministers, Italy's spending on the digitalization of the public administration was among the lowest in the EU as a percentage of GDP – below that of Slovakia.*

Mistrust of the new is not confined to technology. In recent years, Italy has been strikingly resistant to contemporary art. The country that gave the world the Venice Biennale, Futurism and Arte Povera did not open a national museum for contemporary art until May 2010. Italy produced one of the most internationally feted artists of the late twentieth and early twenty-first centuries in Maurizio Cattelan. Yet no one could say that he or any of his fellow painters or sculptors had found a place for themselves in the life of their country comparable with that of, say, the Young British Artists in the Britain of the 1990s or Andy Warhol in the America of the 1960s. Many of the galleries and institutions in Italy dedicated to

---

* Italy also spent the least of all developed countries on fixing the millennium bug. But that proved to be a shrewd decision.

contemporary art have struggled to prosper, or even survive. In 2012 the head of one such, Antonio Manfredi, the director of a museum near Naples, launched what he termed an 'Art War'. With the consent of the artists who had created them, he set light to a series of paintings in his collection in a desperate protest against official and public indifference.

Just as contemporary art is absent from the mainstream, so the culture of the past – and particularly that of the 1950s and 1960s – is present to a striking degree. Look on any newsstand and you will almost certainly find at least one DVD of a film starring either Totò* or his fellow comic actor Alberto Sordi. Turn on the television in the afternoon (and sometimes even in the evening) and you are quite likely to run across one of their movies. Equally, you will not have to root around for long in a souvenir shop before you find a calendar, postcard or fridge magnet based on a still featuring one or other of these actors. Bars the length and breadth of Italy are decorated with shots of Totò and Sordi in their most popular roles – Totò staring with restrained interest at his co-star's jutting bust† and Sordi playing a provincial motorcycle cop. Now, both men were very funny actors, whose films caught some of the essence of life in Italy. But I know of no other society in which quite so much attention is still being lavished on two dead performers whose best work was first shown decades ago.

One reason for this, I suspect, is that Totò and Sordi were at the height of their careers in the days of Italy's economic miracle and that their genius forms part of the cocoon of nostalgia which surrounds that era of hope and prosperity. But another reason, which is not exclusive of the first, could be that the two actors brightened up the early years of a generation that clung to power and influence with extraordinary tenacity.

Silvio Berlusconi was still prime minister at the age of seventy-five. Mario Monti, who replaced Berlusconi in 2011, took over as

---

* See above, page 33.
† The actor in question was Franca Faldini, his real-life wife.

head of government when he was sixty-eight. His Cabinet, which was brought in as a new broom that would sweep clean and introduce wide-ranging reforms, had the highest average age of any in the European Union at the time. And after the election that followed the fall of Monti's government, the new parliament re-elected a president, Giorgio Napolitano, who was eighty-seven.

For truly untrammelled 'grey power', however, nothing compared with the universities. A study published as Monti and his ministers were settling in behind their highly polished desks found that the average age of Italy's professors was sixty-three and that many were still clinging to their positions and the vast patronage they afforded when they were well over seventy. Their average age was the highest anywhere in the industrialized world.

The importance of this cannot be overstated. It meant that young Italians were not just imbibing the theories and attitudes of the previous generation, which is natural, but of the one before that, and, in extreme cases, even the one before that. The appointment of two younger prime ministers, Enrico Letta in 2013 and Matteo Renzi in 2014, has led to a rejuvenation at the highest levels of government. Renzi became Italy's youngest-ever prime minister at the age of just thirty-nine, and set about naming a Cabinet that included a party colleague who was only thirty-three at the time of her appointment. But it remains to be seen whether the process will extend to other areas of Italian life, and particularly to higher education. The role played by the elderly in the formation of Italy's future elite continued to represent a formidable obstacle to innovation, modernization and the rethinking of established ideas.

This may have some link to the enthusiasm with which so many young Italians embrace the culture of their parents. Perhaps the most striking example of this is to be found in the area of rock music, where, at the time of writing, three of the most popular singers are fifty-two, fifty-six and sixty. Ageing rock stars have kept going in other countries: the Rolling Stones, for instance. But whereas Stones' fans are in the main men and women of more or less their own generation, drawn to their concerts by memories of their youth, those of Italian stars such as Vasco Rossi are often in their twenties, if not their teens.

The importance in contemporary Italy of older people and their ideas may be light years away from the images radiated through the media of careering sports cars and models stalking down Milan cat-walks in the outrageously over-the-top outfits of designers such as Donatella Versace and Roberto Cavalli. But then so is a high level of risk aversion.

Traditionally, the dream of Italian parents has been to fix up their sons (and, more recently, daughters) with a nice, safe, undemanding job, preferably in the public administration, from which it was vir-tually impossible to be sacked. The verb for 'fix up' in this sense is *sistemare*, which is the same as that which used to carry the meaning 'marry off'. By the early 2000s there was evidence to suggest that the children were no longer content to be herded in this way into a job that lacked excitement, challenges and – in many cases – prospects. In 2001 the international employment agency Adecco carried out an extensive survey of Italian workers which found that the most favoured career choice was self-employment. Entering the public administration was barely more popular than becoming a road sweeper or a factory worker. Ten years later, however, when the firm commissioned another poll after a period of prolonged economic stagnation, the picture had changed radically: the single most popular calling was that of state employee.

Until the years of weak growth punctuated by recession began to take their toll, Italians had one of the developed world's highest rates of household savings. It was consistently double or more the rate in Britain and often several times the level in the US. The only comparably enthusiastic savers in a major Western economy were the Germans, who, perhaps not coincidentally, live in the middle of Europe and have a similar history of acute vulnerability to foreign invasion.

Where Italians put their savings is also telling. Traditionally, they preferred the safety of bonds to the potentially higher returns and risks associated with shares. For a long time this was put down to the favourable risk–return ratio on Italian government bonds. Because of the ever-present danger of devaluation before Italy entered the euro zone, the state had to offer high rates of interest to attract foreign investors. But for Italians, who were largely insulated from the effects of devaluation – their lire would continue to be worth the same in Italy – the high yields on government bonds were a bargain. Even more attractive to the members of Italy's huge middle class was the short-dated, zero-coupon bond known as a BOT (*Buono Ordinario del Tesoro*). BOTs do not offer interest payments: the return comes in the form of a final repayment higher than the cost of the bond. But the difference between the final repayment and the cost price nevertheless reflects prevailing interest rates. The millions of Italians who stuffed them away in their portfolios came to be known humorously as the 'BOT people'.

Even after Italy adopted the euro and interest rates fell sharply, the preference for less volatile fixed-interest securities remained. Ten years later bonds accounted for a fifth of all household financial assets. In the US the proportion was less than a tenth. And in Britain it was under 2 per cent.[3]

Italians' appetite for financial assets of all kinds pales in comparison with their investment in land and houses. According to the OECD, in 2008 they had eighteen times as much invested in real estate as they did in securities of all kinds. In the US the ratio was only two to one. One reason for this is that families have clung on to properties in the countryside they left when they moved to the cities in the years of the economic miracle. Another is that parents often buy flats or houses to give to their children when they marry and hold them off the market until they are needed. In some cases Italians buy property purely as an investment and do not even bother to rent it out, believing that prices will inevitably go up and that the profit they make in the end will compensate them for any loss of income in the meantime

All these factors have the effect of boosting the number of empty dwellings. In 2011 there were almost 5 million scattered across Italy – 17 per cent of the total. In Britain the same year the figure was barely

3 per cent. This huge and continual withholding of real estate from the market has helped to keep prices high and rising, thus confirming Italians in the belief that property is the best possible investment. But after more than a decade of economic stagnation, with some families urgently needing to raise cash, the market began to weaken and there was a risk that the apparently virtuous circle just described could reverse.

Just as risk aversion is characteristic of Italians' approach to investment, it can also be discerned in their approach to football. Wary prudence has long been the hallmark of Italian soccer. The traditional form of play began to develop in the 1930s when the then national coach, Vittorio Pozzo, led Italy to two successive World Cup wins, in 1934 and 1938. His strategy leant heavily on a robust – and, at times, ruthless – defence. But it was not until after the Second World War that Italian coaches embraced the style of play that was to typify Italian football for decades – *catenaccio*. The word itself means 'bolt' or 'padlock', an appropriate term for the deployment of a virtually impenetrable defence, the aim of which is to prevent losing at all costs.* Though Italian teams are still capable of boring, highly defensive football, *catenaccio* as such has faded from the scene and in recent years the way in which soccer is played in Italy has become more adventurous.

That is not the only sign that Italians may be casting aside their customary caution. At the election that preceded Enrico Letta's appointment as prime minister in 2013 most of the established parties put forward younger candidates. But the election also saw the eruption into parliament of the Five Star Movement (M5S), led by the comedian Beppe Grillo. The average age of its deputies and senators was the same as that of Letta's youngest minister. Overall, the

---

* *Catenaccio* was not, in fact, invented by Italians. It was first used by the Swiss national team and for several years was known by the French word *verrou*. It entered Italy by way of the Milan team Inter, which used *catenaccio* to win the League title, known as the *scudetto* ('little shield'), in the 1951–2 season.

average age of Italy's lawmakers dropped from fifty-six in the previous parliament to forty-eight.

Recent years have also seen the Italians shoot into the ranks of the world's most enthusiastic gamblers – a clear sign of increased readiness to assume risk. By 2010, according to figures compiled by Global Betting and Gaming Consultants (GBGC), Italy's gross gambling yield (the amount staked less the amount paid out in winnings) was almost $21 billion. That represented annual losses of $345 for every man, woman and child in the country. Excluding the mostly small countries that are specific gambling destinations – places such as Macao and the Netherlands Antilles – Italians' per capita spending was the fifth-highest in the world, behind that of the Australians, Canadians, Japanese and Finns. Their average losses were significantly more than those of the Spanish, who have traditionally been southern Europe's most ardent gamblers. Spokespeople for the Italian gambling business claimed it had become Italy's third biggest industry.

The origins of this abrupt transformation go back to the mid-1990s. Until then, Italians had a narrow choice. They could have a flutter on the lottery, bet on the outcome of football matches and horse races or – if they could get to them – try their luck on the green baize tables of Italy's handful of casinos. The oldest – it claims indeed to be the oldest in the world – is the Casinò di Venezia, which was founded in 1638 and moved to its current premises in Ca' Vendramin Calergi after the Second World War. The branch of the Casinò* on the Lido came into existence in 1938. Other casinos were – and are – to be found at Sanremo on the Riviera, Saint-Vincent in the Valle d'Aosta and at Campione d'Italia, a tiny 'exclave' of Italian territory within the Swiss canton of Ticino.

In addition, there was an illegal gambling sector that included neighbourhood raffles and other, less innocent, outlets for the

---

* The translation into Italian of the word 'casino' is one of the subtler traps awaiting English speakers. With the accent (and stress) on the final syllable, it means a gaming palace. Without it, it means a brothel.

wagering instinct. Spanish governments had long realized that the easiest way to get their citizens to pay their taxes was by encouraging them to gamble and taking a share of the profits. Italian politicians were slow to draw this lesson – or, perhaps because of the strong religious influence in politics until the early 1990s, reluctant to do so. The explosive growth of gambling since the Christian Democrats' grip on the nation was eased suggests that the illegal segment of the market was bigger than anyone imagined. To some extent, then, Italy's gambling boom has been a matter of the regulated segment of the market growing at the expense of the unregulated one.

The first step in this direction came with the legalization of scratch-card lotteries in 1994. Three years later Sisal, a private company with a gambling concession from the state, introduced what was to become a hugely popular lottery, the Superenalotto. Its chief attraction is that every so often it showers a vast jackpot on the player who succeeds in picking the six winning numbers. As the weeks pass without a winning combination, the jackpot grows, tempting more and more people to try their luck. Such is the appeal of Superenalotto that it draws coachloads of punters from neighbouring France and Switzerland. In 2009 an unidentified ticket-holder in Tuscany won €140 million after eighty-six draws that failed to produce a winner.

By then, gambling fever had really taken hold in Italy. Over the previous five years the industry's turnover had soared by 73 per cent. In the same period, the world gambling market expanded by only about 10 per cent. What made this increase all the more remarkable was that more and more Italian euros were disappearing into slot machines (the single biggest gambling medium) and being staked in other ways at a time when the economy was pretty much at a standstill. This raises the intriguing question of whether Italians' new-found enthusiasm for gambling really does reflect an increased appetite for risk. There are some indications that this is the case. Many Italians, and particularly younger ones, have become fascinated by the game of poker. Its popularity was given a huge boost by the legalization of online games of skill in 2008 and, subsequently, by the launch of a satellite channel devoted entirely to poker. But it can also be argued that the gambling boom is a perverse outcome of the extraordinarily long standstill in the Italian economy, which began at the beginning of the decade and was still eroding Italians' living standards long after the end. For people unable to find the cash to pay their bills or meet their regular mortgage payments, lotteries in particular hold out a hope, however faint, that all their problems could be solved by a huge win.

One thing is clear, though. The rapid growth in the social acceptance and official encouragement of gambling is symptomatic of an erosion of the power, though still considerable, of an institution which, down the troubled centuries, has been for Italians perhaps the greatest of all refuges and consolations – the Roman Catholic Church.

Holy Orders

'*Molti italiani, pur modestamente credenti, ritengono il cattolicesimo un patrimonio nazionale irrinunciabile: La Chiesa, da parte sua ha assorbito virtù e vizi degli italiani, in un condizionamento reciproco che ha fatto della religione una caratteristica subculturale, più che un'adesione di fede.*'

'Many Italians, even those who are not particularly religious, regard Catholicism as an indispensable national asset. The Church, for its part, has absorbed the virtues and vices of the Italians in [a process of] reciprocal conditioning that has made religion a sub-cultural characteristic rather than a bond of faith.'

– Giordano Bruno Guerri, *Gli italiani sotto la Chiesa*, 1992

From the moment white smoke gushes from the chimney on the roof of the Sistine Chapel to the proclamation of a new pope from the balcony of St Peter's, something like an hour elapses – an awkward pause during which the crowd in the great square in front of the basilica is in a state of keen expectation. When Pope Francis was elected in 2013 it was raining. So those waiting to hear who would be the new spiritual leader of the world's 1.2 billion baptized Catholics were even more in need of distraction. What better, then, than some music?

After a few minutes the Vatican's band – still known as the band of the Pontifical State – duly marched on to the square, its musicians resplendent in grey-blue capes with yellow linings. A detachment of Swiss Guards followed, bearing pikes.

So far, so unexceptional.

But then a new band came strutting through the columns that

encircle the square – that of Italy's semi-militarized Carabinieri police force. Hard on its heels, five honour guards drawn from the Italian army, navy, air force, Carabinieri and Guardia di Finanza. By the time they had all lined up opposite the Swiss Guards on the broad concourse in front of St Peter's, almost two hundred Italian soldiers and gendarmes – more than half of them armed – were standing to attention in a foreign state. The Vatican band played the Italian national anthem. The Carabinieri played the pontifical anthem. The commanders from each side saluted one another. And then the senior Italian officer swapped places with the commander of the Swiss Guards. Both officers raised their swords and cried '*Viva Il Papa!*', drawing the same cry from the troops ranged in front of them.

Italian TV commentators explained to viewers that the Italian armed forces were paying homage to the new pope in his role as head of state, as stipulated by the Lateran Pacts, the agreements that finally reconciled the Roman Catholic Church to a unified Italy in 1929. But if the aim of the ceremony had been to leave the onlookers in the square baffled as to where the dividing line ran between the Vatican and the Italian state, it could not have been better staged.

Foreigners from more secular nations were similarly perplexed by the reaction to a case taken to the European Court of Human Rights in Strasbourg by one Soile Lautsi, an atheist and an Italian of Finnish origin. She argued that the display of crucifixes in school classrooms violated her right to give her children an education free of religious influence. Laws, which like the Lateran Pacts date from the Fascist era, specify that every classroom in Italy must have a crucifix hanging on the wall. Ms Lautsi's suit was contested by the Italian government, whose representatives argued that the crucifixes were symbols of *national* identity. The education minister at the time, Mariastella Gelmini, summed up the government's case when she said that the symbols 'do not mean adherence to Catholicism'. When the court sided with Ms Lautsi, there was outrage. A poll conducted at the time suggested that 84 per cent of Italians were in favour of the crucifixes, which are also widely displayed in law courts, police stations and other public buildings. Two years later, the court's decision was overturned on appeal. More than a dozen countries, including Poland and several Ortho-dox states, had by that time joined Italy in contesting it. The appeal court, known as the Grand Chamber, found no evidence that the display of the symbol on classroom walls 'might have an influence on pupils'.

The frequently blurred distinction between Italy on the one hand and the Vatican and the Church on the other reflects a historical fact: that, until very recently, not only was Christianity Italy's only religion, but Catholicism was to all intents and purposes the only way of practising it. The assumptions that fostered persist in the most unlikely quarters. When, shortly after standing down as Brit-ain's prime minister, Tony Blair converted to Catholicism, the centre-left newspaper *La Repubblica* greeted the news on its website with a story under the headline 'BLAIR BECOMES A CHRISTIAN'.

The Islamic community in southern Italy was virtually obliter-ated at the start of the fourteenth century. The emperor Frederick II* had deported most of his Muslim subjects to the Italian main-land. Their biggest settlement was at Lucera, in modern-day Puglia. In 1300 the French ruler of the Kingdom of Naples, Charles II, attacked the town. Some fled to Albania. But most of the inhabitants of Lucera were either slaughtered or sold into slavery.

That left only the Jews as representatives of another faith. Size-able numbers had lived in pre-Christian Rome, having arrived as traders or slaves. The Jews of the peninsula fared relatively well in the early Middle Ages; those on Sicily outstandingly well under the Normans. But at the end of the twelfth century Pope Innocent III ushered in a period of intermittent oppression that reached a peak of intensity during the Counter-Reformation.

As late as the end of the fifteenth century the Borgia pope Alex-ander VI, who has gone down in history as one of the most infamous of pontiffs, welcomed to Rome thousands of Jews expelled from

* See above, p. 18.

Spain and Portugal. But just a few years later the authorities in Venice confined the Jews of their city to a single area and gave the world a pretty word for an ugly reality: *ghetto*.* In 1555 Pope Paul IV created another ghetto in Rome, ordered the city's Jews to wear distinctive badges and forced them to work as unpaid labourers on the fortifications. A successor, Pius V, decreed that the Jews be banished from the Papal State (though in fact they were never removed from Rome itself). Elsewhere on the Italian peninsula, their fortunes were uneven. The Spanish expelled them from the south and, later, from the Duchy of Milan. But other states, notably the duchies of Ferrara and Mantua, gave them refuge. It was not until the nineteenth century that the situation of Italian Jewry improved more generally, and only after Unification that they were fully emancipated.

Jews played an important role in the Risorgimento, and were to continue to do so in the politics of the late nineteenth and early twentieth centuries. Two of Italy's early prime ministers were Jews (though one, the secular Alessandro Fortis, was said to have undergone a deathbed conversion to Christianity). It is grimly ironic that Jewish intellectuals were also instrumental in the rise of Fascism. Margherita Sarfatti, one of Mussolini's many lovers and later his biographer, made an important contribution to the development of Fascist thinking about the arts.

The common wisdom in Italy is that Fascism was free of anti-Semitic overtones until 1938, when, under pressure from Hitler, the *Duce* introduced legislation that stripped Jews of their Italian citizenship and barred them from public employment and many of the professions. But this is just not true. The Fascists did plenty of racial theorizing, just like the Nazis. And in her diaries[1] Mussolini's mistress Clara Petacci paints the *Duce* as a thoroughgoing anti-Semite. What is true is that the Fascists, unlike the Nazis, never

---

* The Venetians did not, however, invent the concept. German rulers had been confining Jews to particular areas of their cities since the eleventh century.

countenanced the systematic extermination of the Jews. Disaster came with Germany's occupation of much of the peninsula after Italy pulled out of the Second World War. Though many Italians risked their lives to protect Jewish friends and neighbours – a higher percentage of the Jewish population was saved than in any other occupied country apart from Denmark – between eight thousand and nine thousand people were deported to the Nazis' death camps. Few returned.

Today, the Jewish community numbers only about forty thousand. But its contribution to post-war Italy has been out of all proportion to its size. It has brought Italy a Nobel Prize, won by the astonishing Rita Levi-Montalcini, who lived to the age of 103 and was still active in medical research in her late nineties.* Other distinguished Italian Jews have included the writer and painter Carlo Levi and the author and chemist Primo Levi. The founder of the group that owns *La Repubblica* and *L'Espresso*, Carlo De Benedetti, is a Jew, as are two former daily newspaper editors, Arrigo Levi and Paolo Mieli. Among prominent Italians with one Jewish parent are the late novelist Alberto Moravia, the architect Massimiliano Fuksas and the best-selling anti-mafia writer Roberto Saviano. The current head of Fiat and heir to the Agnelli fortune, John Elkann, is also half-Jewish.

For centuries, the only way to worship as a Christian in Italy without following the dictates of Rome was as a follower of the Blessed Waldo. The son of a rich family in the French city of Lyons, Pierre Valdo (or Waldo) gave away his possessions and began preaching the idea that the way to godliness was through poverty. He soon acquired a band of followers, who in 1184 were declared heretics after they refused to accept that, in order to preach, they had to secure the permission of the local clergy. Unsurprisingly, their sect developed an anti-ecclesiastical bias that foreshadowed some of the teachings of Luther and Calvin by more than three centuries. It

---

* Two Italian Jews, Emilio Segrè and Franco Modigliani, also won Nobel Prizes after fleeing to the United States to escape Fascist persecution.

anticipated by many hundreds of years more the ordination of women: Waldensian preachers could be of either sex.

Though given refuge in Piedmont by a Savoyard ruler, the Waldensians were attacked on more than one occasion by his successors. In 1655 the then Duke of Savoy ordered a massacre that appalled Protestant Europe and moved Milton to write a sonnet, 'On the Late Massacre in Piedmont', that alludes to the Waldensians' role as forerunners of the Reformation:

> Avenge, O Lord, thy slaughtered saints, whose bones
> Lie scattered on the Alpine mountains cold,
> Even them who kept thy truth so pure of old,
> When all our fathers worshipped stocks and stones.

By then, the Waldensians had adjusted some of their ideas and become, in effect, the Italian representatives of Calvinism. Despite subsequent persecution and much discrimination, they clung on in their heartland in the Cottian Alps on the border between modern-day Italy and France until 1848, when they were granted full civil and political rights. In the 1970s the Waldensian Evangelical Church united with the Italian Methodist Church to form the Union of Methodist and Waldensian Churches, which has a combined membership of around 35,000. Another 15,000 Waldensians – the descendants of Italian emigrants – are scattered through the Americas. Their biggest US settlement is Valdese in North Carolina.

For other Italians, the sole way to register disagreement with the teachings of the Catholic Church was Freemasonry. English Masons founded the first known lodge in Florence in the eighteenth century. It seems to have been wound up after the publication of the first anti-Masonic Papal Bull in 1738.

With its code of secrecy, Freemasonry was ideally suited to the hatching of plots and played a crucial role in nurturing those that helped to bring about Unification. Garibaldi, Mazzini and Cavour were all Masons. From an early stage, indeed, Freemasonry in Italy was more political, conspiratorial and anti-clerical than in most of the English-speaking world. It was only after the Second World War that one of the two main Masonic movements in Italy gained recognition in America (but not in England, Scotland or Ireland, where the Masonic authorities withheld recognition until 1972).

Freemasonry today constitutes an important, if shadowy, force in Italian society. But it remains seriously compromised by the activities of Licio Gelli, a 'Brother' who gained control of Propaganda Due (P2), the most prestigious lodge, and fashioned from it a covert organization that was implicated in several of the scandals of the 1980s, notably the collapse of Banco Ambrosiano and the still-mysterious death of its chairman, Roberto Calvi. The P2's members included senior figures in the armed forces, the intelligence services, business, politics, the civil service and civil society. One was Silvio Berlusconi.

More recently, Freemasonry in Italy has suffered from internal divisions and claims of southern lodges being infiltrated by organized criminals. In Calabria particularly, senior mobsters of the local mafia, the 'Ndrangheta, are said to have become Masons as a way of furthering their penetration of legitimate business. The heartland of Freemasonry in Italy, however, is Umbria, and especially the city and province of Perugia. When in 1993 the then head of the city's Masons was asked why, he replied, 'It's simple: because we are secular and we have been subject to papal domination for four hundred years.' Every year, Perugia commemorates a massacre by the pope's troops in 1859 after the inhabitants of the city had expelled the papal governor and offered to become part of a unified Italy.

It has often been noted in this context that the regions that once formed part of the Papal State were also the ones which, after the Second World War, constituted the 'red belt', where support for the Communist Party was strongest (though since Tuscany, which was never ruled by the popes, also formed part of the 'red belt', the process of cause and effect may not have been as simple as is often made out).

The fact that the pope's subjects were doubly constrained, by his temporal and spiritual authority, could nevertheless explain why blasphemous swearing has traditionally been widespread in areas that used to form part of the Papal State. And not only there. In Italy, blasphemy goes far beyond the exclamations you hear in English, such as 'Jesus Christ!' or 'Mother of God!' It ranges from phrases such as *'Porco Dio'* (literally, 'Pig God') to more inventive and obscene formulations involving, for example, the sex organs of the Virgin Mary. In Rome itself, there tends to be rather less blasphemy aired, perhaps because in the old days you never knew if a member of the clergy might not be within earshot. Still, the same sentiments are discernible: it is in the capital more than anywhere that you will hear priests referred to as *bacherozzi* (bugs or cockroaches, from the way they seem to scuttle along in their black cassocks).

Immediately before Unification, about one in every seven Italians was a subject of the pope. But the existence of his realm was just one of several ways in which Catholicism exerted a unique hold on the inhabitants of the peninsula and the adjoining islands. The earthly powers of the papacy enabled it – indeed, obliged it – to become involved in the political and diplomatic affairs of the peninsula in a way that did not happen to the same extent in any other part of Europe. Among the constitutional solutions proposed for a united Italy was an idea floated by an influential Piedmontese priest and author, Vincenzo Gioberti, who suggested it should be a confederation, with the pope as head of state. That idea did not prosper, but – thanks, ironically, to the determination of an ardent Mason, Mazzini – Rome became the capital.* That decision, more than any other perhaps, ensured the Church would have a huge influence on the new Italy.

At first, though, that looked anything but likely. The seizure of Rome and the ejection of the pope from his home in the Quirinal Palace led to one of the longest sulks in history. Pius IX shut himself away in the Vatican, and for almost sixty years he and his

---

* Before Rome was occupied, first Turin and then Florence served as the seat of government.

successors refused to have anything to do with the country that had stripped them of their earthly dominions. It was not until Mussolini came to power that the papacy relented. But to achieve reconciliation, Italy's Fascist dictator had to concede extensive privileges. The Lateran Pacts consisted of two documents. One created the Vatican City state and solved what had come to be known as 'the Roman Question'. The other, a so-called Concordat, governed relations between state and Church. It made Catholicism the state religion; made religion – or rather, the Catholic religion – a compulsory subject in schools; and turned the clergy into public employees whose salaries and pensions would henceforth be paid by the Italian taxpayer.

The fall of Fascism against the background of Italy's ultimately disastrous intervention in the Second World War created a vacuum on the right of Italian politics. The Liberals, advocates of free-market capitalism, had played an important role before Mussolini came to power. But their party had long since become that of the upper and upper-middle classes: the southern landowners, northern industrialists and some liberal professionals. The Christian Democrats, on the other hand, had an ideology that appealed to a much broader section of society, and especially the lower middle class, with its legions of peasant farmers, small businesspeople, clerks, skilled workers and civil servants. The Catholics promised moral leadership to a society that for the previous twenty-odd years had been in thrall to a creed that was now thoroughly discredited. They were looked on with favour by the occupying powers. And, not insignificantly, the pope excommunicated anyone who gave a hand to their most dangerous rivals. In 1948 a papal decree cast out of the Church anyone who spread the teachings of communism.

It would be an understatement to say that the Christian Democrats had found a winning combination. Every prime minister from 1945 until 1981 was from the Christian Democrat Party. And it was not until 1994, when Silvio Berlusconi first came to power – by which time the DC had collapsed – that a government was formed without a member of the party in the Cabinet.

The influence of the Church went far beyond government. Between them, the Church and the Christian Democrats created a web of associations that ensured backing in many areas of society for their shared beliefs. There was Coldiretti for peasant smallholders and the Confederazione Italiana Sindacati Lavoratori (CISL), a trade union confederation that split from the Confederazione Generale Italiana del Lavoro (CGIL) in 1950 to offer an alternative for Catholic workers. The Associazioni Cristiane Lavoratori Italiani (ACLI) offered a network of Church-inspired working men's clubs. And the Confederazione Cooperative Italiane (CCI), which had been founded after the First World War, grew to the point that its web of 'white' co-operatives was even bigger than that of the left-wing, 'red' original. The lay association Azione Cattolica also enjoyed a golden age of influence. By 1954 it was running more than four thousand cinemas, showing only films approved by the Church.[2]

The 1950s were the heyday of Catholicism in modern Italy. The economy was booming. And though governments came and went with dizzying rapidity, there was always a Christian Democrat in charge. Already, though, the factors that would loosen the Church's grip on society were present, if not yet identified as such. One was the movement of millions of Italians from the south to the north. Removed from under the attentive eye of the village priest into alienating new environments, the workers who travelled north often abandoned their observance, if not their faith. Another factor was the same creeping secularization that was beginning to gather momentum in other parts of Western Europe. By the 1960s recruitment to the priesthood was falling sharply.

In 1974 Italians voted decisively in favour of divorce and even more emphatically in 1981 against a bid to rescind the abortion law that had been introduced three years before. It was against this background that the Socialist prime minister Bettino Craxi negotiated a revision of the relationship between Church and state. The new 1984 Concordat made Catholicism self-financing. Under the new system, which is still in force, taxpayers can ask for 0.8 per cent of their taxes to go to the Catholic Church or to one of a range of other denominations or religions.* It is still public money, but at least atheists and Protestants can get their taxes diverted to a cause in which they believe.

The collapse of Christian democracy in the early 1990s left the Church without a dominant party to represent its interests. But that did not mean it was robbed of its influence in parliament. Rump Christian Democrat parties formed part of Silvio Berlusconi's governing coalitions in 1994–5 and 2001–2006. More importantly, many lawmakers in the Italian parliament who belong to other, non-confessional parties follow the teachings of the Vatican and vote accordingly. Although there are fewer on the left than the right, there have often been enough to form a cross-party majority to block reforms inimical to the Vatican. Indeed, it can be argued that the Church's direct, political impact has been greater in recent years than it was when the Christian Democrats were in power. The DC was unable to prevent the introduction of divorce and abortion, yet like-minded Catholic deputies and senators have succeeded in restricting *in vitro* fertilization and stem cell research and blocking altogether the granting of legal status to civil partnerships – a reform the Vatican fears could open the way to gay marriage.

For the first time since the Muslim invasions of the ninth century, however, the Catholic Church has to contend with the fact that not everyone who lives in Italy and believes in God is a Catholic. The dramatic increase in immigration in recent years† has brought in hundreds of thousands of Orthodox Christians, Pentecostals and Evangelicals, along with more than a million Muslims.

In several respects, then, Italy is less Catholic than it once was. But it is nevertheless more Catholic than other countries where the Church has traditionally been strong. The most recent edition of the World Values Survey found that 88 per cent of Italians identified themselves as Catholics, compared with 80 per cent of Spaniards.

* The choice has since been extended to include approved charities.
† See below, Chapter 19.

Proportionately, they were more observant, too. In Italy, 31 per cent of the total said they attended a religious service at least once a week. That may be low by contrast with the United States, where the figure was 47 per cent. But it was a lot higher than for Spain, where it was a mere 22 per cent – one percentage point lower than in Britain.

The small farmers' organization Coldiretti no longer wields the vast influence it once did, for the same reasons that Italian agriculture has lost ground to, first, manufacturing and then service industries. But it continues to play a prominent role in Italian life, as do the other mass organizations created by the Church or the DC. The CISL remains Italy's second-biggest trade union federation. The CCI – nowadays sporting the modish appellation of Confcooperative – is still the country's largest co-operative movement by turnover and affiliated enterprises (though not when gauged by the number of its members).

Famiglia Cristiana, a weekly with a distinctly progressive bias owned by the Society of St Paul, is the fifth-best-selling periodical. It has a bigger readership than all but one of the paparazzi gossip magazines and reaches far more Italians than the internationally better-known news weeklies *Panorama* and *L'Espresso*. The daily newspaper of the Catholic bishops, *Avvenire*, is the seventh-best-selling newspaper, and just about the only one to have increased its circulation in the face of competition from the Internet. When *Avvenire* or *Famiglia Cristiana* takes a clear stance on any political issue, the fact is widely reported in other media. There is an almost ubiquitous – and, to some extent, self-fulfilling – perception that the Church will have a powerful effect on the course of events.

That goes hand in hand with a high level of tolerance for interference by the hierarchy in public life. By and large, Italians also accept with remarkable equanimity the involvement of religious fellowships in politics, finance and business. In Spain, Opus Dei and its members have been a source of unending controversy since the dictatorship of General Franco. But until very recently the power of Comunione e Liberazione (CL) went, if not unremarked, then generally unquestioned in Italy.

Inspired by the works of Luigi Giussani, a Catholic priest from Lombardy, CL coalesced in reaction to the student uprisings of 1968. As with Opus Dei, its structure can be seen as a pattern of concentric circles, each reflecting a different level of commitment. In Comunione e Liberazione, the outermost circle comprises lay Catholics who attend a weekly meeting known as the School of Community, where prayers are said, songs or hymns are sung and a text is discussed – often an extract from the works of Father Giussani. Those who seek a closer involvement can join the so-called Fraternity. CL's innermost rings are the Fraternity of St Joseph, a group of laypeople who take vows of obedience, poverty and chastity but follow otherwise normal lives, and the Memores Domini (often referred to within CL as the *gruppo adulto*), who make the same undertakings, but live in community. The women who did the housework and cooking for Pope Benedict XVI, a keen admirer of Comunione e Liberazione, all belonged to Memores Domini. CL also encompasses a fellowship of diocesan priests and an order of nuns. Since it does not keep a register of its members, it is impossible to know the true number of its adherents. But according to the group's website, the Fraternity alone has around sixty thousand members. The organization as a whole is present in about eighty countries.

Unexpectedly, perhaps, Father Giussani also inspired the foundation of a business association, the Compagnia delle Opere, whose growth has been even more remarkable than that of CL's core fellowships. By its own account,[3] some 36,000 firms are now affiliated. In 2012 their combined annual turnover was put at €70 billion.[4]

In Italy, CL's ventures include an annual meeting in Rimini that is a national event, widely reported in the media. Past speakers have included Nobel laureates, foreign prime ministers, leading Italian politicians and the late Mother Teresa. But it is in Milan, Italy's business capital, and Lombardy, the surrounding region, where

Comunione e Liberazione was born, that its political impact has been greatest. For years, the key local conflict has been an undeclared, and mostly invisible, rivalry between the conservative CL and Azione Cattolica, which over the years had become representative of a more liberal Catholicism. In 1995 the *ciellini*, as members of the CL are known, got the upper hand when one of their number, a member of the Memores Domini, Roberto Formigoni (who subsequently joined Silvio Berlusconi's party), was elected governor of Lombardy. He kept the job for seventeen years, during which time the region became a virtual fiefdom of Comunione e Liberazione. *Ciellini* were given key jobs and, said the organization's critics, lucrative contracts were repeatedly steered towards firms belonging to the Compagnia delle Opere. Formigoni's governorship ended in a welter of scandal. In 2014 the governor, who denied any wrongdoing, was put on trial charged with corruption and criminal conspiracy.

Catholicism, though, is present in Italy in many less controversial ways. Because of the activities of the charity Caritas, the lives of many a homeless man or woman are a lot less miserable than they would be otherwise. The Church runs about a fifth of the health service, though how long that will remain the case is in doubt. Catholic hospitals rely heavily on the services of nuns. And nuns in Italy, once ubiquitous, are becoming increasingly scarce. By 2010 Italian convents still housed almost a third of all the nuns in Europe. But many of the women were elderly or foreign, and their total number had plunged by more than 10 per cent in the previous five years.

The Catholic Church also teaches about 7 per cent of the country's school students, a lower proportion than in many other European countries. But since the public educational system has been obliged to provide religious instruction, devout Italian parents have had less incentive to pay for a specifically Catholic education.

Italian Catholicism has also given rise to one of the most unusual players in international diplomacy: the Rome-based Sant'Egidio

Community. Founded by a group of school students* amid the political and ecclesiastical turmoil of 1968, it takes its name from a church in the Trastevere quarter of Rome alongside the former convent where it is based. Whereas Comunione e Liberazione reacted against the student revolts and much else the 1960s represented, the Sant'Egidio Community set out to put into practice the ideals of the reforming Second Vatican Council, which had closed three years earlier. It began by working among the poor and still runs Rome's biggest soup kitchen. As the group expanded internationally, however, its members found that in many areas there was little point in attempting to tackle the poverty they encountered unless they tried to end the violence that was at the root of it.

Sant'Egidio's greatest success was one of its earliest. In 1992 members of the community brokered a peace deal in Mozambique that ended a civil war in which more than a million people died. Four years later they played a role in halting the civil war in Guatemala. Since then, it is fair to say the group has found the going tougher. But diplomats will say that Sant'Egidio's peacemakers supply a valuable channel for informal contacts and discussion, and that because of the need for confidentiality some of its achievements go unreported.

Catholicism is woven so thoroughly into the fabric of life in Italy that even the most secular Italians pay lip service to its role – literally so, by employing words and phrases wreathed in incense. Journalists routinely describe any meeting behind closed doors as a conclave and, if it produces a result, tell readers it ended with a *fumata bianca* (an emission of white smoke). When Italians want to communicate the idea that nobody is indispensable, they say '*Morto un papa se ne fa un altro*', which translates as 'When one pope dies, you choose another.' Tellingly, the equivalent of 'to live like a lord'

---

* The leader of the original group, Andrea Riccardi, went on to become a university professor. He was a minister in the non-party government of Mario Monti from 2011 to 2013, responsible for overseas development and racial integration.

is *'vivere come un Papa'*: 'to live like a pope'. Police and prosecutors refer to mafiosi and terrorists who have turned state's evidence as *pentiti* ('penitent ones'). And anyone who has a narrow escape immediately becomes *un miracolato*. If, on the other hand, he wins the lottery, his friends will say, not 'Lucky you!', but *'Beato te!'* ('Blessed you!'). If he loses, the response will not be 'What a shame!', but *'Peccato!'*, which translates literally as 'Sin!'

The closeness of the relationship between Italians and the Church, however, owes much to factors that have nothing to do with religion. One is gratitude for the services the Church provides. Another is pride in the papacy. For more than four hundred and fifty years, until 1978 when the Polish cardinal Karol Wojtyła was elected to be John Paul II, all the popes were Italians. And they not only commanded great respect but wielded immense power.

The Catholic Church in Italy also benefits from a fair amount of inertia. Many Italians are Catholic in the way that many Britons are monarchists: it is part of the accepted order of things, and since the affairs of Italy have always been so thoroughly entwined with those of the Church, it can seem vaguely unpatriotic and rather un-Italian to challenge it. Parents, for example, are free to have their children opt out of the religious studies classes provided in Italian schools (which, of course, deal only with Catholicism). Yet relatively few do so. In the school year 2011–12 the overall participation was above 89 per cent, which is clearly far higher than the percentage of parents who are practising Catholics. Unsurprisingly, the highest drop-out rates were in the big cities of the north. The Mezzogiorno returned the sort of figures you would otherwise expect to see in a Central Asian referendum: the average participation rate was 97.9 per cent. The figure for Italy as a whole had dropped steadily in the nineteen years since a reliable study was first made, but by barely more than four percentage points. That could be explained almost entirely by the increase in non-Catholic immigrants.

The reflexive or unthinking element in the relationship of many Italians with the Church often prompts Catholic intellectuals to fret about the quality of their compatriots' faith. In 2006 Famiglia

Cristiana commissioned a poll of practising Catholics. They were asked if they had ever sought heavenly intercession (71 per cent said they had) and, if so, from whom. Which is where the surprises came in. Only 2 per cent said they had asked Jesus to intercede with his Father, while just 9 per cent had invoked the help of the Virgin Mary. Far and away the most popular choice – of nearly a third of those questioned – was Padre Pio, the Capuchin friar who died in 1968 and whose purportedly supernatural powers remain controversial.

Father Tonino Lasconi, an authority on Catholic education, was appalled by the results of the poll. 'The fact that Jesus and Our Lady are so little invoked; that the saints are preferred, and that people don't understand that the two concepts are different is a sign our Christians are extremely ignorant, [even] after years of catechesis and religious study classes,' he said.

Padre Pio was said to have levitated, wrestled physically with the devil, experienced visions and borne the stigmata, the wounds inflicted on Jesus during his crucifixion. What is certain is that for years he had gaping holes in his hands and feet. But he has been accused of mutilating himself, perhaps with acid. For a long time, the Vatican refused to accept his injuries as evidence of saintliness, and even at one point stopped him from saying Mass in public. But in 2002 Padre Pio was made a saint at the behest of Pope John Paul II and the friary in which he lived at San Giovanni Rotondo in the south-east is today the world's second-most-visited Catholic shrine. The Capuchin Friars also run a Padre Pio TV channel, available via satellite.

You come across the friar's bearded countenance on cards tucked away on the shelves of bars and the dashboards of taxis. You glimpse it unexpectedly on medallions in the wallets and handbags of people you would have thought would shrink from the kind of devotion he inspires. And you wonder why Padre Pio has such an appeal to Italians, many of whom have not been near a church in years. Is it because they identify with his humble origins as the son of a peasant farmer? Or because he embodied a tradition of mysticism in Italy that stretches back to St Francis of Assisi and St Catherine of

Siena? Is it merely that he offered a simple message of reassurance that is more welcome to Italians than the severe and complex injunctions emanating from Rome? His most famous saying – *Prega e spera non agitarti* ('Pray and hope. Don't get upset') – is certainly one with great appeal to a fundamentally optimistic people. Or could it be that Padre Pio's special appeal was – and is – more pagan? This is a man, after all, who was said to be able to read minds, foretell the future and be present in two places at once. Could it be that people see him, perhaps unconsciously, as more of a wizard than a saint? And that those cards and medallions are not so much objects of devotion as amulets?

At all events, it is highly likely that somewhere nearby you will also find a *cornicello* or *cornetto* – a horn-like charm, often made of red coral or plastic, and employed throughout Italy to ward off the evil eye. Italy's Catholicism coexists with a remarkable amount of superstition. Tarot reading is hugely popular.* Near the main square of most Italian cities you will usually find a lane in which figures are sitting hunched on fold-away stools as they turn the cards for their anxious clients. Several minor TV channels show nothing but Tarot readings for hours on end. Naturally enough, since it is constantly at risk of a volcanic eruption, the capital of superstition is Naples. The city is home to a unique race of ghosts, known as *munacielli* or *monacielli*, and probably the birthplace of the *Smorfia* (which means 'grimace', though the word may derive from the name of Morpheus, the classical god of dreams). The *Smorfia* is a table of numbers from one to ninety, each of which is assigned to a variety of objects, creatures, body parts, actions, concepts and types of person. It is widely used in Naples to place lottery bets according to what crops up in real life or the punter's dreams. Corresponding to the number eighty-eight, for example, are 'ebony', 'revenue stamp', 'a dance with children' and 'the testicles of His Holiness'.

---

* The first Tarot packs appeared in Italy in the fifteenth century, but they were used for playing games. It was not until more than three centuries later in France that they were employed for divination.

Some members of the clergy may agonize over the disparity between Catholicism as it is taught from the catechism and the beliefs of a nation that overwhelmingly defines itself as Catholic. But there would seem also to be a considerable gap between official Church teaching and its interpretation by the pope's representatives on the ground in Italy. In 2007 *L'Espresso* sent reporters to twenty-four churches around the country with instructions to confess to what the Vatican would doubtless consider sins. A journalist posing as a researcher who had received an offer to work abroad on embryonic stem cells was told that 'of course' he should take the job. And when another claimed to have let a doctor switch off the respirator that kept her father alive, the response was 'Don't think any more about it.' The only issue on which the confessors toed the Vatican's line was abortion.

It is a moot point, though, whether the magazine's findings were evidence of insubordination, doctrinal illiteracy or the simple humanity of men faced with moral dilemmas that they themselves would never have to confront in person. By and large, Catholicism makes greater allowance than Protestantism for human frailty, and it has doubtless contributed towards much that is commendable in Italy: compassion, a reluctance to judge and a readiness to forgive; all themes that will recur in later chapters.

But Catholicism also infantalizes (and not just in Italy). One of the bones of contention at the origin of the Reformation was whether the faithful had a right to seek their own salvation through direct access to the scriptures or whether, as the Catholic Church insisted, they needed the mediation of priests. The man who is ultimately responsible for telling you how to live your life is God's personal representative on earth. And in Italian he is known as *il Papa*, which is a mere accent and a capital letter away from being *il papà*, 'the father'. His bishops talk of their flocks, with the implication that the faithful are sheep. And priests address parishioners who may well be older than them as 'my son' or 'my daughter'.

Italy has been exposed to Catholicism more than any other country, so it is hardly surprising that, for example, Italians have no word for 'accountability' or that the phrase in Italian that equates most closely to 'Something will turn up' is '*Qualche santo provvederà*': 'Some saint [or other] will take care of it.' Nor is it surprising that relations between the sexes in Italy still bear the imprint of a religion that has long held strong views on the roles that are suitable for men and women.

10.

Le Italiane – *Attitudes Change*

'Italy is such a delightful place to live in if you happen to be a man.'
– E. M. Forster, *Where Angels Fear to Tread*, 1905

When she was seven or eight years of age, a young girl was taken by her parents to a pretty mountain village east of the city of Trento, near to the blurred line that separates Italian speakers from German speakers in that part of the far north of the country. The girl's family still owned the house in which her great-grandparents had lived, though by then it was unoccupied. In a corridor hung the photograph of a young woman. Her father explained to the girl that it was Clorinda, her great-aunt, who 'had been killed in the war'. As the years went by, the girl often thought back to that fleeting encounter with the past until, one day when she was at school, by then in her mid-teens, she put the name of her grandmother's sister into an Internet search engine. It was only then that she discovered that Clorinda Menguzzato had been a heroine, posthumously awarded her country's highest award for valour.[1]

Clorinda's story would make a Hollywood movie. A farm girl from the picturesque village of Castello Tesino, she joined the Gherlenda partisans' battalion and was given the *nom de guerre* of Veglia. Whereas most of the women who joined the Italian Resistance made their contribution as nurses or messengers, Clorinda actually fought alongside the men, including the man she loved, Gastone Velo. When he was wounded, she and Velo decided to make for a hamlet where Clorinda's family owned a house. But they were stopped on the way and arrested. What happened then would not make for the sort of happy ending beloved of Hollywood producers.

The Germans and their Italian Fascist associates tortured the nineteen-year-old girl for four nights in succession. But nothing they did would get her to reveal the whereabouts of her comrades-in-arms. According to the citation that accompanied her Medaglia d'oro al valore militare, towards the end of her ordeal Clorinda told her tormentors: 'When I can no longer bear your torture, I'll sever my tongue with my teeth so as not to speak.' The commandant even unleashed his Alsatian dog on her. But Clorinda – 'the lioness of the partisans', as the citation called her – never broke. In the end she was taken out of the village, more dead than alive, and shot. Her body was tossed over a cliff, where it landed in the branches of a tree. It was recovered by the parish priest of Castello Tesino, who had Clorinda dressed for burial in the sumptuous traditional garb of her village.

The contribution of those such as Clorinda Menguzzato* to the partisan campaign on which the new Italian republic claimed to have been founded, together with the influence of the Communist Party in the period immediately after the war, meant Italian women could not be sidelined quite as rapidly and comprehensively as some would no doubt have liked.

Historically, the condition of women in Italy has varied enormously from one part of the peninsula to another, over time and between social classes. The seventeenth – and, even more, the eighteenth – century offers plenty of evidence for believing that the freedom available to upper-class women in Italy was at least as great as that enjoyed by their peers in other parts of Europe, and perhaps even greater. A high-born Venetian, Elena Cornaro Piscopia, is held to be the first woman ever to be given a PhD – by the University of Padua in 1678. The first woman to be offered an official teaching position in a European university was also an Italian – Laura

---

* Altogether, nineteen women partisans were awarded the Medaglia d'oro al valore militare.

Bassi, who became a professor at the University of Bologna in 1732 while still only twenty-one years of age. The eighteenth century in Italy also produced the poet, philosopher and physicist Cristina Roccati and another polymath, Maria Gaetana Agnesi, whose name lives on in that of the Witch* of Agnesi, a geometric curve. Agnesi also shares with Laura Bassi the distinction of having a crater named after her on Venus.

One of the most memorable characters to emerge from the pages of Goethe's *Italian Journey* is a provocative young noble-woman† he met in Naples in 1787, as sassy and assertive as any contemporary feminist. Yet when another traveller, Norman Douglas, journeyed through Calabria more than a hundred years later, he formed a rather different impression of the condition of women in southern Italy when he decided to take a short cut over the hills above Bagnara:

> A porter familiar with the tracks was plainly required, and soon enough I found a number of lusty youths leaning against a wall and doing nothing in particular. Yes, they would accompany me, they said, the whole lot of them, just for the fun of the thing.
>
> 'And my bag?' I asked.
>
> 'A bag to be carried? Then we must get a woman.'[2]

The history of the women's cause in Italy is similarly uneven, spells of rapid progress alternating with long periods of stagnation. The first Italian book that could be considered a feminist tract, Anna Maria Mozzoni's *La donna e i suoi rapporti sociali*, did not appear until 1864, seventy-two years after Mary Wollstonecraft's *Vindication of the Rights of Woman* and seventy-three years after Olympe de Gouges's *Déclaration des droits de la femme et de la citoyenne*. Thereafter,

---

* 'Witch' seems to have been a mistranslation into English of the Italian *versiera*, the term for the sheet or rope used to trim a sail and the one Agnesi used to describe the curve.

† Identified, though not by Goethe, as Princess Teresa Ravaschieri di Satriano.

however, the women's movement in Italy caught up swiftly. By the early years of the twentieth century Italy had its own suffragette movement and, around the time that Douglas was touring Calabria, middle-class women in Rome and Milan were campaigning for the legalization of divorce.

What stopped the women's movement in its tracks was Fascism. Mussolini summed up his ideas in 1932: 'My opinion on [women's] role in the state is in opposition to any sort of feminism. They ought not, of course, to be slaves, but if I were to grant them electoral rights I would be ridiculed.' A few years later, just before the outbreak of war, a leading intellectual of the Fascist era, Ferdinando Loffredo, wrote that 'women must go back to absolute subjection to men' and, in case his readers failed to get the message, he explained that that meant 'spiritual, cultural and economic inferiority'.

Italy's Fascist lawmakers and officials had long been practising what Loffredo preached. Under Mussolini, women were banned from applying for senior posts in secondary education; the proportion of women on the staff of public and private enterprises was capped at 10 per cent, and if a company had less than ten employees it could not hire women at all.

After the Second World War, all that Mussolini had stood for became suspect, if not wholly unacceptable, and one of the ways in which the dictator's erstwhile adversaries could undo his legacy was by improving the status of Italian women. In 1945 women were given the vote, just one year after women in France. But, as the Christian Democrats gradually established ascendancy over the Communists, Catholic ideas on the role of women became steadily more influential. For Pius XII, who had been elected pope in 1939, 'the traditional limitation of female activity to the family circle was fundamental to public health and morality'. He explained that one reason why the Church was ready to back workers seeking higher pay was so as to 'redirect wives and mothers to their true vocation of tending the domestic hearth'. From the late 1940s to the early 1960s successive governments worked hand-in-hand with the Church to propagate an ideal of Italian femininity akin to that which radiates from the plaster statues of the Madonna to be found in many a Catholic church, eyes raised towards the Lord and hands clasped in pious fervour.

Try as they might, though, the monsignors in the Vatican and the Christian Democrats in government never quite succeeded in turning back the clock. From an early stage, in fact, there was a striking dichotomy between, on the one hand, the ideal of Italian womanhood disseminated inside the country by its priests and politicians and, on the other, the altogether more complex images projected to the outside world, largely through the medium of film. The explosive Anna Magnani – *La Lupa*, the 'she-wolf of Rome' – first brought to life in the neo-Realist films of the late 1940s a kind of Italian woman who was anything but meekly submissive. Magnani's *italiane* were passionate, courageous, forceful and even sometimes violent. Giulietta Masina, an actor who became Federico Fellini's wife, gave perhaps her greatest performance as a tragically misused elfin prostitute in her husband's Oscar-winning *Le notti di Cabiria*. The voluptuous Sophia Loren, whose career began to gain momentum as Magnani's was reaching its height, added a further ingredient – explicit sensuality.* In 1951, two years before the founding of *Playboy* magazine in the United States, Loren was acting in the nude for the French version of a film with the singular title *Era lui, sì, sì!* And over the next twenty years, Italian women stars, including Gina Lollobrigida, Silvana Mangano, Monica Vitti and Claudia Cardinale, sashayed and smooched their way across the silver screen, leaving behind quite a lot of their clothing on the way.

The Cold War years also saw improvements in the legal status of Italian women. But they were limited. In 1950 employers were forbidden from sacking mothers in the first twelve months of their first child's life, and in 1963 they were banned from dismissing

---

* Magnani won the 1955 Academy Award for Best Actress for her performance in *The Rose Tattoo*. Loren was awarded the same Oscar six years later for her role in an Italian-language film, Vittorio De Sica's *La ciociara* (shown in English-speaking countries under the title of *Two Women*).

women on the grounds of their getting married. Arguably more important was the admission for the first time in Italy's history of large numbers of girls to secondary education, following the introduction in 1962 of compulsory schooling to the age of fourteen.

More ambitious reforms had to wait until after the 1968 student revolt and the social earthquake it detonated throughout Europe. One of its effects was to generate an exceptionally vigorous feminist movement in Italy. Initially, campaigners for women's rights identified themselves closely with the New Left. But they soon discovered that a lot of young, male revolutionary socialists were as *maschilista** as their fathers and grandfathers. Many of Italy's feminists began to form a view that Marxism and its philosophical underpinnings were, if not irrelevant, then certainly inadequate to the realization of their aims. As early as 1970 the *Manifesto di rivolta femminile* was proclaiming that 'We question Socialism and the dictatorship of the proletariat.' The same year, one of the authors of the *Manifesto*, Carla Lonzi, published a pamphlet entitled *Sputiamo su Hegel* ('We Spit on Hegel').

Looking at the Italy of today, it is hard to credit that this is the same country that once gave rise to such a pugnacious brand of feminism. The public debate on gender and language that took place years ago in other societies has scarcely begun in Italy. Married Italian women have always kept their surnames, it is true. But most of the words for jobs or professions that carry with them power and authority still exist only in the masculine. A woman lawyer, who would be an *abogada* in Spain, for example, remains an *avvocato* in Italy. The same is true of several other professions: there are no widely used feminine equivalents for *notaio* (notary), *ingegnere* or *architetto*. One of the few exceptions is *dottoressa*, which is applied to female graduates and also used by women who become medical doctors. The term *avvocatessa* also exists, but most women lawyers eschew it, perhaps because they feel that the specifically female

* The equivalent in Italian of 'macho'.

version has the same, arguably diminutive, connotations as the English word 'actress'.

The situation, in other words, is a muddle. And nowhere is this truer than in politics. Until recently the few women who made it into the Cabinet were known as *ministri* and were written and spoken about as such. On occasions people would try to square the circle by referring to a female minister as *la ministro*. But since the arrival of a more numerous female contingent in government, the word *ministra* has begun to crop up, both in print and speech. Even so, at the time of writing the Italian government's own website continues to use *ministro* to describe those who head the foreign affairs, defence, economic development, education and health ministries, even though all five are women.

Turn on the television and you will sooner or later find yourself watching a variety or quiz show in which women are used in ways that have been considered unacceptable in many other countries since the 1970s. If there is a female presenter, she will almost certainly have big hair, glossy lipstick and an outfit that reveals more than it conceals. And in many cases the only women on the set will be so-called *vallette* or *veline*, whose role is almost entirely decorative. At most, they will be required to do a few dance steps or hold up a placard that shows, say, the answer to a quiz question or the amount won by a contestant. Often their job will be just to stand to one side looking pretty and smiling vacantly. The first *veline* appeared in 1988 in *Striscia la notizia*, a satire and investigation programme on one of Silvio Berlusconi's channels. Their duties involved bringing in the news items (*veline*, in journalistic slang) around which the programme revolved and draping themselves alluringly over the (male) presenter's desk.* *Striscia la notizia* is still a mainstay of

---

* The most famous former *velina* is Elisabetta Canalis, who had an usually long run on *Striscia la notizia*, from 1999 to 2002, before embarking on a career as an actor. She became internationally famous when she was the girlfriend of the Hollywood star George Clooney.

Mediaset programming, and the extended competition to choose a set of *veline* – one has to be blonde and the other brunette – for each new season is pivotal to the calendar of every aspiring Italian showgirl.*

In the same way, advertisements on hoardings and in the written media often use women in various degrees of undress to advertise products that have no connection with sex, beauty or the female body. One of the few that aroused genuine controversy appeared in 2008. Commissioned by a ferry company to advertise a new and faster connection between Naples and Catania, it showed a woman's hands clasped over her abundant breasts and was accompanied by the caption: 'Vesuvius and Etna – never this close.' Unabashed by the row over its ad, the ferry company ran another the following year featuring a long line of young women heading towards the open rear doors of one of their ferries. They were mostly wearing shorts that, in some cases, barely covered their bottoms. This time, the slogan was 'We have Italy's most famous sterns.'

Each year, the World Economic Forum (WEF) publishes its Global Gender Gap Report, which aims to assess women's status in each country according to a variety of criteria, including economic participation, political empowerment, educational attainment and various health-related indicators. In recent years Italy has bobbed up and down in the rankings, but its position as of 2013 was close to the mean: the WEF put it at seventy-first place. That was twenty-six places below France and, perhaps more surprisingly, forty-one places below Spain. Women in Italy were reckoned to be getting a worse deal than those in Romania and eleven African states.

The area in which Italy scored worst was economic participation. Recent EU and OECD figures have put the number of women in employment at around half the total female population – the lowest proportion in any large EU state. Inevitably, that also means a much

---

* Not that Italy is the only country in which women's bodies are exploited in the media. No Italian newspaper has ever published anything similar to the topless 'page three' shots in British tabloids.

higher proportion of housewives. But since there are twice as many women as men who say they are keen to work but have given up looking for a job, it is clear that many of the 5 million women who work only in the home in Italy do so reluctantly. A survey carried out in 2011 indicated that Italian housewives were not just reluctant but desperate: their level of dissatisfaction was significantly higher than that of women in either Spain or France.

Unsurprisingly, very few women are to be found in Italy's board-rooms. By 2013 they accounted for only about 8 per cent of the directors of leading Italian firms – once again the lowest share in any big European economy. In Spain, the figure was 10 per cent, in France 18 per cent and in the UK and US it was 17 per cent. A detailed illustration of how women are squeezed out of the labour market as their careers advance emerged the same year in a study of higher education.[3] By then, well over half of the graduates being turned out by Italian universities were women. But the proportion of associate professors was barely a third and the share of full professors one in five.

Those figures doubtless owe something to the age profile in academia, and to a higher 'drop-out' rate among women. The full professors tended to be older and belonged to generations in which female graduates were less common and in which it was more unusual for women to pursue a career outside the home. But the universities also feature repeatedly in allegations of what is known as *ricatto sessuale* (sexual extortion).

This is a difficult phenomenon to gauge with any precision, and certainly not one confined to Italy. But the anecdotal evidence – the frequency with which cases come to light in the media or are alluded to in private conversations – gives an impression that it is relatively widespread. The cases that surface in the media usually involve university teachers alleged to have asked a student or PhD researcher for sex in return for a pass or high marks. It is reasonable to infer that a lot of *ricatto sessuale* goes unreported and indeed unmentioned: in the cases in which the blackmail succeeds, neither party has much interest afterwards in drawing attention to what has happened. To judge by the accounts of foreigners who have worked in higher education in Italy, the exchange of academic favours for sex may not be typical, but nor is it uncommon.

Not that all the *ricatto sessuale* takes place in academia. According to a study by Istat, in 2010, 3.4 per cent of the women interviewed said they had been asked for sex in connection with their work, either as a condition of being hired or in return for promotion or – in the worst cases – as an alternative to being dismissed. So is *ricatto sessuale* any more prevalent in Italy than in other countries? If that figure is accurate, then perhaps not.

But my subjective impression – backed up by just a shred of objective evidence – is that *ricatto sessuale* has come to be regarded by quite a few Italian women as a regrettable, but unavoidable, fact of life. I found it striking, a few years ago, that one of the first comments by a newly elected Miss Italy was 'I will never sell my body for the sake of success.' And it set me to wondering how often the winners of national beauty contests in other countries begin their 'reigns' by making that clear at their inaugural press conference. The shred of evidence is a poll – with a sample that was less than statistically significant – commissioned by a women's association, Donne e Qualità della Vita. It involved asking 540 female university students if they would be ready to give sexual favours to advance their careers. Only one in five gave an outright 'no'. Almost 20 per cent said 'yes', with the remainder – roughly three out of every five – giving a coy 'don't know'.

How has a country that once had a dynamic and assertive feminist movement fallen so far behind? To some extent, what happened in Italy after the heyday of feminism is what happened throughout the world. A generation came of age in which the women no longer wanted to minimize the differences with men. Glamour came back into fashion and street demonstrations in support of women's rights began to seem outmoded. That, however, was partly because women in the 1970s had secured, if not all of their aims, then enough of them to satisfy a large percentage of the female population. Italy stood out inasmuch as the outstanding conquest – the legalization of abortion – was so unexpected and complete. Maybe, having won such a resounding victory, the warriors on the female side in Italy's battle of the sexes were all the more disposed to rest on their laurels.

The verdict of some Italian feminists, however, is less charitable. They feel that the movement took a disastrously wrong turn. Partly because of their disillusion with the men of the New Left, Italy's leading feminist thinkers shifted the emphasis to a greater extent than in most other countries away from the demand for equal rights and towards the analysis of gender differences and the exaltation of female qualities. According to this interpretation, women's liberation was sacrificed on the altar of what might be called women's pride. Certainly, that explanation would help explain the ease with which Silvio Berlusconi was able to use his growing influence in the media to spread a very different view of female sexuality, beginning in the 1980s: he was like a general marching on to a battlefield that had been deserted by his enemies.

What is incontestable is that the Berlusconi years saw very little resistance to the imposition of the values that the media tycoon represented – and indeed lived out in his own life, both public and private. Though the former prime minister has always insisted that he 'loves women', his attitude towards them has often been condescending and sometimes downright contemptuous. When Spain's Socialist leader José Luis Zapatero appointed a Cabinet in which half the ministers were women, Berlusconi called it 'too pink'. His own idea of bringing on women was made abundantly clear when he appointed Mara Carfagna, a former showgirl who had posed as a topless model, to be his minister for equal opportunities. It was only when the scandal over his bunga bunga parties reached its height in 2011 that Italian women finally reacted with demonstrations that eventually spread to more than two hundred and fifty Italian and foreign cities, under a slogan inspired by the title of Primo Levi's novel of wartime resistance, *If Not Now, When?*

Plans for the revival of a broader women's movement on the back of those demonstrations fizzled out. But, in retrospect, it can be seen that If Not Now, When? marked a turning point. At the time, only a fifth of Italy's lawmakers were women. According to a study by the Inter-Parliamentary Union, that was a lower proportion than in either Iraq or Afghanistan. At the next general election, in 2013, most of the leading parties made a serious effort to promote female candidates. In the lists submitted by Beppe Grillo's Five Star Movement, which selected its candidates in an online poll of its members, almost four in every ten were women. When the results of the election came in, it could be seen that female representation in the new legislature was going to be close to a third. The government that emerged from that election also had an unprecedentedly strong female component. And when Matteo Renzi ousted Enrico Letta the following year, he formed a Cabinet in which women occupied half the seats.

Other changes have been taking place, but without attracting the publicity that Renzi's female ministers received. While the figures given earlier for the proportion of female board members may seem paltry, they nevertheless represented a considerable increase in a brief period. This is doubtless because of legislation introduced in 2011 that made it compulsory for at least one in every five of the nominees put forward for a place on a board to be a woman.

There is also a growing awareness of the violence suffered by women and increasing censure of the men who perpetrate it. In 2013 the campaign to promote that awareness and censure received a huge boost from an unlikely quarter – a monologue delivered on St Valentine's Day by a comedian during the Sanremo song festival. The comedian, Luciana Littizzetto, is herself a symbol of changing attitudes. Stand-up comedy was until quite recently an exclusively masculine preserve in Italy. And the diminutive, impish Littizzetto has used humour to get across feminist messages that her many male fans might otherwise find hard to accept. Her monologue at the Sanremo song festival discourse was not funny at all. But it is worth quoting at length, not just because it was a wonderfully eloquent speech, but because of the huge impact it had on public opinion.

In Italy, a man kills a woman – a partner, daughter, lover, sister or 'ex' – on average once every two or three days, and probably at home, because the family isn't always and necessarily that magical place in which all is love. He kills her because he considers her his property; because he cannot imagine that a woman might belong to herself, be free to live as she wants and even fall in love with another man. And we [women], because we are naïve, often mistake all sorts of things for love. But love has damn all to do with violence and blows . . . A man who beats us up does not love us. Let us get that into our heads. Let us save it on to our hard disks . . . A man who beats us up is a shit. Always. And we must understand that straight-away, at the first slap, because then the second will come along, and then a third and a fourth. Love creates happiness and swells the heart. It does not break ribs and it does not leave bruises on the face.

Yet another sign of change – just as significant in its own way – has been a steady fall in the popularity of the Miss Italia contest. Time was when it was no exaggeration to say that this was one of the great events of the national year: a pageant celebrating the end-less supply of beautiful girls to be found in Italy that was televised for hours on end, night after night, for up to four days at a time on the flagship channel of RAI. There were few higher accolades than to be asked to join the panel of judges. Some of the most illustrious names in modern Italian culture – men like Giorgio De Chirico, Luchino Visconti and Marcello Mastroianni – agreed to duties that included scoring the curviness of the contestants' behinds. As recently as 2001 Miss Italia was winning an audience share of 85 per cent. But since then its popularity has sunk dramatically. And to such an extent that, in 2013, RAI announced that it would no longer be televising the contest. It was taken over by the La7 channel, where it notched up a share of less than 6 per cent.

Sniffing a change in the air, even *Striscia la notizia*, the programme that invented the *velina*, decided it was time for a less sexist approach. A couple of attractive young men – *velini* – were brought into the programme to flaunt their bare chests while two women did the presenting. But the result was a sharp fall in the show's audience ratings, and the *veline* were hurriedly reinstated.

Whatever else may have changed, the cult of the *mamma* in Italy has shown itself to be extraordinarily durable. The respect shown towards mothers – or rather, the lip service paid to motherhood – is well-nigh boundless. And the importance of having – and enjoying – children is impressed on women at all turns. It begins in church, with the worship of Mary. Their elders, their peers, the advertisements girls and women see in magazines and on television and radio all reinforce the message that there is no more important job in life than that of being a *mamma*. Since it is tantamount to blasphemy in most circles in Italy to assert that children are anything but an unmitigated blessing and delight, a childless woman is usually an object of pity.

One of the problems with all this is that it provides employers with the ideal justification for getting rid of workers who would otherwise have to be maintained through their unproductive maternity leave. Whatever the law may say, the practice of dismissing women who become pregnant is still all too common. The way in which some employers get around legislation that, as we have seen, dates back to the 1960s, is to tell a female job applicant that she will be hired, but only on condition that she signs an undated letter of resignation. The employer then files it away to be retrieved and dated whenever it is required in the future. These appalling documents are known as *dimissioni in bianco*. Employers who force them on women risk a heavy fine. But the offence is almost impossible to prove and has survived, particularly in smaller firms.

Italian society otherwise appears to practise what it preaches. In the WEF's surveys, the one category in which Italy has always excelled is that relating to maternity. The provision for maternity leave is among the most generous in the developed world. But once her maternity benefit expires, a young Italian *mamma* finds that the state offers her little help in balancing her role as a mother with her other duties at home and work (if, that is, she has kept her job; *dimissioni in bianco* apart, the social pressure on women to give up work after they have their first child is considerable). What the British call crèches and the Americans day-care centers are in short supply. Free, publicly funded ones are even rarer. Less than one child in five below the age of three goes to an *asilo nido* (literally, 'nest refuge').

That said, it would seem that the shortage of nurseries is a function of demand as well as supply. For one thing, the unusually low number of women in work in Italy means there are more mothers in a position to take care of their children during the day. Pollsters commissioned to carry out a survey for Istat in 2011 found that other factors played a role. When they interviewed a cross section of mothers who did not put their children into nurseries, they discovered that more than a third preferred to leave them with relatives instead, while a similar proportion said they felt their son or daughter was too young.

As children grow up, another factor emerges to keep their mothers tied to the home: the hours in secondary schools have not changed since the days in which almost all mothers were housewives. Lessons are squeezed into the morning on the assumption that children can then go home to a lunch cooked by *mamma*. In reality, that often nowadays means a sandwich left for them in the refrigerator.

Perhaps the most important factor of all, though, is that Italian husbands – like Spanish ones – have proved deeply reluctant to share the burden of looking after the house. According to official statistics dating from 2011 considerably less than half helped prepare meals and barely a quarter washed up. But the real no-go area for *l'uomo italiano* is, apparently, ironing. Whatever the reason – it remains intriguingly elusive – the proportion of men prepared to help with the ironing was one in a hundred.

Faced with the difficulty of reconciling the three roles they are nowadays expected to play, women are forced to choose. The upshot in most cases is that they curb their interconnected roles as wives and mothers. A similar response can be read in the statistics for countries right across southern Europe.

In Italy, ever since the late 1970s women have been pushing back the age at which they marry. They began limiting the number of their children even earlier. Since then, other factors have come into play, notably the erosion of job security, as more and more young people join the labour market on short-term contracts with no guarantee of permanent employment at the end. The birth rate has plunged from a peak of over twenty per thousand in the mid-1960s to less than ten in the mid-1980s. Since then it has fallen away more gently, touching a low of nine for the first time in 2011.

There are few areas of society in which the contrast between rhetoric and reality is so blatant: on the one hand, the glorification of the *mamma* and the worship of the Madonna, and on the other a society in which only children are becoming almost as common as siblings and in which the mothers waiting at the gates of primary schools are often women in their forties. And behind the statistics is another yawning gulf – between the way the Church would like Italians to conduct their sex life and the way they actually do.

Lovers and Sons

'Italians do it better.'
> – Lettering on T-shirt worn by Madonna* in the
> video of 'Papa Don't Preach' (1986)

You see them everywhere – often in the most improbable places. You see them painted on walls and chalked on pavements; you even see them occasionally marked out painstakingly in shells on beaches. They are particularly common at the gates of schools. Declarations of giddy, dizzyingly impassioned love, placed in such a way as to catch the attention of the object of desire as she (or, occasionally, he) goes about daily life, are one of the more delightful aspects of the Italian landscape and a counterpoint to the prudent reserve that characterizes much of Italian life. Some of these *graffiti d'amore* are poetic ('You are the dream that begins the moment I wake'); some are touching ('Anna, come back to me, I beg you').

'Laura, I love you more than life,' declares another I saw recently. And, indeed, some suitors put their love before their lives in their attempts to demonstrate the intensity of their passion. I have glimpsed messages written in giant letters at who-knows-what risk to the writer on bridges spanning motorways. A few years ago a town near Milan woke up to find that someone had scaled the scaffolding around a tower block under construction to hang on it a

---

* Born Madonna Louise Ciccone. Her paternal grandparents, Gaetano and Michelina Ciccone, emigrated to the United States from Pacentro, a mountain village in Abruzzo.

40-square-metre banner with a giant red heart and the name of the woman he loved.

'*Al cuore non si comanda*' runs an often-heard proverb: you cannot govern your heart. But, traditionally, as in other Mediterranean and Catholic societies, matters of the heart have been very strictly controlled, and particularly insofar as they developed into matters of the body. In recent years the grip of the Church and social tradition on the private and sexual lives of the young has loosened considerably. A recent study[1] which looked at the median age at which Italians had their first sexual encounter found that among women it had fallen sharply from twenty-two years in the generation born at around the time of the First World War to eighteen and a half among those born in the 1980s. Among men, however, the figure had scarcely changed over the years, oscillating between seventeen and a half and eighteen and a half. As the author of the study noted, that was because in the generations born in the first half of the twentieth century the sexual initiation of men and women took place in very different ways. For boys in their late teens, it was a rite of passage usually experienced 'with older, non-virginal women or prostitutes'. By contrast, most of the women were either virgins when they married, which was usually in their early twenties, or they 'had their first encounter with their future husband a short time before their wedding'.

Since the 1970s there has been a revolution in the sexual habits of southern Europe. According to the same study, only about one in ten of Italian women born in the late 1960s were virgins when they reached the altar. But the impact – or perhaps it would be more accurate to say the legacy – of Catholic influence can still be read in the few reliable international comparisons in this area.

One of the more recent, commissioned by the manufacturers of Durex condoms, looked at the average age at which people of all ages in different countries said they had first had sex.[2] The figures showed a discernible pattern. The highest averages were, predictably, in countries in the developing world that have robust social taboos on pre-marital sex. Next came a group that included most, though not all, of the Mediterranean Catholic countries, including Italy, where the 'mean age at first sex' was 19.4 years. That was fractionally lower than in Spain, but significantly higher than in the UK or US, where the figures were 18.3 and 18.4 respectively.

An even greater divergence can be seen in figures relating to female sexuality. The image of Italian womanhood projected to the outside world in movies and advertising is often that of a sultry, sensuous and, by implication, sexually voracious she-cat. Yet there is evidence to indicate that, on the contrary, Italian women are relatively inhibited. At a conference in Rome in 2010 figures were presented for the percentage of the adult population in various countries that acknowledged having masturbated at least once in their lives.[3] Among men, the levels were roughly the same in southern as they were in northern Europe – in all cases, 90 per cent or above. But among women there was a striking difference. Whereas in the Nordic countries roughly four out of five said they had pleasured themselves, in Italy the proportion was under half.

Casual sex among Italian teenagers is clearly more common than it was in the days when the influence of the Vatican – and the Christian Democrats – was all-pervasive. But a boy will often still refer to his girlfriend using the same word that was used then, as his *fidanzata* ('fiancée'), even if they are not engaged to be married. And it is quite possible that she will refer to him in a similar way, as her *fidanzato*. The terms *il mio ragazzo* and *la mia ragazza* have become increasingly popular to refer to boyfriends and girlfriends, especially among urban, middle-class youngsters. But the words *fidanzato* and *fidanzata* have shown remarkable staying power, and that is perhaps because they reflect more accurately the nature of the relationships that many young Italians form: virtual engagements that can last ten years or more before they lead seamlessly to marriage or – more commonly these days – long-term partnerships.

Madonna's T-shirt echoed a view of long standing: a perception of Italians, and particularly Italian men, as great lovers – 'Italian stallions'. It is a view that has run through the collective subconscious of the Western world from the days of Giacomo Casanova to those of Marcello Mastroianni: a view that says that Italians are not just among the world's best-looking people but also the most romantic, seductive – and exciting in bed. Fact or myth?

Another of Durex's polls[4] found perplexingly contradictory evidence. Two thirds of the respondents in Italy said that they always, or almost always, experienced an orgasm during sex, which was one of the highest proportions in the world. As in other countries, the share of women who consistently reached a climax was lower than the percentage of men who did so. But the proportion in Italy was still one of the highest registered in any of the countries surveyed. Italian couples had sex relatively often and, on average, they spent more time on intercourse than in most other countries. The overall picture, then, was that – even if Italians did not 'do it better' than everybody else – they certainly did it pretty well. Except that when the same respondents in Italy were asked if they were content with their sex lives, fewer said they were fully satisfied than in almost any other country. Maybe there is another factor that is not showing up in the statistics. Or perhaps the Italians (like the French, who also registered a low level of contentment) suffer from unreasonable expectations.

While disapproving strongly of pre-marital sex, particularly for women, the Catholic Church has always taken a more relaxed attitude towards extra-marital dalliances, especially when the adultery is committed by the husband and provided that the family remains intact – at least when seen from outside. So while being restrained in their sexual encounters before marriage, Italians have had a much more varied sex life afterwards. Or, rather, that is the impression left by a long literary tradition going back to Boccaccio's *Decameron* (in which, strikingly, many of the adulterers are not men, but women like Monna* Ghita).

The curmudgeonly Tobias Smollett, visiting Tuscany in the 1760s, described the custom among wealthy Florentine ladies of

---

* An archaic honorary title for a woman that was used in the same way that 'Mistress' once was in English. 'Mona Lisa' is, correctly, 'Monna Lisa'.

maintaining what we would today call a toy boy. In those days he was called a *cicisbeo*. The relationship between them was known to – and accepted by – the woman's husband. Though it was regarded as bad form for a *cicisbeo* to show any sign of affection to his mistress in public, he accompanied her everywhere. 'Just without one of the gates of Florence, there is a triumphal arch . . . and here in the summer evenings, the quality resort to take the air in their coaches,' Smollett wrote. 'Every carriage stops, and forms a little separate *conversazione*. The ladies sit within, and the *cicisbei* stand on the foot-boards, on each side of the coach, entertaining them with their discourse.'[5]

In some cases the *cicisbeo* was a gay man whose role was restricted to that of an amusing companion. But in others he was the woman's lover.

That Italians take a less than earnest view of marital infidelity was also the conclusion drawn by a psychology magazine, *Riza Psicosomatica*, from a light-hearted poll it carried out in 2006. The aim was to discover which vices and defects caused Italians to feel most guilty. Top of the list came gluttony and overspending. At the very bottom was sexual infidelity. It prompted fewer qualms than neglecting one's physique.

Until recently the figure of the mistress also featured more prominently in Italian culture than it did in those of many other countries. The fact that famous men had a second partner (sometimes even a second family) was often common knowledge, and when he died it was not uncommon for journalists to seek a quote, not just from the bereaved widow, but also from her rival in love. Another figure who crops up quite frequently is the middle-class Italian man who drifts away from his marriage once the children have been born and embarks on a string of affairs before returning to spend his declining years with his wife.

But entertaining girlfriends costs money. Keeping mistresses – let alone second families – costs even more. This sort of cheating was always confined to the better-off, who, by virtue of their social position and financial standing, were more likely to come into contact with foreigners and shape their perceptions of what was typically Italian. So it is legitimate to ask whether, in fact, Italians as a nation are as unfaithful in marriage as their reputation would suggest. The only international comparison I know of dates from 1994 and concerns attitudes rather than habits. People in more than twenty countries were asked their opinions on extra-marital sex. The proportion in Italy who answered that it was 'always wrong' was 67 per cent, which was exactly the same as in Britain. It was a substantially lower figure than in the US, where four out of every five respondents condemned adultery unconditionally, but a much higher one than in formerly communist states: in Russia, the disapproval rate was a mere 36 per cent.[6]

Less well-off Italian males looking for sex outside marriage (and, as mentioned earlier, before marriage) turned to prostitutes. In 1958, however, a law sponsored by a Socialist, Lina Merlin, made it illegal to profit from prostitution and led to the closure of the many brothels that had existed up until that time. The result of that still-controversial measure was to force prostitutes on to the streets, where the majority remain to this day. Some, it is true, work undisturbed from home. They traditionally advertised their services in newspapers, often beginning their ads with a string of capital A's designed to ensure that they secured first place in the personal column. Nowadays, a growing number use the Internet. According to figures compiled by *Corriere della Sera* from a variety of sources and published in 2013, there were 45,000 prostitutes active in Italy of whom only 8,000 were Italians. Of the rest, well over half were walking the streets, more often than not protected – and exploited – by pimps, and less likely perhaps to be subject to the medical check-ups they might get in a brothel.

The effect of the Legge Merlin has been to make prostitution in Italy even more sordid than in other societies and increase the health risks for all concerned. But it may have made it less widespread. If the figure given earlier is correct, then the number of prostitutes in Italy is a fraction of that in Spain, where estimates begin at around 200,000. That discrepancy is another reason for wondering if the Italian male is as wayward as he is reputed to be.

Perhaps the area where the influence of the Church can be seen clearly is contraception. The manufacture, sale and advertising of contraceptives were all at one time crimes in Italy, punishable by up to a year in prison. The prohibition was lifted in 1971, notwithstanding the publication only three years earlier of Paul VI's encyclical *Humanae Vitae*, which reaffirmed the Vatican's opposition to artificial methods of birth control.

As in other majority Catholic societies, the Vatican's strictures are widely ignored. Contraceptives of all kinds can be bought in Italy and, in some cases, the cost can be recovered from the state. Yet because the whole issue remains so sensitive, contraception is treated with a mixture of benign neglect and discreet omission. In 2013 the International Planned Parenthood Federation published a survey that aimed to measure the ease with which young women could access forms of contraception in ten European nations. Each was scored on a range of criteria that included the development of policies by the government, the availability of sex education and the provision of individualized counselling. Italy's average score was barely half that of Spain and less than a third that of France. It was one of only three countries in which policies to promote sexual and reproductive health and rights were either given a low priority or were 'practically absent from institutional agendas'.*

Successive governments have done nothing, moreover, to bring down the high prices of condoms, which, according to a survey in 2009,[7] cost almost double the global average. That may go some – albeit very small – way to explaining why another study a few years later found that less than half of sexually active young Italian

---

* One of the few areas in which Italy was given a high rating was sex education. But, as several gynaecologists and obstetricians pointed out, that was no thanks to the state. Their own professional body had taken the initiative to promote sex education in the classrooms. Italy remains one of the few countries in Europe where it is not a mandatory subject at school.

men in their late teens or early twenties took steps to prevent an unwanted pregnancy. The rest of the explanation would seem to consist of a mix of inexperience, irresponsibility and perhaps, too, a reluctance – whether conscious or unconscious – to use those artificial means of contraception that are so repugnant to the Catholic Church.

At all events, a similar disinclination can be seen in the figures for female contraceptive use. Italian women are less likely to take the Pill than those in other European countries, even though it remains the most widely used method. But in a survey conducted in 2006 the third most popular method was still *coitus interruptus* – and that was using the results of an online poll that gauged the preferences of only a relatively sophisticated cross section of the population that used the Internet.[8]

All this would seem to point in the direction of a higher level of unwanted pregnancies which would lead in turn to a high abortion rate. Instead, it signposts a mystery. One of the surveys mentioned earlier[9] found that unplanned pregnancies were less common in Italy than in any of the thirty-six other countries surveyed. The abortion rate is also comparatively low.

What we have, then, is a society in which a lot of young men are not taking precautions, but without the results you could reasonably expect. Something here does not add up. To some extent, the circle can be squared by the rapidly increasing popularity in Italy of the morning-after pill, but it may be that the frequency of sexual relations between young Italians who are not in stable relationships is still low and that promiscuity is rare. Another reason for believing this is that the opportunities for sex between young people are more limited. Italian parents today may not have the same conservative attitudes as their mothers and fathers. But going to college or university in your home city and not leaving your family home until your thirties does not exactly encourage an active sex life, let alone a promiscuous one.

It is a peculiarity of Italian that it has two ways of saying 'to love'. There is *amare*, but also *volere bene*. Not even Italians themselves can agree on the precise difference between them, and the way in which they are used can differ from one person to another. Very broadly speaking, *volere bene* denotes a less intimate, less erotic kind of affection (though when Italians want to say that they 'love', say, sailing or hunting, they sometimes use *amare*). If you were to use *volere bene* in connection with your partner or spouse, people might think something had gone wrong with your relationship. Applied to friends or colleagues, it can mean no more than 'to be very fond of'. And it is the term normally – though not always – used when speaking to or about relatives. '*Mamma*,' goes a popular song from the 1940s[10] revived by Luciano Pavarotti, '*Quanto ti voglio bene!*'

The lyrics of that, and many other songs written in Italian, attest to what other Europeans tend to regard as a uniquely strong bond between Italian sons and their mothers. The final words of '*Mamma*' are: *Queste parole d'amore che ti sospira il mio cuore/Forse non s'usano più, Mamma!/Ma la canzone mia più bella sei tu!/Sei tu la vita/E per la vita non ti lascio mai più!* (These words of love that my heart sighs/Are maybe not used these days, *Mamma!* But my most beautiful song is you!/You are life/And for the rest of my life I shall never leave you again!)

Small wonder that when non-Italians have covered this lovely ballad, they have either sung it in Italian – a language incomprehensible to the vast majority of their audiences – or in a translation with a very different slant. In the Italian version, an adult son is returning to his beloved mother and swearing never to leave her again. In the English adaptation,[11] he is regretting the distance between them: 'Oh Ma-ama/Until the day that we're together once more/I live in these memories/Until the day that we're together once more.' Tellingly, perhaps, the song in its English version had its greatest success when sung by a woman, the Italo-American singer Connie Francis.*

A son tied to his mother's apron strings is known in Italian as a

* Born Concetta Rosa Maria Franconero.

mammone. Equivalent terms can be found in other languages. In English, he would be a 'mother's boy'. Like 'mother's boy', *mammone* is not a term any man would take as a compliment. But Italian is possibly unique in having a word to describe the phenomenon of sons unduly dependent on their mothers: *mammismo*. It is a fact sometimes put forward as evidence that the stereotype is correct and that a uniquely intimate – some would say unhealthy – relationship links a disproportionate number of Italian males to their mothers.

But is *mammismo* an intrinsic and immutable aspect of the Italians' national character? In 2005 a historian, Marina D'Amelia, published a book[12] that argued that *mammismo* was what historians Eric Hobsbawm and Terence Ranger dubbed an 'invented tradition',[13] similar to other legends conjured into existence for a specific political, social or other purpose such as nation-building. D'Amelia found that the term *mammismo* dated only from 1952. The journalist and novelist Corrado Alvaro first used it as the title of an essay in his collection *Il nostro tempo e la speranza*. The way Italian mothers brought up their sons to believe that they had 'a right to everything' was 'at the origin of Italy's traditional amorality, lack of civic education and political immaturity', he argued.

For D'Amelia, this was just a way of loading on to women the responsibility for the perceived defects that had led Italy into its adoption of Fascism and the disasters that befell it during the Second World War. But it is one thing to coin a term and another to invent the syndrome it describes. And, as D'Amelia's own book makes clear, examples of an unusually strong bond between sons and mothers can be found earlier in Italy's history. One of the most celebrated is the relationship between the leading ideologist of the Risorgimento, Giuseppe Mazzini, and his mother, Maria Drago.

Mothers remain close to their son in most, if not all, Mediterranean societies. Robbed of any real economic or political clout, women in southern Europe (and North Africa) have traditionally sought to capitalize on the fact that they are nevertheless revered as mothers – and all the more so if they have given their husbands a son – by lavishing attention on their male offspring. Their sons have responded with a mother-worship that carries much the same subtext as son-adulation: that a mother's best place is in the home with her children.

Much is made of the exclamation *Mamma mia!* as evidence that *mammismo* has infiltrated even the Italian language. But *Madre mia!* is heard almost as often in Spanish. And it would be hard to come up with a more forceful, over-protective parent than the stereotypical Jewish mother.

Mammismo may be a unique word. But the difference between what it describes and what happens in other Mediterranean societies is one of degree rather than kind. That said, it would be rash to dismiss *mammismo* as no more than a myth. There is just too much evidence of it on all sides, even if that evidence is often more visible to foreigners and Italians who have lived or worked abroad than it is to those who have never had first-hand experience of another society. Stories abound of wives who discover after their wedding that their mother-in-law is going to be living in an adjoining flat; of Italian men who habitually spend part of the weekend by themselves with their mothers, or who return to live with their mothers after the break-up of their marriage. For the author of another, less scholarly recent study,[14] *mammismo*, far from being a legend, has become a 'pandemic'.

In an interview for *Psychology Today*,[15] a Genoese psychotherapist, Roberto Vincenzi, disagreed with that conclusion. He thought the syndrome was less widespread than it once was. But he acknowledged that 'one of the problems from which many of my patients – and their relatives – suffer' was one of husbands putting their mothers before their wives in their affections and priorities.

In a healthy family, a 'generational barrier' ought to exist between parents and children; that is to say, the recognition of the existence of two different sorts of love: the love that unites the parents [and] the love of the parents for the children and of the children for the parents. If, on the other hand, a parent loves a child with a love that is too strong and thereby prevents him from growing up, you get a breach of the generational barrier, which is a sure sign of pathology.

The British writer Tim Parks, who married an Italian and wrote a fascinating account of family life in Veneto,[16] observed that in the Anglo-Saxon world 'complicity traditionally, or at least ideally, resides in the relationship between the parents. In Italy it is crucially shifted towards the relationship between mother and child.' Everyone knows that the Madonna has traditionally served as a model for Latin mothers. But what is less often noted is the similarity between the roles of the Latin father and that of her husband. As Parks remarks, 'Joseph is merely a stand-in. God is the father, and that fellow's most distinguishing trait has always been his absence.' Some of the most memorable passages in Parks's book are the bitter-sweet ones in which he describes how his wife's relationship with their children swiftly becomes of a quite different quality and substance to his own. It is impossible to read them without wondering whether they do not offer at least a partial explanation for the phenomenon referred to earlier, of the Italian husbands who detach themselves from the family as their children grow up and return much later to spend their old age with their wife.

Among the many paradoxes of Italian life is that it has room for both *mammismo* and *maschilismo* – and, what is more, a high level of gender stereotyping. Pink, for example, continues to be regarded as an exclusively feminine colour, not to be worn by boys or men unless they wish to be regarded as homosexuals. Some years ago I returned from London with what I considered to be a rather elegant pale pink tie bought in Jermyn Street. The first time I wore it to the office one of my female Italian colleagues swept past me in the corridor. 'No Italian man would *ever* wear that tie,' she muttered. To this day, I do not know whether she was applauding my sartorial courage or deploring my cultural ignorance. At all events, I took the hint and did not wear it to work again.

Silvio Berlusconi is far from being alone in using the word 'pink' to characterize something that pertains to the female sex, in the way he did when describing Zapatero's Cabinet.* Women also routinely use it: a statutory percentage of women created for the purposes of affirmative action, for example, is universally termed a *quota rosa*, or 'pink proportion'. The If Not Now, When? demonstrations were advertised with a poster that had a pink background.

One of the effects of this, I suspect, is the enthusiasm in Italy – as in Spain – for transvestite and transsexual prostitutes whose defiance of gender division offers an escape from the straitjacket of stereotyping. It was estimated in the late 1990s that more than one in every twenty prostitutes in Italy was either a transvestite or, more commonly, a transsexual.[17] It is a moot point whether the men who frequent them are deceiving themselves as to their own sexual orientation.

Homosexual acts between consenting adults have been legal throughout Italy since the entry into force of the first post-Unification penal code in 1890.† Yet until recently the taboo on homosexual sex was very strong indeed. Even today attitudes towards gay people are relatively conservative. A recent Istat survey[18] found that a quarter of the respondents believed that homosexuality was an illness. Only 60 per cent thought it was acceptable for people to have a sexual relationship with a member of the same sex, and half that number were of the opinion that 'the best thing for a homosexual is not to tell others that he or she is one'. A lot of gay people, it would seem, follow that advice: the same survey suggested that only a quarter of the gay people who lived with their families had 'come out' to their parents.

By contrast, an overwhelming majority of respondents condemned discrimination on the grounds of sexual orientation. And

* See above, page 147.
† Weirdly, homosexual acts had until then been illegal in the north of the new kingdom, yet legal in the south.

almost two thirds agreed that gay partnerships should have the same rights in law as married couples.

Recent years have seen several members of the lesbian, gay, bisexual and transgender (LGBT) community rise to prominence in national and regional politics. Intriguingly, all are from the Mezzogiorno. Nichi Vendola, who was first elected to parliament in 1992, has never disguised the fact that he is gay. It seems to have done nothing to hinder his career. He was elected as governor of Puglia in 2005 and four years later became leader of the radical Left, Ecology, Freedom Party (SEL), which won more than forty seats in the national parliament at the 2013 election. Rosario Crocetta was Italy's first openly gay mayor – of the Sicilian city of Gela – in 2003 and has since gone on to become president of the island's autonomous government. In 2006 the entertainer and writer Vladimir Luxuria* became only the world's second transgender national lawmaker. And two years later, in the election that saw Luxuria lose her seat, Paola Concia from the Abruzzo, a leading activist for lesbian rights, was elected to parliament.

Yet, because of the influence exerted by the Vatican, parliament has made no progress towards outlawing the harassment of LGBT people or providing gay couples with even limited rights. Catholic lawmakers prevented homosexuals from being included among those covered by hate crime legislation introduced while the centre-left was in office in the late 1990s, and an attempt to provide a legal status for civil unions (involving both heterosexual and homosexual couples) was blocked in the same way during the centre-left government of 2006–2008† – all in the name of that most sacred of Italian sacred cows, the family.

---

* She was born Vladimiro Guadagno. Though physically male, Luxuria has long lived as a woman and prefers to be referred to as such. Her use of the women's lavatories in parliament elicited protests from some of her fellow (if that is not too inappropriate a term in this context) female legislators.

† See below, page 172.

12.

Family Matters

'La famiglia è la patria del cuore.'
'The family is the homeland of the heart.'
       – Giuseppe Mazzini, *I doveri dell'uomo*, 1860

I described earlier how Italians, in general, have been slow to embrace certain new technologies. But there is an important exception. In one respect they were, to use the jargon of the trade, 'early adopters'. When mobile telephones started to become affordable (and useable) with the introduction of the digital GSM standard in the early 1990s, Italians leapt at the chance to buy them. Even though the service providers in Italy baulked at offering easy payment facilities for the handsets, so customers had to buy them outright, cellphones were soon more widely owned than in either Britain or the United States. By the end of the decade Italy had proportionately more subscriptions than any other country in the European Union.

You could not walk down a street or travel on a bus without someone roaring *'Pronto!'* into one of those early, bulky handsets. But what was particularly interesting was what came next. As often as not, it was *'Ma dove sei?'* ('But where are you?'), which seemed odd. The whole point of mobile telephones was that you could speak from anywhere to anywhere, so why would a caller care where the other person was? I did not hear people in other countries asking this question.

It was the first hint at the main reason why, in a country otherwise deeply suspicious of technological innovation, cellphones were spreading at such an extraordinary rate: many Italians were using them to keep in contact with (and keep tabs on) the members of their family. According to an Istat study published in 2006, more than three quarters had bought their mobile telephone because of 'family demands'. On the list of other possible reasons, 'work' came fifth.

Cellphones have reassured any number of solicitous Italian *mamme* and, no doubt, frustrated any number of juvenile escapades, not to mention trysts. Far from allowing people to escape from the intimacy of family life, in Italy the mobile telephone has enabled the family to remain intimate even when its members are scattered over a wide area.*

I vividly recall an interview I once did with a prosecutor whose job was to oversee investigations into Italy's most dangerous mafia, the 'Ndrangheta of Calabria. To get to see him, I had been frisked and then led through a maze of corridors, put into a lift, taken up an indeterminate number of floors, then marched down several flights of stairs and finally steered along more passageways in what was clearly an attempt to obscure the location of the prosecutor's office. Halfway through our discussion, his cellphone rang and he broke off our conversation.

'*Pronto! Sì . . . Sì . . . Sì . . .*'

Turning away from me, he cupped his hand over the lower half of his mobile phone and lowered his voice. I imagined that on the other end of the line was maybe a Carabinieri captain with a hot lead, or else a frightened man insisting on protection if he were to turn state's evidence. The 'yes's turned to increasingly peremptory 'no's. I signalled that I would leave the room if he wanted. But it was too late. He exploded with:

---

* Italy has maintained its position as a mobile telephone operator's heaven, notwithstanding the introduction of more sophisticated handsets. By 2010, according to figures compiled by the market research company Nielsen, 28 per cent of Italians had bought a smartphone, compared with 17 per cent of Americans and only 12 per cent of Britons. Interestingly, the country with the second-highest level of smartphone penetration was Spain, another Latin nation with a largely oral culture and strong family ties.

'Yes! But not *now, Mamma!*'

The strength of the Italian family and its importance in Italian life would seem to be beyond question. More than anything, it has been the refuge in which Italians have traditionally found protection from the turbulence and vicissitudes of life on the peninsula and its adjoining islands. The family has become so fundamental a part of the national identity that it even affects Italian grammar. If you want to say 'my book' or 'my pen', you say *il mio libro* or *la mia penna*. But when you refer to a member of your family, you drop the article before the possessive adjective, so 'my wife' is *'mia moglie'*, just as 'my brother' is *mio fratello*. As soon as you again step linguistically beyond the confines of the family, however, the article reappears – even in the case of close friends and lovers. Your best friend is *il mio/la mia migliore amico/a* and your fiancé/fiancée (or boyfriend/girlfriend) is *il mio/la mia fidanzato/a*.*

The family is praised and honoured at every turn. No campaign speech is complete without an account of what the candidate intends to do for *la famiglia*. Media reports and official documents speak of *famiglie* in situations where, in English, one would use 'households', the subliminal message being that all households must consist of families. Prelates refer to *la famiglia* as something endorsed from on high; unchanging and untouchable.

However, like the commercials on Italian TV – many of which still depict large families gathered around a dining table, all expressing delight at whatever mass-produced or deep-frozen food the advertisers are trying to push – they are indulging in nostalgia. For while it is true that family loyalties in Italy do remain extremely strong (and may even be getting stronger), the traditional family is fast declining. A huge gap has opened up between what is said and what is done. In fact, the day may not be far off when the traditional

---

* There are, however, two important exceptions: *la mia mamma* and *il mio papà* (or *babbo*), even though you say *mia madre* and *mio padre*. The article is also used for plural constructions, such as *le mie sorelle* ('my sisters').

Italian family will be a legend, albeit one in which many Italians will still want fervently to believe.

Let's start by going back to the most recent World Values Survey. Respondents were asked about the importance of the family in their lives. Fully 93.3 per cent of Italians answered 'very important', four percentage points more than in Spain and seven percentage points more than in France. So far, so unexceptional: the replies show that Italians are more family-minded even than their Latin neighbours. But the proportion of Britons who gave the same answer was higher still, if only by 0.3 of a percentage point.

The idea of family, it is true, affects every aspect of Italian national life. As will be seen in later chapters, it has a huge impact on such disparate issues as the role of immigrants and the size of the government budget deficit. It influences crime and corruption. And, for as long as Italians continue to believe in it so passionately, it will continue to have great importance.

Yet the family as an institution has undergone immense changes in recent decades. The most controversial was the introduction of divorce. Its approval, at a time when Italy was still comprehensively dominated by the Christian Democrats, owed much to the spread of feminist thinking following the student uprisings of 1968. Despite furious opposition from the Catholic Church, the bill to legalize divorce was passed by both houses of parliament at the end of 1970. The battle, however, did not stop there. Lay Catholic organizations collected the signatures needed for a referendum, which was finally held in 1974. The outcome was a ringing endorsement of the new law and a spectacular demonstration of the distinction that Italians draw between their attachment to Catholicism and their obedience to Church leaders. Of those who cast a ballot, 59 per cent voted in favour of divorce.

Paradoxically, this huge step towards the modernization of Italian society came at a time when other aspects of family law remained thoroughly antiquated. It was not until the following year that family law was given a comprehensive overhaul. The principle that husbands were the rulers of the household disappeared. Wives were given new freedoms. Children born outside wedlock acquired the same rights as those born inside. Mothers were granted the same rights as fathers to decide how their children should be brought up. Dowries were abolished. And the law was changed to ensure that women continued to own whatever property they had brought into the marriage – a reform of paramount importance now that they could leave it whenever they chose.

Though the introduction of divorce was hailed (or deplored) as a turning point in Italian history, for many years its effects were limited. As late as 1995 the so-called crude divorce rate (the number per thousand of the population) was the lowest in Europe, after the former Yugoslav Republic, which at that time had other preoccupations. Since then, the rate has almost doubled, though it is still low by the standards of the rest of the European Union. Proportionately, more than twice as many Britons – and more than three times as many Americans – put a full stop to their marriages.

Just as there are more Italians leaving wedlock, there are fewer entering it. As early as the late 1990s the number of marriages each year was proportionately lower than in Britain, a country often criticized – not least by Britons – as insufficiently family-minded. By 2009 the rate of weddings per thousand of the population in Italy had shrunk from around 5 to 3.8. It had fallen in Britain, too, but marriage continued to be significantly more popular there than in Italy.

Recent years have also seen a rapid growth in households that are not traditional families: single parents and their children, non-widowed singles without children, same-sex unions, and so on. By the end of the 2000s there were some 7 million of these non-traditional families, and they accounted for 20 per cent of Italy's households, even though households continued to be described as *famiglie*. An important reason for this veritable revolution in Italian life was a sharp rise in the number of men and women who intended to get married but had decided to live together first. By the end of the decade 38 per cent of marriages took place after a period of cohabitation.

Even so, Italian law remains almost exclusively oriented towards the protection of rights and the enforcement of duties within a traditional family. Civil partners lack the most basic of entitlements. They have no right, for example, to be with their dying partner in hospital. If the partner has been married, but is not divorced, as is often the case in Italy, the most he or she can receive is a fraction of the dead partner's overall worth. Italian law stipulates that when a man or woman dies a quarter of his or her property must go to the legitimate spouse, together with the home in which the spouse is living. Half the inheritance goes to the children, with only the remaining quarter available for bequest in a will.*

The short-lived government headed by Romano Prodi between 2006 and 2008 tried to put civil partnerships on a legal footing. But it ran into fierce and ultimately successful opposition from the Catholic Church and was, more than any other, the issue that sealed the government's fate.†

The traditional family has been at the root of much of what Italy has achieved. Family-owned businesses were at the very heart of the country's economic transformation in the 1950s and 1960s. Brothers and sisters, fathers and sons and mothers and daughters were prepared to work harder, longer and more conscientiously for each other than they would ever have dreamed of working for a boss.

And that, of course, is how things have remained. Italy, its economy dominated by small businesses, is still the fortress of the family firm: a land of 'mom and pop stores' and tiny workshops where *papà* toils shoulder to shoulder with his sons while *mamma* keeps the books. Or is it? Here again, if you paid attention only to what

* In the case of a couple with only one child, the proportions are one third each for spouse and child, leaving the remaining one third to be disposed of by a will.
† The late Giulio Andreotti, a former Christian Democrat prime minister who wielded a vote in the upper house as a senator for life, cast the decisive ballot in a no-confidence vote. According to one version, Andreotti, arguably the Vatican's most loyal friend in Italian politics, was given his instructions by an envoy from across the Tiber early one morning at Mass in a church in the centre of Rome.

the politicians and prelates said, you would think so. But the figures tell a different story. In 2007 the international non-profit organization Family Business Network surveyed eight Western European countries. What its researchers found was that the proportion of family businesses in Italy – 73 per cent of the total – was lower than in all but two other countries. The true citadel of family enterprise, where 91 per cent of firms were family owned and managed, was Finland.

Italy did stand out in two other respects, though. First of all, a high proportion of family-business owners in Italy – the second highest percentage after Spain – said they had no intention of transferring the ownership of their companies in the future. Among those who said that they were contemplating a transfer, a high proportion – the highest, along with Germany, in the countries surveyed – said they envisaged their company going to a member of their family. Not coincidentally, perhaps, Italy was also the country with the highest percentage of bigger family firms (those with annual turnovers of more than 2 million euros). In other words, Italians appeared to be exceptionally keen to keep things in the family, and a large number of those who succeeded in expanding their business managed to do so without losing control to either banks or outside shareholders.

Many of Italy's biggest corporations, in fact, including several that are quoted on the stock exchange, remain family businesses at heart. The Agnelli family still has the biggest shareholdings in FCA, the automotive manufacturing group which emerged from Fiat's takeover of Chrysler in 2009. Ferrero, the makers of Nutella, is a private firm owned by Michele Ferrero, the son of the founder and the father of the CEO. Luxottica, which crafts most of the world's designer sunglasses, is still run by its founder, Leonardo Del Vecchio, and steps have been taken to ensure that control passes to his six children on his death. Silvio Berlusconi's business empire will, likewise, continue to be a family affair: his daughter by his first marriage runs the holding company Fininvest; her brother is the deputy chairman of Berlusconi's television group, Mediaset. Italmobiliare is a fiefdom of the Pesenti family. And so on, and so on. Most of the great Italian fashion empires also grew up around families: the Benettons, the Ferragamos, the Guccis, the Versaces, the Fendis and the Missonis.

Because the nuclear family has been so central to Italian society, its decline has potentially limitless effects. Yet they are rarely discussed. Few politicians or commentators, for example, have an appetite for confronting the fact that the contribution of Italy's biggest provider of welfare services is starting to shrink at a time when Italian governments, like those in the rest of southern Europe, are being forced to slash their health and social services budgets to balance the public accounts.

One of the reasons why Italian health authorities have so far had to pay for fewer hospital nurses than in other countries is because of a universal assumption that in-patients will be cared for by their relatives. Until now, moreover, Italian governments have had to spend far less than others on homes for the elderly. Originally, that was because aged parents continued living in, or very near, the same house as their children, grandchildren and, in some cases, great-grandchildren. But, as that system has broken down, particularly in the cities, another was devised – one that allowed the elderly to remain at home and, at the same time, removed a burden from the state. You can see it in action on most crowded urban streets: somewhere amid the passers-by there will often be a white-haired man or woman leaning on the arm of a Filipino, or a Latin American or an Eastern European, as he or she shuffles along on an undemanding walk around the block. The immigrant is a *badante*, or carer, hired by the family so that the women, who have traditionally cared for the elderly in Italy, can get on with their careers. What would have happened if millions of immigrants had not poured into Italy just as the old way of doing things was becoming untenable is a question that is seldom asked in public and studiously avoided by the right-wing parties, whose middle-class voters are the ones with big enough disposable incomes to pay for a *badante*.

One of the Italian family's most important contributions is one that is hard to pin down with facts and figures. It has, I think, made for a generally less alienated society than those to be found in many European countries. Italy may be plagued by organized crime syndicates (which, to some extent, reflect a family ethic), but most of its inner cities are relatively safe places and, as will be seen later, the level of violent crime is much – but *much* – lower than in other, comparable nations.

Go to the railway station in any big Italian city and you will no doubt find a runaway or two preparing to bed down for the night amid the usual assortment of tramps, alcoholics and drug addicts. But their numbers are considerably fewer than in, say, London or New York.

The problem, if there is one, is not of runaway sons and daughters but of stay-at-home children who are still in the family home long after their counterparts in the rest of the world have struck out on their own. In this respect, the family is becoming stronger, not weaker. The phenomenon began to make itself apparent in Italy and other southern European countries as far back as the late 1980s. By 2005, 82 per cent of Italian men between the ages of eighteen and thirty were still living with their parents. The equivalent figure for the United States was 43 per cent, and in none of the three biggest European nations – France, Britain and Germany – was it higher than 53 per cent.

The rise in the number of stay-at-home kids is an important reason why the marriage rate has declined so steeply, despite the fact that young Italians can count on a degree of support from their parents that would be unthinkable in many other societies. It is, for example, common for the parents of newly-weds to get together to buy them their first home. According to a survey published in 2012 two thirds of Italian couples help their offspring in this way.

That means their children do not have to save up to get the deposit for their mortgage, nor do they have to make painful sacrifices to meet the repayments while wondering all along, as do so many British and American newly-weds, how on earth they will get together the money to start a family of their own. For a lot of middle-class couples in Britain the uphill road is even steeper, because they feel they are duty-bound to send their children to private schools. In Italy, as in most other continental European countries, the norm is for children of all classes to attend the local state school, so only parents with a desire to have their children brought up in a particular religion or according to a particular philosophy opt for private education.

As for babysitting, that, too, will probably be taken care of. If the grandparents have bought the young parents' house, it is a euro to a *centesimo* they will have bought one just round the corner from where they live. That way, Granddad and Grandma – *Nonno* and *Nonna* – are conveniently on hand to look after the young ones while *Mamma* and *Papà* slip off to the movies or enjoy a night out with friends. In many cases, the grandparents' role goes further: 30 per cent provide day care for at least one grandchild.[1] In this respect, too, the strength of family bonds is removing a burden from the government.

Though often referred to in the media by the pejorative term of *bamboccioni*, Italy's stay-at-home offspring enjoy a remarkable degree of public tolerance. When the late Tommaso Padoa-Schioppa, the finance minister in the Prodi government of 2006–8 who popularized the word, dared to suggest that parents should kick them out of their homes, he ran into a firestorm of national indignation. The conventional wisdom in Italy is that they only stay at home because of the country's skewed labour market. The financial uncertainty generated by the spread of short-term contracts has made it all but impossible for young people to make their way on their own. Children, it is felt, have no option but to stay at home and their parents have no choice but to put up with them.

There is, unquestionably, some truth in these arguments. But in 2005 two (Italian) researchers, Marco Manacorda and Enrico Moretti, published a study that challenged popular wisdom on the subject.[2] For a start, older Italians were not for the most part making any great sacrifice by agreeing to live together under the same roof as their offspring. 'Italian parents report that they are happier when living with their adult children,' the two academics wrote in a summary of their findings. 'This is the opposite of what happens in Britain and the United States.'

And if parents are happy living with their offspring, most children are happy to live with their mother and father. Surveys consistently reflect good relations between teenagers and their parents. But perhaps the most striking finding emerged from a poll carried out among 33- to 37-year-olds, which was published in 2005 under the telling title *Inizio dell'età adulta* or 'The Start of Adult Life'.[3] It found that, among these thirty-somethings, about 12 per cent of the women and 17 per cent of the men were still living with their parents. The rest had left home. When asked why, some said it was to get married or live with a partner; others cited work or study. But less than one in ten of the total said they had moved out because they wanted to be independent. Older but still young Italians will often tell you with a slightly guilty air that it is pretty convenient having *Mamma* do the washing. And these days many a parent will agree to let his son's girl-friend or his daughter's boyfriend stay the night.

The main reason for Italy's legions of *bamboccioni*, Manacorda and Moretti concluded, was that their parents were 'bribing' them to stay at home. Increased parental incomes coincided with almost identical rises in the level of cohabitation, as the older generation passed on to the younger one a share of the new wealth sufficient to keep them at home.

It hardly needs to be said that such an approach robs young Italians of a sense of responsibility for their own lives. The Italian language both reflects and reinforces this. The word for boy/girl – *ragazzo/a* – continues to be applied to those who, in other societies, would long since have qualified as men or women. The age at which Italians cease to be referred to as *ragazzi* (and cease to be addressed in the familiar *tu* form) is ill-defined, but a fair guess would put it at around twenty-seven.

The equanimity (or enthusiasm) with which Italian parents contemplate the prospect of their children remaining at home raises the intriguing question of whether it is not another reason for

Italy's increasing tendency to gerontocracy. By keeping their children at home – and, in many cases, out of the labour market – parents are consciously or unconsciously reducing the natural pressure that would otherwise be exerted on their generation to move aside in favour of younger men and women.

The *bamboccioni* are young, but not hungry. Since they do not have to find the rent for a flat, or to pay for their own meals, they also have fewer incentives for taking a job that is not commensurate with their qualifications – or aspirations. Manacorda and Moretti concluded, in fact, that it was not the high rate of youth unemployment that was breeding the *bamboccioni*, but rather the *bamboccioni* who were, in part at least, responsible for the high rate of youth unemployment. Once they do get a job, moreover, young men and women who choose to remain at home have fewer reasons to push for a higher salary, and that in turn means they will have fewer reasons to take on greater responsibility and work longer hours. Crucially, too, they will be loath to accept a post elsewhere in the country. All this undermines Italy's economic competitiveness.

However, there is, I think, another and subtler way in which cohabitation between the generations holds the country back. The 2005 study concluded that the single most important advantage that the parents derived from having their children at home was 'the opportunity they have to get their children to conform to their precepts'. Imbued with the ideas of a previous generation, *bamboccioni* are less likely to launch initiatives of their own, whether they be dotcom start-ups, sandwich-delivery businesses or garage bands.

The closeness between parents and children may help explain why there are so few sullen and resentful hoodies on the streets of Italian towns. But it is also the reason why Italy is not spawning other, more innovative youth movements. Punk, hip-hop and the Goth phenomenon all began elsewhere. When they surfaced in Italy, they did so as very pale reflections of the originals. Some young Italians, it is true, find their way into the so-called *centri sociali* that often began as squats and which usually have a far-left- or far-right-wing ethos. Every so often, there is an eruption of angry street violence, invariably featuring rioters from the *centri sociali*. But, on the whole, young Italians just do not 'do' rebellion. I remember a magazine photo caption that ran '*Sporca, ruvida anima rock*' (Dirty, rough rock soul). It was next to a photograph of a young man in an impeccable jacket with a designer-frayed scarf around his neck.

The two academics cited earlier are not the only Italians in recent years to have questioned whether the strength of family affiliations always works to Italy's benefit. It may have been that its family businesses enabled Italy to catch up with some of the more prosperous nations in Europe, but they also help to explain why it has since fallen dramatically behind.*

Inheritance is not necessarily the best way to ensure dynamic management. And family firms have a poor record of investment in research and development, which is becoming increasingly vital for businesses in the twenty-first century. It is one thing to think up an elegant new design for shoes or sweaters. It is altogether another to develop an innovative new digital or electronic product. Small may once have been beautiful in industry. But that is no longer the case.

The most serious charge levelled at the Italian family, though, is of a quite different nature. And it has been around for much longer than doubts about the family's impact on prosperity. In 1958 an American sociologist, Edward Banfield, published a study of peasant farmers in the southern region of Basilicata. He entitled it 'The Moral Basis of a Backward Society'. And if that sounds pretty damning, then a lot of what was in the book was pretty damning, too. Banfield argued that the villagers he studied were unable to

---

* In 1987 the Italian government claimed that Italy's GDP had overtaken that of Britain in absolute terms – an event that came to be known as *il sorpasso* ('the overtaking'). Some economists challenged the claim at the time, but the dispute over the authenticity of the *sorpasso* gradually lost relevance as it became clear that Italy had fallen back in relative terms. By 2011, almost twenty-five years later, Italy's GDP per capita at purchasing power parity, as calculated by the International Monetary Fund, was 16 per cent lower than that of the UK.

progress because they were incapable of acting together for their common good. They were in the grip of what he termed 'amoral familism': their loyalty to their immediate family transcended any considerations of right and wrong. And since they assumed – correctly – that the members of other families would share their outlook, they preferred to undermine them rather than attempt to find a basis for mutually beneficial action. Loyalty to the family superseded loyalty to any wider grouping, be it the village, the province, the region or the nation.

The correlation that Banfield proposed, between strong family ties and antisocial behaviour, has since been challenged. In 2011 a Danish academic, Martin Ljunge, published a study based on findings from more than eighty countries. It concluded that, on the contrary, strong loyalty to the family was more likely to be associated with civic virtues such as disapproval of corruption, tax dodging and benefit cheating.[4]

That may well be true generally. But I have to say that I have my doubts about its application in Italy. Anyone who has borne witness to the interaction of modern-day Italian families in a *condominio* (the tenants' association which has to approve decisions affecting an entire apartment block or residential estate) will know what I mean. My wife and I once lived in Rome and rented a flat in an old palazzo just beyond the ancient walls. Year in, year out, the owners of the various apartments would meet to discuss the deplorable state of the common parts, which appeared not to have seen a lick of paint since the 1940s. Year in, year out, they failed to agree and the issue would be postponed.

Finally, not long before we left, rumours swept the building to the effect that an agreement in principle had been reached to repaint the hallway and the stairs. Some days later I ran into the flat owner who had held out with the greatest resolve. I asked him about the meeting of the *condominio*, which I knew had taken place the night before. Were the dismal, putty-coloured common parts finally going to get a coat of paint?

'No!' he wailed. 'They wanted' – and here he rolled his eyes

to heaven in horrified recollection of his neighbours' prodigality –
'*colours!*'

Since Banfield's day other commentators have taken the opposite
view to that of Ljunge and argued that 'amoral familism' is endemic
not just to rural Basilicata but to Italy as a whole, and has been for
centuries. Family and clan loyalties were at the root of the clashes
between rival factions that bloodied the streets of many Italian cities
in the Middle Ages. Attitudes identical to those described by Banfield can be found in the writings of the fifteenth-century Florentine
polymath Leon Battista Alberti, a renowned intellectual who is
often cited as the archetype of a 'Renaissance man': the editors of a
1974 edition of his work *I libri della famiglia* remarked that it was
impossible to find 'in the entire body of Leon Battista's work a
"cluster" of families that come together and manage to form a
civitas, a society'.

It would be wrong, all the same, to assume that amoral familism
has been an unvarying characteristic of Italian life. The southern
countryside in the mid-twentieth century may have been reminiscent of the Tuscany of the fifteenth century, but modern-day
Tuscany has precious little in common with the Mezzogiorno of
four or five hundred years ago. Over the centuries the farmers of
central Italy developed a complex system of mutual assistance, providing help to each other at times of the year when they needed
extra labour. They also cultivated a tradition known as the *veglia*,
where entire families would visit one another on winter evenings to
while away the hours playing cards, telling stories, and so on. The
greater social consciousness of the people of Tuscany, Umbria,
Emilia and the Marche may be a better explanation than papal rule*
of why so many of them embraced communism after the Second
World War.

Nor in the Mezzogiorno was the story always one of unremitting
mistrust. From time to time, sections of the peasantry formed common cause to challenge the enclosures by landowners of what had

---

* See above, page 123.

once been common land. In the late 1940s tens of thousands of people banded together in Sicily, Calabria, Basilicata and Abruzzo to occupy estates in support of land reform.

Since then, countervailing forces have been at work. On the one hand, it can be argued that the scramble for a better, richer life triggered by Italy's 'economic miracle' promoted a renewed, more family-centred approach. On the other hand, industrialization and urbanization thrust Italians into trade unions and vastly broader networks of relationships than they had known in the villages or towns from which they had migrated. People whose only previous attachment had been to their immediate family joined sporting clubs, leisure groups and sometimes charitable associations. At the same time the Catholic Church shifted the emphasis of its teaching further from an almost exclusive stress on the value of the family to encompass a recognition of the importance of society as a whole.

These forces remained finely balanced until the early 1990s and the arrival of Silvio Berlusconi. In a very real sense, he has been the paladin of a new brand of amoral familism. From the outset, his speeches – rich in allusions to the family – carried an implicit message: that his listeners had a right to advance their family's interests while paying only limited heed to the needs of society.

As the Italian family declines, there is a risk that amoral familism will dissolve into simple egocentricity, broadening and strengthening what Italians call *menefreghismo* (from *me ne frego*, or 'I don't give a damn'). *Menefreghismo* is the bartender who pushes your coffee across to you as he looks the other way; the cashier who stares through you as she takes your money. It is also the driver who bears down on you at such a speed as you step on to a pedestrian crossing he would run you over if you did not pull back in time. By itself, *menefreghismo* is usually little more than irritating. But, mixed in with *furbizia,** it forms a distinctly toxic blend that helps explain a phenomenon that influences much else in Italian life – a high level of mistrust.

* See above, page 33.

13.

People Who Don't Dance

'*Fidarsi è bene, non fidarsi è meglio.*'
   'To trust is good; not to trust is better.'
                                    – Italian proverb

Walk down any street in Italy, and what is it that makes the scene different? Obviously, there will be shopfronts and signposts that are specific to Italy. But another difference even from what you see in other countries fringing the Mediterranean will, in all probability, be the number of people wearing sunglasses. It is the middle of the winter, but you can be sure that some of those walking down the street, peering into shop windows or sitting outside a bar, will be wearing them.

Why?

For much of the year – it is true – the light in Italy is bright. And doctors will tell you that wearing dark glasses is advisable to protect against ultraviolet radiation. But the light in our hypothetical street is perfectly bearable. Some of those you can see – or, in truth, only half see – may be wearing sunglasses for cosmetic reasons: to hide the bags under their eyes caused by too late a night or perhaps too early a morning. In other cases, the dark glasses are simply a fashion accessory. But none of this fully explains why you see so many more people shielding their eyes in Italy than in, for example, Spain, where the light is, if anything, even more dazzling in winter because of the generally higher altitude. Could it be that some Italians like sunglasses for the same reason that poker players do? Could it be that they have more reason to want to see while remaining only half seen?

'*Ut imago est animi voltus sic indices oculi,*' wrote Cicero: 'The face is a picture of the mind as the eyes are its interpreter.' And certainly anyone who can hide the expression in their eyes is giving him- or herself an advantage in the delicate interactions that are the stuff of life in Italy.

Unsurprisingly, the world's biggest manufacturer of dark glasses is Italian. Nothing, you might imagine, is more American than a pair of Ray-Bans. But, in fact, the brand is owned by a company started in 1961 in Agordo, a little town in the shadow of the Dolomites. Its founder, Leonardo Del Vecchio, spent much of his childhood in an orphanage. His company, Luxottica, which now has its headquarters in Milan, also owns Oakley and makes the sunglasses that bear the names of many of the world's most celebrated fashion houses: Versace, Dolce & Gabbana, Chanel, Prada, Ralph Lauren and Donna Karan.

The image of themselves that the Italians are happiest to foster is that of a warm-blooded, warm-hearted, smiling, laughing people, whistling their way through life in an attitude of carefree bonhomie. This is the Italy of the joking waiter who flirts outrageously with the women diners. It is the Italy often projected by Roberto Benigni, the quick-fire Tuscan comic whose movie about the Holocaust, *La vita è bella*, won him the 1999 Oscar for best actor. And it is real. One of the Italians' most engaging characteristics is their optimism, backed by a determination to put their best foot forward in even the most daunting circumstances. It is an important, and delightful, part of what Italy is about.

However, before deciding that this is what Italy is *all* about, foreigners would do well to learn about two almost untranslatable Italian words. One is *garbo*, which dictionaries translate as meaning either 'grace' or 'courtesy'. But that only hints at its connotations. Certainly, a man or woman with *garbo* is one who behaves elegantly. But it is also a quality essential to any kind of decision-maker in Italy: it is the one needed to keep open your options without appearing to be indecisive; the quality required to impart unwelcome news in a way that is not too hurtful; but also the one needed to keep face as you imperceptibly shift your position.

The other quintessentially Italian noun is *sprezzatura*, which was coined by Baldassare Castiglione in *Il cortegiano*, a manual for early-sixteenth-century courtiers. His book makes clear that life at court was no soft option. Renaissance courtiers were expected to speak eloquently, think clearly and have not just extensive learning but also the accomplishments of a warrior and athlete. *Sprezzatura* was the key to how all this should be presented to the world with a studied insouciance, as if it had all come naturally, even if it was the result of long nights spent reading by candlelight and exhausting days spent practising swordsmanship.

If we go back now to our hypothetical street and look around carefully, we can see the spiritual descendant of Castiglione's courtiers; of those unnervingly composed young men you see whispering conspiratorially in one another's ears in the corners of Renaissance masterpieces. He is there, sitting in that convertible outside the bar, staring at a hostile world through those ubiquitous shades. His hair seems to be tousled. But, in fact, it has been carefully teased that way: it is as much a product of artifice as his perfectly toning shoes and belt. Our modern-day courtier is probably waiting for a beautiful young woman who is as elegant as he is. Yet it is more than possible that he is there for an appointment with someone who can fix an *appalto*, a contract, or perhaps tell him on whom he needs to make a good impression if he is to get on to the slate of candidates for the upcoming local election. His is a world of elegance and machination but, beyond his family and perhaps a handful of friends from school or university, it is probably one of isolation. It is the isolation that was so vividly brought to life by the actor Marcello Mastroianni in the knowing, lonely characters who wander through some of the films of Federico Fellini. But it can also be seen in, for example, the cool gaze and absurdly precocious, lounging pose of little Giovanni de' Medici* as he stands at his mother's side in a celebrated portrait by Agnolo Bronzino. It sends a message: that even

---

* Giovanni was later made a cardinal – at the age of sixteen. He died of malaria two years later.

toddlers, if they come from Medici stock, are possessed of daunting emotional self-control.

Perhaps the most paradoxical aspect of the Italians, and the one that most deceives others, is their apparent impulsiveness. Their animated facial expressions, their energetic hand movements and their seemingly emotional outbursts coexist with a deep, under-lying caution and discretion. Their troubled history and guileful compatriots have taught Italians to be intensely wary.

One of the first things to strike any foreign correspondent arriv-ing in Italy is the reluctance of ordinary people to supply their names, let alone other details such as their profession, age or home town. They may talk loudly into their mobile telephones about the most intimate details of their private life – their problems with their brother-in-law; even their medical examinations – but if you go up to them and ask them how they are going to vote, for example, they will often decline to answer. Or they will tell you but refuse to give you any details of their identity. I have found the same is true when Italians are asked to comment on an almost infinite range of issues, from what they witnessed at the scene of an accident to who they thought might win Saturday's match. Even when assured their remarks would not be published in Italy, they will often turn away with a wag of their upheld index finger, usually muttering a word imported from English: *privacy*.

Perhaps the most remarkable example of caginess occurred one evening after I had been rung by a colleague in London. The paper was putting together a table showing the prices of similar items in various European capitals. One of them was a McDonald's Big Mac. I asked my assistant to call the nearest branch in Rome.

'Who wants to know?' came the reply when she did so.

My assistant said it was for a British newspaper.

'In that case, I can say nothing.'

My assistant said she did not need a comment, let alone a name. And she pointed out that, if she were to walk down the street and go into McDonald's, she would be able to see the price of a Big Mac on display above the counter. All she wanted was for the person at the other end of the phone to repeat the figure that was presumably emblazoned on an illuminated sign just above her head. No dice. In the end, my assistant had to leave the office and walk a quarter of a mile through Rome to find out something that could not have been more fully in the public domain.

But then, reticence about providing information can even extend to the media, whose entire reason for existence – you might think – is to provide information. The news you get on television may be biased but, like the news on radio, it is normally communicated in a clear and comprehensible manner. Italian magazines and, to an even greater extent, Italian newspapers, on the other hand, often need to be decoded rather than read. This is particularly true of political reporting. All too frequently, the impression you are left with at the end of an article is that the reporter has been indiscreet enough to lift a corner of the veil covering the story so that you have been let in on some, but certainly not all, of the secrets to which only he or she is privy.

To be fair to my Italian fellow journalists, much of this is done to protect sources. In other instances, circumlocution is employed – usually on orders from above – as a way of not upsetting the politicians concerned. It hardly needs to be said that the politician with the most intimidating media power has long been Silvio Berlusconi. While he was in power the Italian media often got around the problem by reprinting criticism that had appeared in foreign publications and which they were loath to air in quite such bald terms.

'For centuries, we used to call in foreign armies to fight our battles for us,' one of Berlusconi's ministers remarked to me at dinner one evening. 'Now we invoke foreign correspondents instead.'

Fear, wrote Luigi Barzini in his classic study of his own people, has taught Italians 'to go through life as wary as experienced scouts through the forest, looking ahead and behind, right and left, listening to the smallest murmurs, feeling the ground ahead for concealed traps'.

Pinocchio is not just a moral parable about the perils of lying. It is also a cautionary tale about the dangers of innocence. When the puppet runs into the Fox and the Cat, they persuade him to take his gold coins to the Field of Miracles and plant them in the ground. The money, they assure him, will soon grow into a tree laden with cash. What happens next scarcely needs to be spelt out.

One of the most common mistakes made by foreigners who arrive in Italy, convinced they are among carefree, genial Latins, is to go around saying '*Ciao*' to everyone. But *Ciao* is the equivalent of 'Hi' in English, and while in America you might be able to say 'Hi' to someone you do not know well, in Italy you do not. *Ciao* broadly corresponds to the familiar *tu*. But if you would normally use the formal *Lei*, then the appropriate greeting will be *Buongiorno* ('Good morning') or *Buonasera* ('Good afternoon/evening'), depending on the time of day – and there are also significant local variations in the time at which you switch from one to the other; it is one of the many tell-tale signs by which Italians can detect outsiders. In some parts of Italy you also hear *Buon pomeriggio* for 'Good afternoon.' Somewhere in between *Ciao* and the more formal greetings is *Salve*, which can be used when you are not quite sure whether you are on *tu* or *Lei* terms with the other person. Use *Ciao* too freely and you will sooner or later be brought up sharp with a *Salve* or even an icy *Buongiorno* or *Buonasera*. Used in this way, they are the linguistic equivalents of cold water. They say: 'You are over-stepping the mark. I am not your friend. So don't treat me as if I were.'

Other cultures, of course, have their way of marking social boundaries. In Europe, there are *tu* and *vous*, *du* and *Sie*, *tú* and *Usted*. But Italy, like Germany, is also keen on placing additional signposts along those boundaries, in the form of titles.

These are not just for use on business cards. An *ingegnere*, *avvocato* or *architetto* will expect to be addressed as such by all and sundry. But the same is also true of a *ragioniere* or *geometra*,* even though a

---

* A member of a uniquely Italian profession whose practitioners combine some of the attributes of surveyors and architects, but without having to attain anything like the same educational qualifications. If you have ever wondered why, in

university degree is not required for entry into either of their professions. Anyone who has a degree qualifies to be addressed as *Dottore* – a term that is used scrupulously for journalists, medical doctors and, more surprisingly perhaps, senior police officers.

If you are not a graduate, and neither a *ragioniere* nor a *geometra*, you can always aspire to one day being addressed as *Presidente*. Vast numbers of Italians preside over something, be it a multinational or the local tennis club, and they all revel in the title of *Presidente* and the pleasure of being addressed as such.

So, if you think of yourself as belonging to the professional classes, chair the parent–teacher association or at least make a habit of wearing a collar and tie, you will start to feel slightly offended if, after the first few visits, the staff at your local bar continue to address you as merely *Signore* or *Signora* (even though those two terms originally meant 'Lord' and 'Lady'). Once firmly established as a *dottore* or *dottoressa*, you will be in position for the next big leap. Every so often, when the need arises for you to be flattered, you may be elevated temporarily to the rank of *professore* or *professoressa*.

It goes without saying that people who really do lecture college students expect to be addressed in the appropriate fashion. After the French decided to do away with the term *Mademoiselle*, which, like 'Miss', had become one you might use to choke off a rather-too-insistent young saleswoman, there was a debate in Italy about whether to ditch *Signorina*, too. *La Repubblica* commissioned an article on the subject from an unmarried female academic.

'*Signora* or *signorina*?' it began. 'I don't know. It depends. At times, it's just a matter of context, even though, in general, I really don't like being addressed in that way. For my friends, I'm simply Michela. For other people, I'd always like to be just *Professoressa* Marzano.'

The educational world holds more than one trap for the unwary. *Professore* and *professoressa* do not denote a professor in the sense in

---

a country renowned for its beautiful architecture, there are so many hideous modern buildings on the outskirts of towns, it is because in many instances their design was entrusted to a *geometra*.

which that term is understood in the English-speaking world. University lecturers qualify. So, too, do secondary or high-school teachers. Primary or grade-school teachers are referred to as *maestro/a*. But they are not addressed as such, except by their pupils, who call them *Signor(a) maestro/a*. Used as a form of address, *Maestro* (I cannot recall a *Maestra* in this sense) is for distinguished musicians, especially conductors, and – to a lesser extent – other renowned figures in the arts.

At the very top of the honorific pyramid rests the virtually unattainable title of *Commendatore*. Formally, it is used for Commanders of the Italian Republic's Order of Merit and some other dynastic and pontifical orders.

Part of the importance that Italians attach to titles is, I think, due to the need to assess the standing of the person in question and thus how much leverage he or she could exercise. Nowhere is this truer than among the Romans, who for centuries depended for their well-being on calibrating with pinpoint accuracy the exact status – and clout – of the various dignitaries at, or accredited to, the papal court.

After the death of John Paul II the *Guardian* sent its then religious affairs correspondent to share the huge workload of reporting the funeral and the election of his successor. One morning in a taxi to the Vatican I realized that my colleague would need to get into *Corriere della Sera*, where the *Guardian* had its bureau. So, using my cellphone, I telephoned Milan, where *Corriere* has its main office, to get the number of the security officers who guard the entrance to the Rome office and then called to authorize them to let in my colleague. As I rang off, I noticed the taxi driver was studying me attentively, and admiringly, in the rear-view mirror.

'*Dunque*,' he said. '*Lei è un qualcuno*.' ('So then! You're a somebody.')

When it comes to pigeonholing strangers, foreigners present a particular difficulty. Their accents hold no clues and the Romans have learnt that, even if they dress a bit scruffily, it does not necessarily mean they are impoverished or unimportant. In the bar I went to for breakfast when I first lived in Italy as a correspondent, they began by addressing me as *Signore*. But after they saw that I owned suits and ties, I was upped to *Dottore*. Then they began to ask seemingly innocent questions that might yield a clue as to why I had come to live in a part of Rome where my wife and I were pretty much the only foreigners. I took a mischievous pleasure in giving non-committal answers. There was a faculty of the Sapienza university nearby, so one day the barman tried out *Professore*. But I told them I was no sort of academic. The resulting disappointed frustration was written all over his face. Summer turned to winter, and one morning I was out walking the dog – an intimidating-looking Staffordshire bull terrier – when the rain started bucketing down, and I dodged into the bar for a warming cappuccino. I had on a long raincoat with a military look.

'*A domani*,' said the owner as he took my money.

'No,' I said. 'I won't be in tomorrow. I'll be in Naples.'

'Not at this conference on organized crime?'

The whole of Italy was aware that a big international gathering had been arranged.

'Yes,' I said. 'That's why I'm going.'

'So,' said the bar owner, as he clicked his heels and gave me a jocular salute. '*A presto, Comandante.*'

He had finally solved the mystery. From that moment on in the *quartiere*, I was *il Carabiniere inglese*, perhaps attached to the British Embassy or seconded to *i servizi*.* But clearly someone to be wary of.

Another use for formal titles is that they keep people at arm's length. A '*Buongiorno, Ragioniere*' uttered with just the right mix of respect and condescension is enough to make sure he doesn't start asking you in a familiar way about your connections or – horror of horrors – your finances.

Italians, like everyone else in the world, have friends, and some friendships are so close as to be as intimate as, if not more intimate

---

* The colloquial term for the intelligence services, both military and civilian.

than, relationships within the family. But, if the findings of that mine of social information the World Values Survey are to be believed, that is unusual. One of the questions that respondents were asked concerned how much they trusted people they knew personally. In the UK, the number who answered either 'completely' or 'a little' was fully 97 per cent. In the US, it was 94 per cent. In Spain, it dropped to 86 per cent. But in Italy, it did not even reach 69 per cent. What is more, the number who said they trusted completely their friends and acquaintances was less than 7 per cent – the lowest proportion in the world after Romania. Perhaps that remarkable finding offers a way of resolving the clash of views over 'amoral familism' mentioned in Chapter 12: that the cause of the antisocial attitudes identified by Banfield is not an unusual degree of family loyalty but rather an exceptional level of distrust that may have little or nothing to do with the family.

Widespread mistrust is all of a piece with the absence of a term in Italian that would equate to 'let your hair down'. *Lasciarsi andare* ('to let yourself go') lacks the distinctly positive connotations of the English phrase. But then you are less likely to see people break spontaneously into a dance in Italy than in any other Mediterranean country I know.

I have been in North African hotels at the end of Ramadan when local diners leapt to their feet and swirled into movement for the sheer joy of being alive. I have been in a restaurant on the Bosphorus in Istanbul when, after emptying a bottle of wine and each downing a shot of raki, a couple got to their feet, the woman holding up her arms and gyrating her hips in a display that combined elation with eroticism. In Greece, people need little encouragement to join arms in a dance that can soon become frenetic. In Spain, it is not at all uncommon to see a group of young revellers leave a bar on a Saturday night (or more often on a Sunday morning) and break into *palmas* – that mesmeric, rapid clapping on and off the beat that soon has one of the women gracefully twirling her hands and spinning her body in the joyous, flamenco-inspired style known as *sevillanas*. But in all the years I have spent in Italy I have never seen anything similar. The young go to clubs and discos, like the young everywhere. But Italy is perhaps the only country in the Mediterranean that does not have a characteristic dance form.

There are some regional folk dances. But they are mostly stiff, disciplined exercises, not unlike Scottish Highland dancing or square dancing. There are traditional Piedmontese dances that involve swords. The Sardinian *ballu tundu* has elaborate rules concerning who may hold whose hand – and how. The only dance that can be compared to the ecstatic physical expressions of joy to be found elsewhere in the Mediterranean is perhaps the tarantella from Puglia (though it is danced elsewhere in the south). But it is worth noting that the tarantella, like some parts of the flamenco canon, traditionally served a quite different purpose: not as an expression of happiness but as a refuge from misery. The dancers spun themselves into a trance-like state that allowed them to escape from the unrelenting poverty and systematic oppression of their lives in the rural south.

Elsewhere, release has seldom seemed to be in demand. Italians are by and large very moderate drinkers. Look over at the table where a group – perhaps an extended family – is enjoying dinner. It is quite likely there will be no more than one bottle of wine for every four adults and, by the end of the main course, it is a fair bet that some of the bottles on the table will be a quarter or more full. The Italian language has no word for 'hangover'. And in no other country I know do so many people refuse your offer to pour some wine into their glass, usually with a polite '*Grazie. No. Sono astemio.*' ('No, thank you. I'm teetotal.')

Italians will often say that this is because they do not need to drink in order to relax, and I think there is a lot of truth in that. But relaxing is one thing and losing control, even to a modest degree, is something else. In a society where it pays to keep your wits about you, people are, quite understandably, reluctant to take that extra step.

In 2008, the latest year for which the OECD had comparable figures at the time of writing, Italians over the age of fifteen drank an average of just over eight litres of pure alcohol per capita. This was, unsurprisingly, lower than consumption in Germany and the United Kingdom (just under ten and eleven litres respectively). But it was also much less than in Spain and Portugal, where the figures in both cases were between eleven and twelve litres.

I have only once seen a genuinely drunken Italian. And only once have I been with an Italian who drank rather more than was good for him at dinner. In both cases, it was in the north-east of the country, and that is where statistics indicate that alcohol consumption is highest. It is also where penetrating winds blow up the Adriatic, through the lanes of Venice and across the dank, flat expanses of the Veneto. Beyond Venice and the Veneto lie the Alps, where a shot of grappa never goes amiss in winter.

Elsewhere, the emphasis, especially at parties, is less on the drink than the food, which is invariably delicious. One of the first Italians I met after arriving in Rome had been brought up in Britain. When she left school her parents decided that she should get back in touch with her roots by going to university in Italy. It was not long before she was invited to a student party, where she realized, to her dismay, that the only drinks on offer were non-alcoholic ones. Her experience dates back several years. Since then, young Italians have become more relaxed about alcohol. But drunkenness is still rare.

Drugs are quite another matter. Surprisingly little is said or written about them in the media, but the consumption of narcotics in Italy is high. Two recent surveys indicated that the percentage of adults who had used cannabis in some form in the previous twelve months was the highest or second-highest in the EU (and significantly higher than in Spain, which has a long history of cannabis use because of its proximity to Morocco). The consumption of synthetic narcotics was less widespread. But acknowledged cocaine use in Italy was well above the European average (though not as widespread as in Spain).

In 2005, however, doubts were raised about official and other estimates of cocaine consumption when a research institute took a different approach to the issue. Instead of getting pollsters to question people, it took samples from the River Po. What its researchers were looking for was a substance known as benzoylecgonine, the main urinary byproduct of cocaine. The amounts detected suggested that consumption in the north of Italy was almost three times the officially estimated national average.

The following year a satirical-cum-investigative TV show tried out a quite different methodology. Reporters from *Le Iene* ('The Hyenas') tricked fifty politicians into taking drug tests. Four were found to have used cocaine in the previous day and a half. But they were never identified, and the report was never shown. The reason? *Privacy.*

14.

Taking Sides

'*Quella del calcio è l'unica forma di amore eterno che esiste al mondo. Chi è tifoso di una squadra lo resterà per tutta la vita. Potrà cambiare moglie, amante e partito politico, ma mai la squadra del cuore.*'

'Football love is the only sort of love on this earth that is eternal. The fan of a side will remain one for the whole of his life. He may change his wife, his lover or his political party. But he will never change his favourite team.'*

– Luciano De Crescenzo, *I pensieri di Bellavista*, 2005

When my wife and I moved back to Italy we lived for a while in a flat in EUR, the adjunct to Rome that Mussolini began in the 1930s. It was intended for the 1942 World's Fair (hence the initials, which stand for Esposizione Universale di Roma). In the event, the *Duce* and his ally Hitler were busy with other things when 1942 came around. Today, there are government offices in EUR as well as the headquarters of some of Italy's biggest banks and corporations. The problem is that when the office workers go home the place becomes a morgue. Apart from a concert venue, just about the only evidence of life is offered by the numerous prostitutes – many of them transvestites – who hang around on street corners near the parks. But EUR has its attractions. It is within easy reach of the coast. It is home to one of the finest twentieth-century buildings in

---

* 'Favourite team' is the only – but hopelessly inadequate – translation into English of '*squadra del cuore*'. It does not even begin to convey the passion, anguish and blind, unquestioning loyalty that is wrapped into the Italian term.

Europe, the Palazzo della Civiltà Italiana, better known as the Square Colosseum. And EUR also has a splendid man-made lake surrounded by acres of lawns and hedges.

For most of the year this pleasant spot is the preserve of joggers, local dog-walkers and office workers taking a stroll in their lunch hour. But there comes a time in the spring when the park around the lake, which is known as the *laghetto*, fills to bursting. It remains that way for two or, at most, three weekends. Then the droves of people from elsewhere in Rome disappear as abruptly and conclusively as the swifts at a certain point in late July.

There is a logic to this. The weather is not yet hot enough to encourage a visit to the beaches at Ostia, but it is sufficiently warm to make a walk by the lake a pleasant experience. Even so, the unanimity with which thousands of Romans reach the decision to go to EUR for a walk and an ice cream is astonishing. It is as if an order had gone out: 'This is the weekend that we *all* go to EUR.' And it is not too much of an exaggeration to say that something a bit like that has indeed happened.

Extensive consultations will have taken place in hundreds of circles of friends and acquaintances all over Rome. And the 'wisdom of crowds' principle means that each of those circles is likely to reach a similar, if not identical, conclusion. So at a certain point in the spring, the consensus will be 'Let's all go to EUR.'

The crowds you see as a result are the tangible evidence of *il piacere di stare insieme*, which can be translated as 'the joy of being together':* a love of communal social action that points up one of the many paradoxes that characterize life in Italy. Ask any group of Italians for their outstanding national character trait, and it is highly likely that at least one, if not most, will tell you it is *individualismo*. This does not mean individualism in the sense that Britons or Americans mean it. *Individualismo* combines 'independence of action' with 'self-interest'. Yet the vast majority of Italians are

---

* In a different context, *stare insieme* means 'to go steady'.

instinctively – almost compulsively – gregarious. So they may all prefer to go their own way, but they often end up in the same place.

When foreigners look around for a country with which to compare Italy, they usually light on Spain, or maybe France or Portugal, where the cultures are actually very different. No one ever mentions Japan. Yet it has often struck me that *il piacere di stare insieme* is one of several things that link the Italians to the Japanese. Both cultures put a high value on the appearance of things. The Japanese, like the Italians, have a recent history of wielding an economic power that far exceeded their influence on the world stage. Both have traditionally had a high level of savings. Both have a tendency to form anti-competitive, cartel-like structures and, partly for that reason, have engendered seemingly indestructible organized crime syndicates.* Japan, like Italy, is highly seismic. And both are long, narrow countries where the vast majority of the population is crammed into river valleys and narrow strips of land along the coast. You only have to look at the hinterland of Naples or the near-endless conurbation that follows the Po to the sea to realize how accustomed Italians are to living cheek by jowl.

Italians are great joiners-in. The reason why, as mentioned in Chapter 13, there are so many *presidenti* is because there are so many clubs, associations and federations – noticeably more than in Spain. Even youthful rebels join *centri sociali*, which are more like communes, even though that idea went out of fashion in the rest of the West sometime between the 1970s and the 1980s.

I have never quite fathomed whether this powerful associative tendency among Italians exists because they are trying instinctively to replicate a family structure, or because they are attempting subconsciously to pull themselves free of the family's tentacles. Perhaps there is an element of both. At all events – and this is where we get to a paradox within the paradox – it coexists with a formidable tradition of querulousness.

The political conditions in central and northern Italy throughout

---

* See below, Chapter 16.

the Middle Ages gave full rein to a combination of mutual collaboration and antagonism. The papal government of most of the centre of the country, though sporadically cruel, was rarely strong. Further north, there was no administration – or rather, there were many administrations. First came the self-governing communes. Later, they were replaced by a patchwork quilt of principalities, duchies and counties. For a period of centuries Rome and the cities to the north of it were wracked by vicious fighting between factions based on loyalty to a noble family, a clan or a neighbourhood. This is the world of Romeo and Juliet; of the Montagues and Capulets. In Siena these bitter rivalries can be seen today, channelled more or less harmlessly into the twice-yearly Palio horse race.

The factions, with their stores of weapons and fortified towers, lent themselves naturally to being subsumed into a broader conflict between the papacy and the Holy Roman Empire. In the twelfth century this crystallized around the rivalry between two German noble houses, each aspiring to the emperorship: on the one hand, the Welfs, and on the other the Hohenstaufens, with their battle cry of *'Waiblingen!'* Since it was the Hohenstaufen candidate who got the job, the opponents of the empire and supporters of the papacy (who were not always the same) later adopted the Italianized name of *Guelfi*. Their adversaries came to be known as *Ghibellini*, from a clumsy Italianization of the war cry of the Hohenstaufens. Entire cities were one or the other: Orvieto was Guelph, whereas Todi, just a few miles away, was Ghibelline; Cremona was Guelph, but Pavia, upstream on the River Po, was Ghibelline. Other cities, such as Parma on the other bank of the Po, went back and forth between the two sides. Over the years, clashes in and between cities belonging to different factions left thousands dead. In 1313 fighting between the two parties in Orvieto went on for four days. Florence, a Guelph city, and Ghibelline Siena were intermittently at war for decades.

The tendency for entire societies to split into two camps along a fault line is scarcely confined to Italy. But few divisions have lasted as long as that between the Guelphs and the Ghibellines. Several Italian writers have seen in their bloody rivalry a legacy that can still be discerned today. According to one theory, it was re-enacted throughout the Cold War in the stand-off between the Christian Democrats and the Communists: the former, allies of the papacy, had the same essential characteristic as the Guelphs; the latter, like the Ghibellines, aligned themselves with a foreign power (just as the Ghibellines had taken the side of the empire, so the Communists looked to the Soviet Union for support).

But that interpretation has to be squared with another two-sided conflict that was suppressed at the end of the Second World War and never quite went away – between the supporters and opponents of Fascism. It is argued, mostly by right-wing intellectuals, that the Second World War in Italy did not end cleanly in a popular rebellion against the Nazi occupiers (which was the version of events that underpinned the post-war years). Instead, the Allied invasion put a stop to a messy civil war between Mussolini's diehard supporters on the one hand and a predominantly communist partisan force on the other. Seen from this standpoint, the conflict resurfaced in the murderous street fighting that erupted between young neo-fascists and left-wing revolutionaries in the 1970s. And it was resolved only after the Christian Democrats and Communists were swept aside by history in the late 1980s and early 1990s, when Silvio Berlusconi brought the far right into an alliance and from there into government. In doing so, it might be argued, he also put an end to the age-old enmity between the Guelphs and the Ghibellines: his success in the 2000s eventually forced most of his adversaries, including both former Communists and ex-Christian Democrats, into a single centre-left movement, the Democratic Party (PD).

The issues at stake between the Guelphs and the Ghibellines may have long since become irrelevant, but the scars left by their conflict nevertheless run deep. In 2007 a banner – fully sixty metres across – was draped from the terraces at the ground belonging to AC Siena (also known, from the original name of its footballing section and the date of the club's foundation, as Robur 1904). The banner, which stayed there for three years, read: 'Ghibellini Robur 1904'. A message posted on a fan website explained that it summed up in a phrase 'the soul of the *Senesi*: [their] pride in being Ghibellines and love of Robur 1904'.

Some Italians, of course, are indifferent to football. Some – and progressively more – follow other sports, including a few that are very much minority interests elsewhere. Fencing, for example, has a wider following than in most other countries. And Formula One motor racing is immensely popular, largely because of Ferrari's achievements over the years. On Sundays from spring through to autumn, the high-pitched whine of Formula One engines can be heard issuing from TV screens in bars the length and breadth of the country.

Yet it is still football more than any other sport that captures the imagination and fires the passions of Italians. No other country in Europe, except possibly Spain, is quite as soccer crazy. Nor has any other been as successful on the pitch. Italy's national side, Gli Azzurri (the Blues),* has taken home four World Cups, more than any other country except Brazil.

Football in Italy began with the British, and specifically with British expatriates living in the industrial and commercial cities of the north at the end of the nineteenth century, when the Italian economy was growing fast. The oldest surviving club is Genoa, which still uses the English version of the city's name rather than the Italian Genova. It was founded in 1893 as the Genoa Cricket and Athletic Club (later renamed the Genoa Cricket and Football Club). Cricket never caught on with the Italians (though that could have been because they were not allowed to join the original, Genoese clubs). Football, on the other hand, spread rapidly. By 1898 there was a league of four sides, the other three – all in Turin – with Italian names. But though a growing number of the players were locals,

---

* If you have ever wondered why the national sporting representatives of a country with a red, white and green flag all wear blue, there is a reason: it is the colour of the House of Savoy, which provided Italy with its kings until after the Second World War. Italy's footballers wore blue shirts for the first time for a game against Hungary in 1911. Even after Italy became a republic the *azzurro* strip remained.

the coaches – then called managers – were still usually British. Even today, the man in charge of an Italian team, regardless of his nationality, is referred to as the 'Mister' and addressed as such by players, journalists and officials. AC Milan, which has also kept its English name, dates from the final years of the nineteenth century, as does Juventus, whose full name in Italian remains Juventus Football Club. FC Internazionale Milano – usually known as just Inter – came into being later, as the result of a dispute and split at AC Milan.

Genoa dominated the early years of the game in Italy, but its fortunes declined in the 1930s. The club won its last *scudetto** in 1924. By then, Mussolini was in power and keen to exploit Italians' gift for soccer to reap glory for his young Fascist state. As a first step, he had to give what was by then the national game an Italian origin. In the sixteenth century one Antonio Scarino had written about a game that was then popular in Florence known as *calcio*, which means 'kick'. In fact, *calcio* had little resemblance to modern football, but it provided Mussolini with an exclusively Italian name for the sport that has survived to this day. The Fascists also strong-armed Genoa and AC Milan into dropping their English names in favour of Italian ones. They reassumed their original names after the Second World War.

Enthusiastically backed by Mussolini and his regime, Italian soccer went from strength to strength. In 1934 and again in 1938, the national side carried off the World Cup. On the second occasion, Italy's captain gave a Fascist salute – albeit a rather hesitant one – before accepting the trophy.

Back home, the emblematic team of the Fascist era was Bologna (ironically, since the city would later become a communist stronghold). Bologna FC won the league five times between 1929 and 1941. Inconveniently for Mussolini, two of those titles were won with a

---

* 'Shield-let', a synonym for the league championship. The winners acquire the right to wear on their shirts a little shield bearing the Italian colours throughout the following season.

Jewish coach, Árpád Weisz. He was fired in 1938 after the regime brought in anti-Semitic legislation. Weisz left Italy and found work in the Netherlands. But after the Nazi occupation, he was deported to Auschwitz, where he and his family were killed.

The recovery in Italian football after the Second World War was much slower than in either the arts or the economy. During the late 1940s Torino dominated the league in a way no side has done since. It took five titles in a row and Italy's national team was sometimes composed almost entirely of Torino players. But on 4 May 1949 a plane carrying eighteen members of the squad crashed into the wall of the Superga Basilica on a hill overlooking Turin. Everyone aboard was killed. It was not until 1963, when AC Milan won the European Cup, that an Italian side again triumphed internationally.

The 1960s were a sparkling decade for both the big Milanese sides. Coached by an Argentinian, Helenio Herrera, who earned the name of *il mago* ('the magician'), Inter won the next two European Cups. The club continued to collect trophies in the 1970s and 1980s. But, starting in 1990, and for the fifteen years that followed, one of Italy's greatest sides was unable to win a thing. It was as if Inter, the club once bewitched by *il mago*, had fallen under a curse. Imitating the Inter fans' chant of *Non mollare mai* ('Never give in'), rival supporters would taunt them with choruses of *Non vincete mai* ('You never win').

The dominant team of the 1970s and 1980s had been Juventus. The Turin side carried off the championship nine times before Silvio Berlusconi bought AC Milan in 1986 and then hired Marco van Basten, the first of three Dutch stars who helped pilot the club to a string of league and then European victories. As in many other instances, events on the pitch in Italy reflected and perhaps influenced developments in other areas of the country's life: Berlusconi stormed to an unexpected victory in the 1994 general election as his team was clinching its third successive Serie A* title.

---

* The top division in the league, and another of Fascism's contributions to Italian football, it was inaugurated in 1929.

Sir Winston Churchill is credited with having said, 'Italians lose wars as if they were football matches, and football matches as if they were wars.' Apocryphal or not, there is certainly some truth in that quip, and it is often quoted by Italians themselves. Soccer is accorded a degree of respect Italians certainly never give to their politics. But then, for the most part, those involved in football behave with a lot more dignity, consistency and overall seriousness than Italy's politicians. Matches, like Masses, begin on time, even in parts of the country notorious for their lack of punctuality. Football is played with a tactical complexity that would baffle the coaches, let alone the spectators, in many other countries. It is analysed by professionals and amateurs alike with a sophistication that is far greater than that to be found in most other societies. And, though there are exceptions, the players themselves approach their calling in a spirit of resolute earnestness. They train hard. Most drink sparingly, if ever. They eat sensibly. And it is almost unheard of for an Italian player to be caught up in a night-club affray (even if that also has something to do with the deference shown by the media). At all events, Italy has seldom produced a tumultuous character like George Best or Eric Cantona.

The criticism most often levelled at Italian players is not that they are unprofessional but rather that they are *too* professional: that, on the pitch, defenders all too often resort to professional fouls; attackers make exaggerated use of the dramatic arts when robbed of the ball in a legitimate tackle – and that players of all kinds try to intimidate the referee with repeated specious protests. Such criticism, though, is seldom heard in Italy itself. On the contrary, as John Foot observes in his history of the Italian game,[1] fair play does not really come into it:

Italian defenders have always tried to anticipate forwards . . . If the anticipation went wrong, then a well-placed and well-timed foul was always a key part of the stopper's armoury. In Italy this became known as the 'tactical foul' in the 1990s, and was taught to defenders as part of the game. They all knew when to foul and when not to, and how to foul without picking up a booking. Often, Italian foot-ball commentators will praise a defender for a foul, sometimes adding that 'Maybe it isn't fair play, but . . .' Allied to this concept of the useful or tactical foul is the idea of the *useless* foul. Hence the parallel notion that being sent off for a useless offence is stupid, and unprofessional, whilst being called up for a *useful*, tactical foul is not only good practice, but deserving of praise as it represents – if the player has been booked or sent off – an individual sacrifice for the greater good of the whole team.

Soccer is part of the fabric of Italian life in a way that not even motor racing can rival. One of its archetypal figures was the anxious father with a transistor radio pressed to his ear on a Sunday after-noon as he listened to the progress of his *squadra del cuore* while his wife and children relaxed on the beach or enjoyed a walk in the country. Nowadays, he is more likely to be seen on afternoon televi-sion in old comedy movies. He was conjured out of existence by the arrival in 2003 of Rupert Murdoch's Sky TV, which made available live coverage of all the Serie A matches. These are nowadays split between Saturday evenings, Sundays and even some weekdays. But Italian fans were never satisfied with just going to a Sunday match and then reading about it in the newspapers the next day. Soccer has long been available in one form or another throughout the week.

La Gazzetta dello Sport was originally published to provide cover-age of the first modern Olympics in 1896, but it evolved into what was virtually a football daily. *Corriere dello Sport* followed in the 1920s and *Tuttosport* after the Second World War. At the height of its influ-ence in the early 1980s, *La Gazzetta*, with its distinctive blush-pink newsprint, was Italy's biggest-selling newspaper. Its most famous editor, the late Gianni Brera, went on to write for a number of other publications and changed the Italian lexicon.

Brera claimed to think in dialect, yet his Italian prose was enriched with a vocabulary of astonishing breadth. In Brera's writing, for example, Diego Maradona, the legendary Argentinian striker, becomes 'the hyperbolic beast, in the infernal, mythological sense of Cerberus: if you do as much as respect him, out of sporting fairness, he'll plant his teeth in the scruff of your neck, rip off your head and let it fall to the ground like a piece of fruit [torn] from the already sodden petiole'.*[2] Just that passage, in the original, contains two words that would have most Italians reaching for a dictionary, and a third they would not even find there.

When Brera lacked the word or phrase he needed, he would resort either to dialect (not necessarily his own) – or make one up. Among the words he is credited with inventing is *libero* (for a defender not assigned to marking a specific opponent): a term that has passed from Italian into most of the other major languages of the world.

On Monday nights fans who had read their favourite sporting daily from cover to cover could continue to alleviate their withdrawal symptoms by tuning into *Il processo del lunedì*, which started on RAI television in 1980. It soon became a national institution and its presenter, Aldo Biscardi, a national celebrity. *Il processo del lunedì* means 'the Monday trial'. It consisted of a meticulous re-examination of the more controversial moments from the weekend's games, using a device – or rather, a technique – dubbed the *Supermoviola*. Using know-how reputedly developed for military purposes, Biscardi and his team let viewers study each contested episode in slow motion from every possible angle, including even those unavailable to TV cameras at the time. The *Supermoviola* was the ultimate argument settler. It provided apparently indisputable proof that penalties had been wrongly awarded, and that goals disallowed by the referee had in fact been scored by players onside at the time. Biscardi's programme, which has since had many imitators, also benefited from the presence of *vallette*,† whose role was to introduce the studio

---

* A petiole is the stalk that attaches a leaf to a stem. I leave it to the botanists among my readers to judge whether it can also be used in the context of fruit – or whether Brera was just using an obscure term because that was what was expected of him.

† See above, page 143.

guests and announce the commercial breaks, but above all to be stunningly beautiful and alluringly dressed. The combination of soccer and sex is still a winning one, though these days the women with the big hair, high-gloss lipstick and low-cut dresses usually play a more active part. Several female presenters are recognized by even the most *maschilista* fans to be knowledgeable and passionate about the sport.

Not that every Italian woman is. 'Seven out of every ten programmes is about football: it's unreal,' Ilary Blasi, the showgirl and wife of Roma star Francesco Totti, once complained. 'If I happen to watch them, I fall asleep.' Plenty of other wives have expressed similar exasperation with the quantity of soccer on Italian TV. In addition to the replay-and-discussion programmes, pay TV has brought with it channels devoted entirely to individual clubs. Nor does radio necessarily guarantee an escape. Several cities now have FM radio stations concentrating exclusively on the activities of a local team.

Their output – up to fourteen and a half hours a day of it – can be sampled in many a Rome taxi. For anyone whose life does not revolve around the club in question, it is mind-numbingly boring: meandering discussions between experts, punctuated every so often by a phone call from a fan whose state of mind is usually somewhere between indignant and apoplectic. The capital is maybe the most football-crazed town in a football-mad country. Though AS Roma* is meant to represent the city, and Lazio the surrounding region, there is plenty of overlap that makes for searing rivalry between them. Unsurprisingly, it was in Rome that fan radio began. At the time of writing, there are no fewer than four stations focusing solely on Roma (and a fifth with a daily four-hour programme

---

* A latecomer to the league, AS Roma was formed in 1927 by the merger of three existing teams. The capital had a special significance for the Fascists because it was the centre of the empire they sought to emulate. It was felt its soccer team ought to be worthy of the heirs of the Caesars – an example of the way politics and football entwine in Italy.

devoted entirely to the club) and two for Lazio. The most successful of the Roma stations had an estimated daily audience of 150,000. The concept has since been taken up in Florence and Milan.

Fan radio was originally an invention of Rome's formidably well-organized, powerful and wealthy fan clubs. In this, however, the capital is by no means unique. Every Serie A side is followed by one or more groups of die-hard fans generically known as *ultras*. The oldest *ultras** groups date back to at least the 1950s. *Ultras* see themselves as different from – and more disciplined than – British-style hooligans, and as the originators of a style of support that spread from Italy to much of the rest of Europe, featuring the use of drums, flags, banners and, above all, flares. These days, however, they project a mix that is well-known among soccer fans in Britain and elsewhere: a taste for violent behaviour and extremist, usually far-right, politics that routinely comes out in the form of naked racism.

What continues to distinguish Italy's *ultras* from hard-line supporters in other countries, though, is not so much their extremism as the degree of legitimization they get from the managements of the clubs they support. Some *ultras* are even put on the payroll. They often receive subsidized travel to away games. Their leaders are frequently given free tickets. And they can usually get friends into the ground to watch matches for free. But such perks are as nothing to what they can make for themselves by using their symbols – and often those of their clubs – for merchandising. BBC journalists who made a documentary about Lazio's Irriducibili found to their astonishment that the Irriducibili had their own headquarters and stocked fourteen shops in and around Rome.

Ultras leaders routinely have access to the players, and the implicitly menacing influence they exert can lead to changes of tactics, players and club policy. In 2004 Lazio's Irriducibili and AS Roma's Ultras gave a frightening demonstration of their power at a 'derby' between the two sides. In the first half, a rumour went around

---

* The final 's' is correct. The term came from French.

among the spectators that a young Roma fan had been run over and killed by police outside the ground. It is widely suspected that the rumour was agreed upon between the Ultras and the Irriducibili before the match for reasons that have never become clear. At all events, a few minutes after the restart, a delegation of *ultras* from both factions somehow got on to the running track that surrounds the pitch, and Roma's captain, Totti, went to speak to them. Paddy Agnew, the Rome correspondent of the *Irish Times*, who was commenting on the match for RAI, wrote afterwards in his book on the game in Italy[3] that Totti's words to his coach immediately following the incident 'came loud and clear over the effects headset'. They were: *Se giochiamo adesso, questi ci ammazzano* ('If we play [on] now, these guys'll kill us'). With the agreement of Lazio's captain and despite the protestations of the referee, the game was called off.

'Fan power had won,' wrote Agnew. 'Fan violence, too, then ensued as violent elements in both Roma and Lazio camps engaged in a series of running battles with riot police outside the ground.' Over the next few years, football violence went from bad to worse, with clashes between *ultras* and the police becoming considerably bloodier than those between rival groups of fans. In 2007 a police officer died as a result of injuries sustained in a riot during a match in Sicily and a fan was shot dead by a policeman during a clash between supporters of rival teams at a motorway service station. With the public clamouring for a response, the government introduced a programme of restrictions and reforms that has curbed, but not yet eliminated, violence in the game.

If the *ultras'* adversary is the *sbirro* ('cop'), then the enemy of all fans is the referee. In Italy, he is not just short-sighted but an object of almost universal contempt.* Gianni Brera, whose opinions were read by millions, could write that 'in almost every case, we are dealing with either a frustrated person [with a need to show] to himself

---

* A rare exception, who inspired pride, respect and even a degree of affection among fans, was the charismatic, shaven-headed Pierluigi Collina, who refereed the 2002 World Cup final.

that he exists and has free will, or a bully'. Ennio Flaiano, a fellow journalist and writer of fiction – he co-wrote with Fellini the screenplays for *La dolce vita* and *8½* – thought Italians hated the referee for a much simpler reason: 'Because he gives a verdict.'

Over the years a view formed that these detested creatures were susceptible to influence: that consciously – or more probably unconsciously – they favoured the big clubs. A term was even found for the condition from which they were suffering: 'psychological slavery'. Nowhere, it was argued, was this more obvious than in their handling of matches involving Juventus, the side that more than any other exuded power. Rooted in Piedmont, the region that unified Italy, and owned by the Fiat automotive manufacturing firm, the embodiment of Italian industrial pride, Juventus has a *national* character – and a national following – greater than that of any other club. One of its nicknames, indeed, is *La fidanzata d'Italia* (roughly, 'The sweetheart of Italy'). You can go into bars in the wilds of Calabria, at the other end of the peninsula from Turin, and find a black-and-white-striped pennant on the shelf and a notice proudly declaring that the bar is the meeting place for the local branch of the Juventus supporters' club.

The idea that referees subconsciously felt it was unpatriotic to let Juventus lose might seem far-fetched. But fans, and particularly those of clubs such as Fiorentina, Cagliari and Verona who won the championship only once in a blue moon, could nevertheless point to a number of controversial decisions that had gone Juventus's way at crucial moments in the history of the league. In 1981, for example, in the seventy-fourth minute of the vital clash with Juventus, the referee disallowed what would have been a deciding Roma goal that was later shown to be valid. The result was that the title went to Juventus. The same happened the following year, after the referee refused a goal that would have given Fiorentina the championship with only fifteen minutes of the season left. On more than one occasion, moreover, Juventus finished the season with noticeably more penalties awarded in their favour and suspiciously few given against. As the years passed, and suspicions increased, fans of rival teams taunted Juventus supporters with chants of 'You only know how to rob' and 'We'd rather be second than thieves.'

It was only in 2005 that they began to wonder if Juventus's singular good luck might be due to something more than just psychological subjugation. It was then that the first reports appeared of an investigation codenamed 'Offside' being carried out by a prosecutor in Turin. He subsequently concluded that nothing the police had discovered was proof of a crime. But he passed the evidence he had gathered to Italy's main soccer authority, the Federazione Italiana Giuoco Calcio (FIGC), and a few days after the end of the 2005–6 season, extracts from the transcripts of wiretapped telephone conversations were leaked to the press.

It was the beginning of a scandal like no other in the history of football in Italy, or anywhere else, for that matter. From time to time, players or referees are caught out fixing matches. It happens in all countries. Usually, there is a link to some kind of betting ring. But Calciopoli,* as this scandal came to be known, was different. What the transcripts suggested was that Juventus's top managers had created a web of influence that did indeed enable them to secure compliant referees for their games. Some other clubs were in on the system, too, and could benefit from similar favours. The implication was not, as in other scandals, that this or that game was fixed, but that Serie A was fixed; that it was not a tournament between sides that began the season with a theoretically equal chance of winning but a puppet show: a colourful, dramatic performance that lasted from one year into the next for which the script was written by a handful of powerful and conspiratorial men. And that did not just apply to what could be seen in the stadiums. Some of the transcripts indicated that Juventus's general manager, Luciano Moggi, was in contact with Aldo Biscardi,† the presenter of what was by then *Il processo di Biscardi*. The idea was to ensure that the

---

* In honour of Tangentopoli or 'Bribesville', the name given to the cluster of scandals that led to the fall of Italy's political order in the early 1990s.

† See above, page 206.

slow-motion reconstructions on his programme were interpreted in the way that suited Juventus. It was the quintessential demonstration of how, in Italy, what is visible is not necessarily real. Biscardi took his programme off national television after it was caught up in the scandal and he, his *Supermoviola* and his *vallette* were last seen – more than thirty years after the first edition of the programme – on a circuit of minor local stations.

There were two bizarre things about Calciopoli. One was that, while the scandal was at its height, Italy won its fourth World Cup. The other was that no money was ever shown to have changed hands.* The system worked because the managers concerned had created a belief that they were so powerful and influential they could make or break the careers of anyone else in the game. And the very belief that their word was law gave them the power and influence they needed to secure their aims. It was a perfect example of a mafia in the loosest sense of the word; of the sort of inclusive (yet exclusive), anti-competitive and perhaps family-like arrangements that abound in Italy.

---

* Calciopoli gave rise to two sets of criminal proceedings. In the first, Moggi and his son were accused of duress and attempted duress, respectively. They were found guilty at both the trial and appeal stages, and received prison sentences. But in 2014 a statute of limitations quashed the charges against them. The second case, involving charges including conspiracy, had not run its course at the time of writing. After the first of two appeals, Moggi faced a sentence of two years and four months; the former managing director of Juventus, Antonio Giraudo, risked a sentence of one year and eight months. Five other ex-officials and referees were looking at sentences of between ten months and two years. However, because of a retrospective pardon enacted in 2006, it was highly unlikely that any of the defendants, who denied wrongdoing, would see the inside of a prison cell.

15.

Restrictive Practices

'*Per lungo tempo si sono confuse la mafia e la mentalità mafiosa, la mafia come organizzazione illegale e la mafia come semplice modo di essere. Quale errore! Si può benissimo avere una mentalità mafiosa senza essere un criminale.*'

'Mafia and mafia-like mentality; the mafia as an illegal organization and the mafia as simply an outlook on life have long been confused. What a mistake! You can perfectly well have a mafia-like mentality without being a criminal.'

– Giovanni Falcone, *Cose di Cosa Nostra*, 1991

Claudia had been left with several houses when her husband died. She let them out to holidaymakers wanting to spend time in the Italian countryside. We had agreed to meet her at the house of a mutual friend. Claudia had to pick up some guests – non-paying guests who were old friends, as it happens – from the railway station. She said she would catch up with us once she'd dropped them off at her home. As she was coming out of the station, she was approached by a group of local taxi drivers.

'They said that by collecting my guests from the station I was taking business off them,' she said. She was clearly shaken by their intimidating manner and concerned at what might happen if she ignored their protest. This did not happen in Sicily, nor even in Puglia. The station in question is in Tuscany.

I have a friend who lives on one of the Italian islands. She needed a table. She had seen just what she wanted in another part of the island. But there was a furniture shop in her immediate vicinity, owned by someone she had known since she was a child but who was not in any sense a friend. To buy the table anywhere else, however, would be seen not as the legitimate choice of a consumer but as a gross betrayal. She and her partner were *his* customers. He would probably never speak to them again if they went elsewhere. So they ended up buying the table at the shop on the other side of the island and carrying it between them all the way back to their home on a circuitous route so that neither the table nor a delivery van of the rival shop would be seen by the man who regarded himself as *their* furniture supplier.

Anyone who has lived in Italy will no doubt be able to recount similar anecdotes. If you go regularly to a shop, bar or restaurant, you risk arousing possessive instincts (and particularly if you have accepted – and there is really no way you can refuse – an unsolicited *sconto*, or discount). This has been a special problem for me because of the nature of my work. I travel frequently and on my return I have often been greeted in regular haunts with an ever-so-slightly sardonic '*Ben tornato*' ('Welcome back'). If I explain apologetically that I had to go abroad, then everything will be fine. But if I limit myself to the customary – pretty much untranslatable – response of '*Ben trovato*', there is a danger that my coffee will be served with just a tad less care and that the bar owner will remove himself to the other end of the counter to chat with exaggerated warmth to someone he clearly regards as a *genuine* regular.

This desire for the preservation of monopolies – or, in the case of Claudia's disgruntled taxi drivers, a cartel – runs like a semi-visible vein through Italian society. And it has a long history. The enduring strength of the Italian craft guilds and the restrictions they enforced were among the reasons why the Italian economy went into decline during the seventeenth century. One of the most jealously protected cartels was that of the glassmakers on the Venetian island of Murano: anyone who tried to take their skills elsewhere faced severe penalties, or even death.

The spirit of the guilds lives on today in Italy's still-formidable trade unions and in the *ordini* and *collegi* – professional bodies membership of which is essential for anyone who seeks to practise. There are more than thirty of these, and they regulate access to a much wider range of professions than in other EU countries. There are *ordini* for notaries and architects, but also for social workers and employment consultants. There is a *collegio* for nurses, but also one for radiological technicians and another for ski instructors.

The professional bodies are part of a vast web of restrictive practices. One of the most ludicrous examples to surface in recent years was that of the Venetian street artists. It turned out that their licences were inherited. So even if someone had no talent for drawing or for painting, he or she could occupy a pitch that would otherwise have gone to someone with real artistic talent.

It is a moot point as to whether the Catholic Church developed its anti-liberal attitudes because its outlook is essentially monopolistic or because until very recently it was run largely by Italians. At all events, Pius IX's Syllabus of Errors, issued in 1864, anathemized liberalism, along with a long list of other creeds and beliefs. His stance put an even greater distance between the Vatican and the new Italian state, in which liberalism became the dominant ideology.* Early free-market economics, particularly as practised by the governments of Giovanni Giolitti in the period leading up to the First World War, delivered prosperity. The Italian economy surged ahead as the country industrialized. But the liberals became hopelessly – and quite justifiably – identified with official corruption.

The Fascists brought with them an approach to economic organization that fitted more easily with Italian tradition. Whereas Giolitti had wanted wages to be decided by the free interplay of market forces, Mussolini and his associates set about building a corporatist state in which employers and employees were forced to collaborate.

The fall of Mussolini might have given back the initiative to the liberals. But by the end of the Second World War they were not

---

* The Vatican's condemnation was lifted in 1904, but only after it decided that socialism represented an even greater danger.

only tainted with the memory of graft; they had allowed themselves to become the party of a narrow layer of society made up of
southern landowners, big industrialists and financiers. When it
came to electoral appeal, they were no match for the Christian
Democrats. The arrival in power of the DC ushered in a period of
more than forty years in which power would be shared between the
five parties that, to a greater or lesser degree, opposed the Communists. The original idea was to make sure that Western Europe's
biggest communist party never acquired a toehold in government.
To make it work, Italy's post-war politicians evolved the system of
lottizzazione mentioned in Chapter 8.*

One of the many bequests of Fascism was a giant public sector.
Every part of it was shared out in line with the clout wielded by the
parties that made up the *pentapartito*, a generic name conferred on
the five anti-Communist groups. With time, even the Communists
were brought into this cosy system for sharing out power, influence
and the financial sweeteners that often came with them. If, for
example, a Christian Democrat was made head of the civil aviation
regulatory body, a Socialist would get air traffic control. *Lottizzazione* was practised way beyond the bounds of public industry and
finance. Even regional responsibilities within the foreign ministry
were shared out according to party loyalties. The Christian Democrats held sway over Latin America. The Socialists got most of the
Middle East and North Africa. The television channels of RAI were
carved up in the same way. The first went to the Christian Democrats, the second to the Socialists and the third to the Communists.
The effects can be seen to this day. If you meet a veteran journalist
or even technician who works for, say, Rai1 it is highly likely that he
or she will have had a relative who belonged to the DC. Throughout the years that Silvio Berlusconi was in power in the 2000s
Rai3 remained a bastion of critical reporting and analysis (though
increasingly cowed by the media tycoon's influence).

The Liberal Party was one of the five in the *pentapartito*, as was

* See above, page 105.

the Republican Party, which also came to favour economic liberalism. And, as the years passed, the Christian Democrats' Catholic idealism gave way to an easy cohabitation with the market economy. But, straddling the centre, it nevertheless espoused a more collaborative form of capitalism than that which had evolved in the United States and which was to emerge in Britain under Margaret Thatcher in the 1980s.

While Christian democracy flourished, social democracy never succeeded in the way that it did in Germany, where Willy Brandt and Helmut Schmidt dominated politics from the late 1960s until the early 1980s. There was a party of Social Democrats in the *pentapartito*, but it became renowned as the most hopelessly venal of the five. The Socialists under Bettino Craxi finally got to run the government in the mid-1980s. But, by then, they were already deeply immersed in the patronage and corruption that infected Italian post-war politics, and became even more compromised in office. Craxi was the outstanding victim of the Clean Hands investigation.* In 1993, in an incident that has passed into political legend, he was pelted with coins as he left the hotel where he and his cronies held legendarily extravagant parties. Soon after, he fled to Tunisia, where he died in exile and disgrace seven years later.

For most of the post-war period, then, the key choice for voters was between two fundamentally anti-competitive ideologies: on the one hand, Christian democracy; and on the other, communism. It has left a profound legacy.

The fall of the so-called First Republic in the early 1990s was to be the prelude to Italy's recent economic decline (even though it was not until the early 2000s that it was recognized as structural rather than cyclical). Italy's underlying problem is its declining competitiveness. Much brainpower has been expended on attempts to explain and analyse the phenomenon. Yet the point is seldom made that Italy has an exceptionally uncompetitive form of capitalism.

Silvio Berlusconi, who had been Craxi's protégé, entered politics

---

* See below, page 234.

in 1993 as a paladin of free enterprise (even though, as has been virtually forgotten, his political affiliation until the early 1990s was with the centre-left and not the centre-right). Several of the politicians, journalists and intellectuals who rallied to his cause, men such as the flamboyantly brilliant Giuliano Ferrara, his first government's Cabinet-ranking spokesman, were genuine, ideological liberals. But while Berlusconi himself has long described himself as a liberal, he is really nothing of the kind: his approach, to the extent that he has any discernible ideology, has always been a sort of 'national capitalism' that allowed for dyed-in-the-wool protectionism. In 2008 he successfully built an election campaign around saving Alitalia from falling into French hands. Visceral protectionism, however, is certainly not the preserve of the right in Italy. Just the year before, the then centre-left prime minister Romano Prodi torpedoed the sale of Telecom Italia to the US telecommunications giant AT&T.

To a large extent, Prodi and Berlusconi were merely reflecting the views of the public. The takeover of Italian firms by foreign ones is invariably reported in the media as a defeat. The idea that outside firms might be able to bring in know-how or that foreign direct investment (i.e. investment in companies rather than shares) helps spur growth is seldom, if ever, acknowledged. The results can be seen in the figures for the stock of inward foreign direct investment (FDI) compiled by the Organization for Economic Cooperation and Development (OECD). By the end of 2012 the value of FDI in Italy relative to the size of the economy was the lowest of any country in the EU except Greece. For Portugal and Spain, which opened their economies to the outside world long after Italy, the corresponding figures were between two and a half and three times higher. In Sweden and the Netherlands, countries that might be thought to be less in need of foreign know-how than Italy, they were about four times as high.

To encourage investment across national frontiers, the OECD has a 'name and shame' table. It is called the FDI Regulatory Restrictiveness Index and it measures the statutory restrictions that countries put in the way of foreign direct investors. The intriguing thing is that Italy scores really quite well: better, in fact, than Sweden, Denmark or the UK. So either Italians are hindering outsiders in less identifiable ways, or foreigners are baulking at putting their money into a country that has significant drawbacks from the point of view of a prospective investor.

Year after year, Italy has been slipping down the World Bank's ease-of-doing-business table. By 2012 it had fallen to seventy-third place in a list of 185 countries: one place behind Romania and six behind Azerbaijan. It was easier to enforce a contract in Togo than it was in Italy (partly because of the sluggishness of the courts) and harder to get electricity laid on than in India. Then there was the widespread corruption and the danger you might cross paths with one of several organized crime syndicates.

Some years ago I was sitting in the office of an Italian lawyer when the telephone rang. He answered, a mite irritably, saying he thought he had given instructions that he was not to be disturbed. On the other end of the line I could hear the sound of an excited female voice. The lawyer's expression became progressively graver until he said he would take the call in the other room. He returned about five minutes later.

Without giving any clue as to the identity or nationality of the firm, he said that one of his clients was a foreign company that had opened a small plant in the Mezzogiorno. The manager had made it known that if any of his new staff wished to discuss their future with the company they had only to walk through the door of his office. After a short time, one of his employees – an unskilled worker – did just that. He was after promotion, he said. The foreign boss replied he was all for encouraging ambition, but which job did his young employee have in mind?

'Yours,' came the answer. At which point the young man got up and left the room without another word.

Astonished by what had happened, the manager asked around among his staff and was told that the worker was the son-in-law of the local mafia capo. The message was eventually made clear: he would leave the firm if it gave him generous – or rather, exorbitant – severance pay. He left it to the company to imagine what the consequences might be if they failed to agree on a sum. An offer had been made through the lawyer, which, after some haggling, had been accepted. But now the young man had changed his mind and had rung up to say that he wanted half as much again.

For investors who are keen to take a stake in the Italian economy and would rather steer clear of direct investment, there is, of course, the stock market. But if the stake you are after is a big one, then it will mean coming to grips with what the *Financial Times* once described as 'almost certainly the strangest and most convoluted business culture of any of the large Western economies'.[1]

At the core of this culture is a uniquely Italian concept: the shareholder pact. Groups of big Italian investors – usually banks or other firms – get together to establish control of a listed company. Rarely do they need a majority stake. A third or even a quarter of the shares will normally suffice: there is not much chance of any group of investors with a bigger proportion of the total equity voting in unison. The merit of the system is that it can deliver the kind of stability that managers need to pursue a long-term strategy. But if there are conflicting interests among the members of the pact, it can also inflict paralysis.

The latter is especially true if the firm in question is linked into a network of cross-holdings – stakes held by one publicly quoted company in another. These are equally characteristic of Italian capitalism. For many years the Milan investment bank Mediobanca and its publicity-shy president, Enrico Cuccia, sat at the heart of a tangled web of such cross-holdings. The influence of the secretive Cuccia reached into every corner of the clubby world of Italian capitalism, which is summed up in an untranslatable phrase: *il salotto buono*. It moots the existence of a refined drawing room where the giants of industry meet the titans of finance to stitch up deals while keeping outsiders kicking their heels in the hallway. In fact, there is no such place, but if the strands of control over Italian industry and finance converged on any one location, it would have been the offices of Mediobanca.

Cuccia died in 2000, but it was not until thirteen years later that his successors decided, in the wake of the euro crisis, that their exposure to corporate Italy was just a bit too broad for comfort. The bank announced that it would be slowly reducing several of its key holdings. That may have signalled the beginning of the end of the culture of cross-holdings in Italian business. But it will take a while for the skein to unravel, and shareholder pacts will doubtless still be around even after it has. The number of firms listed on the Milan bourse controlled in this way is falling, but slowly.

For an example of a 'mafia' that remains as tenaciously protective (and protectionist) as ever, you need to turn away from the worlds of finance and industry to that of higher education. Italy's universities are among the last great bastions in Italian society of patronage (and a fair number of restrictive practices). Take the case of the *lettori*. When I first came to Italy as a correspondent in 1994, it was already an old story. Twenty years later, it has still not been resolved.

Lettori are non-Italian university lecturers who teach a foreign language in their mother tongue. Back in the 1980s the *lettori* began to lobby for pay and conditions comparable to those of Italian lecturers. But that would have meant giving them open-ended contracts. Those who have campaigned on their behalf believe that the last thing most of the so-called *baroni* – the tenured full professors – wanted was to give security of employment to a bunch of foreigners who might challenge the way things were done in Italian universities.

In 1995, under growing pressure from the European Commission, the Italian government of the day changed the law. It reclassified the *lettori*, not as teachers, but as technicians. Those who refused to accept their new status were sacked (though most were subsequently reinstated at the insistence of the courts). Among other things, the reclassification of the *lettori* has meant that they can no longer set or mark exams. That now has to be done by an Italian who, except in very rare cases, does not have the same proficiency in the language as the *lettori* who, in fact if not in law, have taught the students being examined.

Ever since the mid-1990s those who were dismissed (or who accepted the 1995 terms while reserving their right to contest them) have campaigned for the back pay they believe is their due for the period in which – it is acknowledged by all sides – they were teachers, and not technicians. Over the years the European Court of Justice (ECJ) has ruled six times in their favour, accepting their contention that Italy's treatment of them constituted discrimination on grounds of nationality. On several occasions the Rome government has changed the law in the semblance of an effort to meet the ECJ's demands. But few of the *lettori* have ever been compensated. In 2010 a law was brought in that simply declared null and void the cases in which *lettori* were suing universities for compensation and led to about half of them having their salaries cut – in extreme cases, by as much as 60 per cent.

All this may help to explain why Italians sometimes use a phrase that baffles foreigners, telling them with a shrug: '*Siamo tutti un po' mafiosi*' ('We're all a bit mafia-like'). The son of Bernardo Provenzano, the last undisputed *capo di tutti capi* of the Sicilian mafia, said something like it after his father was arrested in 2006 at the end of an unprecedented forty-three years on the run. The then thirty-year-old Angelo Provenzano was being interviewed by a reporter from *La Repubblica*. 'The Mafia,' he said, 'follows on from *mafiosità*, which is not solely and exclusively Sicilian behaviour.'

To say there is a widely diffused *mafiosità* in Italy (and that elements of *mafiosità* can indeed be found in every society) is one thing. But to claim, as Cosa Nostra's apologists have often done, that the Mafia itself is no more than a frame of mind is quite another. Angelo Provenzano called it a 'mental attitude' and a 'fluid magma with no defined borders'.[2] In so doing, he was consciously or unconsciously echoing an argument that for many years succeeded in bamboozling politicians, investigators and public opinion. But the fact is that the Sicilian Mafia and Italy's other organized crime syndicates exist as something considerably more than an attitude. And their borders are anything but fluid.

Of Mafias and Mafiosi

'Noialtri siamo mafiosi, gli altri sono uomini qualsiasi. Siamo uomini d'onore. E non tanto perché abbiamo prestato giuramento, ma perché siamo l'élite della criminalità. Siamo assai superiori ai delinquenti comuni. Siamo i peggiori di tutti!'

'We are *mafiosi*. The others are just ordinary men. We are men of honour. And not so much because we have sworn an oath, but because we are the elite of crime. We are very much superior to common criminals. We are the worst of all.'

– Antonino Calderone, Mafia *pentito*, quoted in
Pino Arlacchi, *Gli uomini del disonore*, 1992
(trans. Marc Romano as *Men of Dishonor:
Inside the Sicilian Mafia*, 1993)

It may come as a surprise, particularly to readers who have seen the film *Gomorrah* or read the book by Roberto Saviano on which it is based,[1] but Italy is not a particularly crime-ridden country. Definitions vary widely from one country to another, so crime rates are notoriously difficult to compare. And what they show, in any case, is not the true amount of crime, which is unknowable, but the level of *reported* crime, which varies according to the readiness of the public in each country to tell the police. What is more, in Italy, there are sizeable variations between regions. The overall rates for most crimes are nevertheless much lower than in other European countries of the same size. Figures compiled by the European Commission suggest that in 2009, for example, there were less than half as many robberies as in France and only an eighth as much violent crime as in Britain.

Unsurprisingly, then, many Italians feel outraged when foreigners identify their country with the mafia. Back in 1977 the German news magazine *Der Spiegel* put on its cover a photograph of a pistol on a plate of spaghetti. It has never been forgotten. Even today, whenever some foreign journalist is felt to have given a stereotyped view of Italy, someone will drag up that offending cover as evidence of the gross prejudices about the country that are held abroad.

Those who complain also point out that organized crime is found elsewhere. Reference has already been made to Japan's mafia, the Yakuza. In recent years gangsters originating in Russia, Turkey, Albania and Latin America have been active far beyond the borders of their respective countries. Just a few weeks before I began writing this chapter, the Spanish newspaper *El País* publicized an official report showing that the police had investigated 482 organized criminal gangs in Spain in the previous year, mostly of foreign origin.

Nor did Italians invent the concept: the Yakuza gangs probably pre-date Italy's oldest mafia, the Camorra, which operates in Naples and the surrounding region, by about a hundred years. There is evidence, moreover, to suggest that organized crime in Italy is not even home-grown; that it entered the Mezzogiorno from Spain when the south was under Spanish rule. But while it died out in Spain in the centuries that followed, it developed and flourished in Italy and turned into something that is different from, and more than just, organized crime.

Italy has three main criminal syndicates: the Camorra; Cosa Nostra in Sicily, which was the first organization to be designated with the term 'Mafia';* and the Calabrian 'Ndrangheta. There is also, on a much lesser scale, the Sacra Corona Unita ('Holy United Crown')

---

* Hereafter, a capital 'M' is used to designate the eponymous Sicilian Mafia, while a lower case 'm' will be used to refer to Italian organized crime syndicates in general.

in Puglia.* All these groups have at least four characteristics that set them apart from ordinary criminal gangs, including Italian ones.

One is that, like the Yakuza, they are secret societies. In the 1980s a gang known as the Banda della Magliana was active in Rome. But it was not a secret society. It did not, like Cosa Nostra, initiate its members by getting them to hold a burning image of the Virgin Mary. Nor did it have ranks and rituals that mimicked the liturgy of the Catholic Church, like the 'Ndrangheta.

A second characteristic that Italy's four mafias have in common is that their members all feel they belong to something more than just a gang. Though the gang, or clan, is largely autonomous in its day-to-day operations, it forms part of a broader fellowship that – albeit intermittently – has a hierarchical structure.

In the case of Cosa Nostra, the cell or gang is the *cosca* (a telling word: in Sicilian, it refers to the head of an artichoke, with its densely overlapping leaves). Above that is the *mandamento*, made up of several – usually three – neighbouring *cosche*. Each *mandamento* sends a representative to the *commissione provinciale* (known in the province of Palermo, at least to the media, as the *cupola*, or dome). In the six provinces of Sicily where the Mafia is active,† the *commissione provinciale* chooses a representative to send to a *commissione interprovinciale* (or *regionale*). That, on the evidence of most of the *pentiti* (mafiosi who have turned state's evidence), is how things are *meant* to work. But there seem to have been periods in which the structure has fallen apart, because of either police action or internal conflict.

The other point that needs stressing is that Cosa Nostra's hierarchy has never really been a command structure. As far as is known,

---

* In the early 1990s the 'Ndrangheta helped create the Basilischi, an alliance involving members of the 'Ndrangheta and small groups of gangsters in the Basilicata region. Major police operations were launched against this 'fifth mafia', and the threat posed by the organization is thought to have since receded, though not to have disappeared.

† Messina, Ragusa and Siracusa have always been largely mob-free.

the *commissioni* exist – when they do exist – for the purposes of consultation, the resolution of disputes between *cosche* and the agreeing of rules common to the entire organization. They do not usually order specific operations. But there have been exceptions. Among them was the decision by the *commissione provinciale* in Palermo to assassinate two anti-mafia prosecutors, Giovanni Falcone and Paolo Borsellino, in 1992. There was a grim irony in their violent deaths. The killings were in reprisal for the so-called Maxi Trial of 1986–7, in which the two men for the first time succeeded in convincing a court of law that Cosa Nostra had a hierarchical structure and that Mafia bosses could therefore be convicted of ordering crimes they did not themselves perpetrate.

For a long time the situation in the 'Ndrangheta was less clear. It was known that, as far back as the 1950s, a supreme assembly had existed that met every year, when the heads of the various cells, known as *'ndrine*, assembled in and around the village of San Luca for a pilgrimage to the sanctuary of Our Lady of Polsi. The assembly was called, appropriately enough, the *crimine* ('crime'). But in the early 2000s investigators discovered that the *'ndranghetisti* in Reggio Calabria, the biggest province in Calabria, had created a body similar to that of Cosa Nostra's *cupola*. Recordings of conversation between mobsters suggested it was called the *provincia* ('province'). It was assumed the old ways had been abandoned. But in 2010 an investigation established that the *crimine* was still very much in existence. Domenico Oppedisano, an eighty-year-old man who had been almost unknown to the police and who lived quietly as an apparently impecunious peasant farmer, was identified as its president. He was arrested, tried and sentenced to ten years in jail.

The Camorra is less hierarchical and conflicts between clans are more frequent, but its initiates nevertheless feel they are part of a broader whole, which they themselves refer to as the *sistema* ('System').

Like the mafiosi and *'ndranghetisti*, though to a lesser extent, the gangsters of Naples and the surrounding region of Campania look for political 'cover'. This is a third way in which mafiosi differ from

ordinary criminals: they are constantly on the look-out for acquies-
cent lawmakers who can smooth their path in exchange for the
votes they can deliver. Nor is it the only means by which Italy's
mafias subvert the authorities. Yet another distinguishing feature of
its organized crime syndicates is that they attempt relentlessly – and
often successfully – to replace the state. The obsession of every
'boss' is to secure *controllo del territorio* ('control of the territory').
Ideally, nothing should be done on his turf to which he does not
consent, and the people who live there should look to him as the
ultimate arbiter of their fortunes. If their home has been burgled, if
they need a job for their son or daughter, if they need the drains fixing on their housing estate, it should be to the boss and not to the
civil authorities that they turn.

A sociologist writing in the late 1950s might well have concluded
that Italy's mafias were doomed. Cosa Nostra and the 'Ndrangheta
were still essentially rural phenomena, and it would have been
natural to assume that the immense flow of population from the
countryside to the towns would rob them of their power bases. Yet
more than half a century later it can be seen that this is not at all
what has happened. Piero Grasso,* a former national anti-mafia
prosecutor, once wrote, 'As is clear from decades of investigation, in
Italy the mafia is a structural component of large areas of society,
politics and the business world.'

But just how extensive its activities are remains unclear. Year in,
year out, Italian think tanks and other organizations come out with
shocking figures to show that organized crime is the country's biggest industry or that its mafias account for an appallingly high
percentage of its GDP. Their press releases make for a good story,
and they are duly reported in the national and international media.
But the question of how on earth researchers can arrive at these
estimates is seldom asked. In recent years the consensus has been
that organized crime accounts for close to 9 per cent of national
output (though one estimate has put it at substantially more than

---

* In 2013 Grasso went into politics and became Speaker of the Senate.

10 per cent). In 2013, though, researchers from the Catholic University in Milan and the University of Trento presented a study[2] that challenged the established orthodoxy. They concluded that the figure was between about 1.2 per cent and 2.2 per cent of GDP.

The impact of Italy's mafias on the life of the country is nonetheless formidable. There are more than a hundred gangs in the Camorra alone. Figures for the number of mafia affiliates are probably no more reliable than those for their revenue. But most estimates put the total at well over 20,000. According to the shop-keepers' association, Confesercenti, around 160,000 retailers hand over protection money (known in Italian as the *pizzo*). In areas traditionally associated with the mafia, the level of extortion is thought to range from 70 per cent of shops in Sicily down to 30 per cent in Puglia. More surprisingly, perhaps, an estimated one in ten of the retail outlets in Lazio, the region that includes Rome, pays the *pizzo*, as does around one in every twenty in Lombardy and Piedmont.

On Sicily, at least, it can be argued that the mobsters are in serious difficulties. Cosa Nostra has suffered from the shift in the market for narcotics away from heroin, in which it was a big player, towards cocaine, where the dominant importer among Italy's mafias was – and is – the 'Ndrangheta. The arrest in 2006 of Bernardo Provenzano was the third time in thirteen years that a *capo di tutti capi* had been captured. Since then, police have netted a string of second-level Mafia commanders, decapitating the organization at least temporarily. In response, Cosa Nostra has striven to keep as low a profile as possible while continuing to reap the *pizzo* in Palermo and elsewhere in western Sicily.

Because of the Sicilian Mafia's transatlantic connections; because of the Godfather books and films; because of its position as the eponymous Mafia, Cosa Nostra is vastly better known – and more intensively reported – than any of the other Italian organized crime syndicates. Mesmerized by the legend of the Sicilian Mafia, international public opinion has failed to notice the extent to which it has been overtaken by the Camorra and 'Ndrangheta since the 1990s. I know from having interviewed him twice while he was in hiding that one of the reasons Roberto Saviano wrote *Gomorrah* was his frustration at the lack of interest – not just abroad, but in Italy itself – in a trial of more than a hundred *camorristi* comparable to the Maxi Trial of mafiosi in the 1980s. The Processo Spartacus centred on the activities of the Casalesi, a clan based in the town of Casal di Principe, north-west of Naples. It lasted for seven years, yet was virtually ignored by the national media.

Saviano's book achieved its aim of focusing national and international attention on the threat posed by the Camorra. But he paid a high price for the satisfaction that it brought. The Casalesi passed a death sentence on him. He still lives under police protection.

Unlike the Camorra, the 'Ndrangheta remains in the shadows. It has managed to grow, almost unpublicized, into what most police and prosecutors reckon to be Italy's richest criminal fraternity. Several of its clans amassed considerable financial resources in the 1970s by kidnapping rich businessmen and holding them for ransom in the wilds of the Aspromonte, the uplands that form the rocky heart of southern Calabria. One of their victims was John Paul Getty III, the grandson of the oil tycoon. The cash they got from kidnapping was reinvested in drugs. The 'Ndrangheta was the first of Italy's mafias to establish solid links with the Colombian cocaine cartels. And they have since played a leading – perhaps dominant – role in the import of the drug into Europe. They are known recently to have built working relationships with some of the Mexican cartels.

Not that it has done much good for Calabria. It is Italy's poorest region after Campania. And more perhaps even than Campania, the 'toe' of Italy has undergone a process that a priest working there once termed 'Somali-ization'. Large parts of the region are, in effect, outside the control of the Italian state. Anyone who visits Calabria and can understand Italian cannot help but be struck by the number of crimes, obviously linked to the 'Ndrangheta, that are chronicled in the local media but which go unreported in the rest of the country. In recent years the homicide rate in the region has been three times the national average, even higher than in Campania.

Drug trafficking has enriched all three mafias and helped fund their expansion both nationally and internationally. As far back as 1960 the Sicilian novelist Leonardo Sciascia had one of his characters speculate that:

> Maybe the whole of Italy is becoming a sort of Sicily . . . Scientists say that the palm tree line, that is, the climate suitable to growth of the palm, is moving north, five hundred metres, I think it was, every year . . . The palm tree line . . . I call it the coffee line, the strong black coffee line . . . It's rising like mercury in a thermometer, this palm tree line, this strong coffee line, this scandal line, rising up throughout Italy and already [past] Rome.[3]

It was a quite extraordinarily prescient passage, because the mechanism that would allow Cosa Nostra and the other mafias to spread through the peninsula was in its early stages. Migration from the south to the north played a role. But even more important was a well-intentioned but wholly misguided law passed in 1956 that allowed suspected or convicted mobsters to be uprooted from their home territory and forced to live under curfew in the north. It went by the name of *soggiorno obbligato*, or 'required stay', and, according to one estimate,[4] by 1975 some 1,300 mafiosi, *camorrista* and *'ndranghetisti* had been settled within striking distance of the industrial and financial heart of Italy.

Until very recently, nevertheless, there was a generalized perception in Italy that the mafia remained an overwhelmingly southern phenomenon. Northerners, who feel themselves to be several cuts above their fellow Italians from the Mezzogiorno, indignantly denied that organized crime was any part of life in their region. That myth was dispelled for ever in 2010, when police made a wave of arrests in and around Milan after an investigation that found abundant evidence of the 'Ndrangheta's presence in the Italian business capital and the surrounding area. The most striking proof was a video made secretly by the Carabinieri of a dinner summit held by 'Ndrangheta bosses near Milan. The venue they had chosen was a left-wing social centre named after Giovanni Falcone and Paolo

Borsellino. A few years earlier, in fact, a journalist and a prosecutor had collaborated on a book that pointed to evidence that the 'Ndrangheta's activities had penetrated almost every corner of Italy, including even the partly French-speaking Valle d'Aosta in the shadow of the Alps.[5]

But is there any particular reason why the 'Ndrangheta and the other groups should have taken root and grown to such a flourishing maturity in Italy, rather than in, say, Spain, Portugal or Greece? The earliest mafiosi are thought to have been *campieri*, toughs hired to protect the land and interests of an emergent class of tenant farmers, the *gabelloti*. But the early, rural mafiosi soon learnt they could play a useful role.

Like the rest of Italy, Sicily at the time had a judicial system that was slow and frequently corrupt. What is more, the mistrust described earlier was at least as bad as on the mainland, and probably worse.* Which is where the mafiosi came in. They could guarantee a contract with the implicit threat of violence. If a farmer who had promised to sell his neighbour a horse delivered a mule instead, the *uomo d'onore*† and his confederates would pay the farmer a visit of a kind he would never forget.

The problems Sicilians encountered in reaching agreements have endured. In one of the most insightful books written about Cosa Nostra,[6] a social scientist, Diego Gambetta, observed that it was not until 1991 that a radio-dispatched taxi service began operating in Palermo – the last city in Italy to get one. Before the arrival of GPS, which allows the location of each cab to be pinpointed, it was easy to cheat: 'driver B can wait until driver A answers the operator's call and then quote a pick-up time shorter than A's,' Gambetta wrote. And that is exactly what happened again and again in Palermo when the system was tried.

But if, as Gambetta argued, the taxi drivers of Palermo were no

---

* See above, Chapter 13.

† *Onore* in this context does not really translate as 'honour' in the sense that that term is understood nowadays in English: the meaning is closer to 'respect'.

more dishonest than in the rest of Italy, the really interesting question is why they were unable to solve the problem in the same way as in Naples and Milan. There, if one driver suspected another of cheating, he could go to the pick-up address and, if he arrived first, claim the ride for himself. Persistent cheaters were reported and could have their radios disconnected. The implication is that certain drivers in Palermo enjoyed the protection of the Mafia and could therefore cheat with impunity – Cosa Nostra's arbitration is not always of the fair, if intimidating, sort described earlier.

Nor does its historical role as an agency of mediation provide a full explanation for the organization's survival and growth. Another theory rests on the fact that the Mafia came into existence at approximately the same time as the Italian state. The first mention of the term in an official document was in 1865. The simplest – and perhaps the most convenient – explanation for this is that organized crime flourished in the south, where the young state was weak and family and clan allegiances even stronger than in the rest of the country. But there is another way of looking at what happened, which is to see organized crime as, in part, a reaction to Unification. The ideologues of the Risorgimento were mostly northerners, and it was northerners – and particularly Piedmontese – who carried Unification through to completion. Thereafter, the Piedmontese dominated both the government and the armed forces that were sent to deal with the brigandage that plagued the south. At the same time, Naples lost its role as capital and became a provincial city on the way to nowhere very much except Sicily and North Africa. To many in the south, it must have seemed more like colonization than Unification.*

---

* In recent decades a school of revisionist historians has argued that the history of the south has been distorted by having been viewed largely through northern eyes. Some have stressed the relative prosperity of parts of the Bourbon Mezzogiorno and the marginalization of the region after Unification.

Temptation *and* Tangenti

'Non abbiamo sconfitto i corrotti, abbiamo solo selezionato la specie.'
'We have not defeated those who are corrupt. We have merely
identified the species.'

– Piercamillo Davigo, a prosecutor in the *Mani Pulite*
('Clean Hands') team that investigated the Tangentopoli
corruption scandals of the early 1990s

Back in the 1920s Giuseppe Prezzolini expressed a view that was to
remain common until quite recently. 'All the main defects of the
Italians,' he wrote, listing corruption as one of them, 'derive from
Italian poverty in the same way that the dirtiness of so many of
their villages derives from the shortage of water. When more real
money and clean water are running through Italy, its redemption
will be largely complete.'[1]

This is a view I have often heard voiced in respect of other countries in the Mediterranean: that corruption is simply a matter of
economics, or rather poverty. Before Spain or Portugal joined what
was to become the European Union, foreign diplomats and visiting
journalists would often assert as an axiomatic truth that, as soon
as the two countries did so, they would become richer; and that
when their inhabitants were richer they would start to behave in
exactly the same way as people in the North. But, in the case of Italy
at least, time has shown that the relationship between corruption
and wealth – or rather, the lack of it – is not as straightforward as
was imagined.

The 1980s, for example, were a time of rapid economic growth in

Italy. As seen earlier, it is possible that towards the end of the decade Italians were richer than Britons. Yet it was precisely in those years that the tide of sleaze later uncovered by the Clean Hands investigation reached its height. What the prosecutors in Milan uncovered – or rather, brought to court for the first time – was nothing less than a system of ingrained bribery, dubbed Tangentopoli, on which the country's entire post-war political order had come to depend. In essence, the price of everything supplied to the public sector – from airports to the paper table napkins in an old people's home – had been inflated. And the difference between the inflated price and the fair one was siphoned off to provide a *tangente* ('bribe') to the party or parties in a position to award the contract. For the most part, the cash was used to maintain the parties and pay for the patronage they dispensed. But some of it stuck to the fingers of individual unscrupulous politicians.

The clampdown by the prosecutors in Milan seems to have had an effect. Each year, the NGO Transparency International publishes a table that ranks most of the countries in the world according to the level of corruption among politicians and officials as perceived by independent bodies specializing in governance and analysis of the business climate. The higher the ranking, the 'cleaner' the public sector of the country concerned. By 2001 Italy had climbed the ranking to occupy twenty-ninth place – six places behind France. But then it plunged. By 2012 Italy had fallen to seventy-second place, fifty places behind France. Countries ranking higher than Italy included Lesotho, Georgia and Uruguay. Italy was only three places ahead of Bulgaria and six places *behind* Romania, which was deeply ironic since Romania, like Bulgaria, was being kept out of the EU's passport-free Schengen area largely because of concerns about the extent of corruption there.

Italy may be worryingly corrupt, but I have to say that I am sceptical as to whether it is really *that* corrupt. Other soundings, and assessments based on data rather than perceptions, all suggest Romania is still sleazier than Italy. Of itself, that is scarcely anything for a rich nation and member of the elite Group of Eight to boast about, especially since most of the other attempts to measure corruption have given Italy pretty awful marks. In the World Bank's 2012 assessment of corruption control, on a scale from −2.5 to +2.5, Italy was fractionally below zero. Spain and France both scored more than one. Romania was −0.2. The World Economic Forum, using a measure that ran from 1 to 7, gave Italy 3.9 under the heading of 'Irregular payments and bribes' – again better than Romania, but worse than Spain or France. A recent study[2] which looked at the way the EU's structural funds were handled in various countries between 2000 and 2006 found that fraud was suspected or proved in almost 30 per cent of cases in Italy – the highest proportion in any of the seven countries studied.

So what is it that makes Italy so prone to graft? One theory, often put forward in Italy itself, is that it has to do with it being a relatively young country. According to this view, Italians' loyalty to the state is so tenuous that they have a weaker sense of identification with society in general, and are thus more likely to indulge in activities such as tax evasion and the giving or taking of bribes that benefit them individually while undermining fairness and, more generally, the well-being of the broader community. But then what about Germany? Unification there took place in the nineteenth century at almost exactly the same time as in Italy. And, it could be argued, Germany is inherently more divided because of the split between Catholics and Protestants in the population and the separation of East from West during the Cold War. Germany is certainly not free of graft. But corruption is not a problem to anything like the same extent as in Italy.

Another view is that it all stems from the family. Unquestionably, certain forms of corruption can be traced directly to the strength of family ties in Italy. But in recent years – as seen above – a considerable gap has opened up between the levels of corruption in Italy and other countries in southern Europe where family ties are also strong. In the latest survey published by Transparency International at the time of writing, Italy was thirty-nine places behind Portugal and forty-two behind Spain – both poorer countries than Italy, and with less recent experience of democracy.

It would seem that the answer to the question of why some countries are more corrupt than others has to take account of a much wider range of social, cultural and maybe political factors. Italy's still-inflexible bureaucracy is almost certainly among them: one of the ways in which officials wangle bribes is by offering to bend otherwise unyielding rules. It is also probably true to say that, to a greater extent than in Spain or Portugal, Italy remains a society in which many of the most crucial dealings take place between influential patrons and their various clients. Italy developed economically later than the other big countries in Western Europe (though not later than Spain or Portugal) and, as recently as the end of the Second World War, it was still a predominantly rural and agricultural society. Many of the characteristics of that society have survived. Notwithstanding its high-speed trains and glitzy TV shows, today's Italy is in some respects reminiscent of Jane Austen's England or Émile Zola's France – a country where advancement in many areas of life depends less on talent than on your family's position in society and/or the backing of a powerful sponsor.

What is more difficult to explain is the widespread toleration of corruption in Italy. The crisis in the euro zone brought to light quite a lot of graft in Spain, too. But it is noticeable to anyone moving between the two countries that the misbehaviour of politicians in Spain arouses among their compatriots a degree of furious indignation that is often lacking among Italians, many of whom react with a shrug and a comment to the effect that they expected nothing better. On occasions, it goes further than that.

At a party to which my wife and I were invited not long after we arrived in Italy for the first time in the 1990s, I found myself chatting to a woman in her late thirties. At some point, I must have expressed my dislike of a certain politician.

'Why don't you like him?' she asked resentfully.

'Because he's a crook,' I said.

'But I don't want my politicians to be honest,' she replied. 'If they were honest, it would mean they were stupid. I want my country to be run by people who are *furbi.*'

Not long before that encounter a journalist had carried out what became a celebrated test of attitudes to corruption in a sector of the population where you might assume it would incur universal censure. With the Clean Hands prosecutors hard at work in Milan and new scandals involving graft coming to light almost every day, he set off around Italy to visit the confessionals of churches known to have politicians and businesspeople in their congregations. The journalist posed as the secretary of an important Christian Democrat politician and told the priests that for years he had been demanding and receiving illegal party contributions in return for awarding public contracts. With only one exception, his confessors imposed trifling penances.[3]

The journalist's experience touched on a fundamental point: people, of whatever nationality, will get away with what they can. I know of no evidence to show that Italians who emigrate to the United States, for example, are more or less corrupt than Americans of Scandinavian, African or Latin American extraction. But what they all find when they get there are stringent and effective deterrents.

In Italy, the legal sanctions against corruption are much weaker, and in some cases manifestly inadequate. Take, for example, the ban on vote-trading between politicians and organized criminals. The penal code outlaws the payment of mafiosi in exchange for guarantees of electoral support. But votes are seldom purchased with money. Usually, candidates promise favours, confidential information or preferential access to lucrative contracts. And the law does not make that illegal (though, if it can be detected, the supply of favours at a later date is, of course, illegal).

The issue of legal sanctions poses the ticklish question of what does and does not constitute corruption. Italians often point, for example, to the activities of lobbyists in Britain and the US as an example of how the boundaries of the acceptable vary between cultures. There is undoubtedly some truth in this argument: there are activities which are perfectly legal in some other developed nations that would put you in jail in Italy. But, by the same token, there are practices in Italy which, while they may be seen by many as reprehensible, are not actually defined as corrupt.

The very word *corruzione* is often used – and especially in courts of law – in a much narrower way than 'corruption' and its equivalents in other languages. In its legal definition, *corruzione* is what an English speaker would call bribery. Some of the other activities that are corrupt in the wider sense constitute separate offences under Italian law. If, for example, a public official coerces someone into paying him or her for a service, whether in cash or in kind, that is *concussione*. Helping yourself to public money is *peculato*. Taking advantage of public office to inflict damage on another person is *prevaricazione*.

Nepotismo, which is not illegal, covers the giving of jobs to relatives. The word, which derives from the Latin *nepos* ('nephew'),* originated in Italy during the Middle Ages. It was inspired by the privileges and sinecures showered on the 'nephews' – in reality, illegitimate sons – of some highly placed Catholic prelates (and even some popes).

Nepotism is scarcely confined to Italy, but it is certainly rife there. One of the most flagrant cases in recent years involved the founder of the Northern League, Umberto Bossi, who launched his party in the 1980s on the back of a wave of revulsion at the mounting evidence of sleaze emanating from what he termed *Roma Ladrona* ('She-thief Rome'). The whole idea underpinning the Northern League was that honest and industrious Lombards, Venetians and Piedmontese had a right to hold on to more of their wealth, which would otherwise just be squandered or pilfered by the irredeemably corrupt politicians of the capital.

This high moral stance did not prevent Bossi's son being put up for election to the Lombardy regional assembly at the age of

---

* It also meant 'grandson'. The Italian *nipote* has the same dual meaning.

twenty-one. Had Renzo Bossi been a political and intellectual prodigy, his place on the Northern League slate – in a position that guaranteed his election – might have been understandable. But the younger Bossi, whose father conferred on him the unfortunate nickname of *il trota* ('the trout'), had struggled to get even a high-school leaving diploma: he finally passed the required exams at his fourth attempt a few months before his election to the parliament of Italy's biggest region and the one that encompasses its business capital, Milan. Two years later his career in politics came to an abrupt end when he resigned in the midst of a scandal over the Bossi family's alleged misuse of public funds.

While *nepotismo* crops up often in the discussion and reporting of politics in Italy, less is said or written about *favoritismo*. For decades, for example, left-wing local authorities have made sure that contracts of all kinds are steered towards 'red' co-operatives. But this thoroughly incestuous, iniquitous and anti-competitive relationship is widely accepted. Every so often a politician on the right will point to it as evidence that not all the controversial behaviour in Italy can be laid at the door of Silvio Berlusconi and his followers. But no one much seems to care.

Even less controversial is the exchange of favours. This is central to life in Italy and, I would guess, at the root of quite a lot of corruption. A few years ago a social research body carried out a survey to discover how often Italians sought a helping hand from their compatriots.[4] It found that in the previous three months almost two thirds had asked a favour from a relative; more than 60 per cent from a friend and more than a third from a colleague at work. If the favours were given without any expectation of a return then there would be no problem, but there is a well-established tradition in Italy, going back to classical times, that one good turn ought sooner or later to be repaid with another. '*Omnia Romae cum pretio,*' wrote Juvenal ('Everything in Rome comes at a price'), and it is as true today as when he was writing, in the days of Trajan.

Where this culture of reciprocal favours mixes with the prevalence of favouritism and nepotism is in the *raccomandazione*, also known as a *spintarella* and by various other, more innocent-sounding names such as an *indicazione* or a *segnalazione*. In its widest sense, a *raccomandazione* can cover any intervention by one person with another on behalf of a third. There are plenty of more or less innocuous examples: the mayor who calls a local garage, for example, to ensure the son of a friend who has just arrived in town gets good service at a fair price. Significantly less innocuous is the widespread practice of influential people intervening on behalf of their relatives, associates or clients to get them moved up hospital waiting lists or given preferential access to public housing.

So ubiquitous is *raccomandazione* in this wider sense that politicians sometimes openly admit to practising it. It has even been endorsed, albeit somewhat grudgingly, in a sentence of the supreme court. The judges declared that 'The search for a *raccomandazione* is now so deeply rooted in custom and practice as to appear in the eyes of most people to be an indispensable instrument, not only for obtaining that to which they have a right, but for restoring an acceptable degree of functionality to inefficient public services.'

In its narrower and more commonly used sense, *raccomandazione* applies to the procuring of jobs. There was a time when this, too, was pretty innocent. Indeed, it could be argued that, until the 1960s, the system of *raccomandazioni* made a positive contribution to labour mobility and making Italy into a fairer, more meritocratic society. Typically, a villager who had decided to seek work elsewhere would turn to the parish priest or mayor for a *raccomandazione* that could be presented to prospective employers. This would say that he or she was of good character, with no criminal record, and perhaps add some other details. It was what today would be called a character reference. In some cases, the *raccomandazione* might be addressed to someone with whom the priest or local official had influence. But for the most part the only possible exercise of power was negative: the local priest or mayor could deny a *raccomandazione* to someone either out of spite or because of a genuine conviction that he or she was undeserving.

As the parties gradually emerged as the most powerful institutions in Italian society, it was politicians who emerged as the key *raccomandatori*. In a society where now not only the jobs but the job-seekers were largely urban, Christian Democrat bigwigs replaced parish priests as the key arbiters of who was, or was not, worthy of being hired. Several had assistants whose sole task was to collate requests for *raccomandazioni* and decide if they should be acted upon. Giulio Andreotti's sidekick, Franco Evangelisti, was a legendary dispenser of patronage on behalf of his master.

But the criteria that he and others like him applied were significantly different from those that had been used, or were meant to have been used, by priests and local officials. The key requisite for getting employment was no longer moral rectitude or the absence of a criminal record but loyalty to a particular party. What is more, in pretty much every case, the politician or his assistant – unlike the rural priests and police chiefs who once handed out *raccomandazioni* – had the means with which to exert overwhelming influence on the person who was in a position to provide the job or favour requested.

The Clean Hands investigation curbed drastically the power of the parties. But politicians continue to dole out patronage in the form of *raccomandazioni*, as do a slew of interest groups. Various surveys in recent years have concluded that up to half of all Italians owe their jobs to *raccomandazioni*. One of the most detailed investigations was carried out by a publicly funded employment research body, Isfol.[5] It found that 39 per cent of those interviewed had got their jobs through contacts of some kind – relatives, friends, acquaintances or existing employees of the firm. Another 20 per cent had found work in the public sector by way of open competition. But what stood out in the results of the poll was how few Italians had used the recruitment channels that are considered normal in other societies. Only 16 per cent had found their jobs by writing in with a CV, while a mere 3 per cent had responded to advertisements in the press.

Some years ago the news magazine *L'Espresso* discovered that the Italian postal service kept a database specifically for *raccomandazioni*, complete with the names of the *raccomandati* and their corresponding *raccomandatori*. Among the latter was a Vatican cardinal.

Raccomandazioni are inherently unfair. They stand in the way of a more meritocratic society, and spread demoralization. I know personally Italians who have worked hard at their jobs only to be overtaken – or, in some cases, supplanted – by *raccomandati*. In one instance, the *raccomandata* who led to my acquaintance's dismissal was the mistress of the incoming chief executive.

Raccomandazioni mean that people are put into jobs for which they may be unqualified. They lead to contracts being placed with companies that are not the best suited to fulfilling them. They shut out foreign investment. And they encourage corruption: someone who owes his or her livelihood to the munificence of another is in no position to refuse if that other person one day asks for an illicit, or maybe even illegal, favour.

Corruption also holds back the economy and keeps Italians poorer than they need be – a point overlooked by those Italians who shrug at the mention of graft. Just to take one example, a country in which the cost of bribes is routinely added to public contracts is one that is going to have to raise that much extra in the form of taxes. That in turn reduces disposable incomes, lowers consumption, cuts demand and in that way limits growth. Corruption deters competition, making the economy less efficient and productive.

Evaluating the cost of graft is an even more hazardous enterprise than making international comparisons. But according to the latest estimates of Italy's national audit court, corruption costs Italy enough to meet the entire cost of the interest payments on its vast public debts. Ironically, they themselves are, at least in part, the outcome of excess government spending intended to generate *tangenti*.

If we accept Transparency International's view that in the 2000s Italy became steadily more corrupt relative to other countries, there are three possible explanations. One is that the other countries became progressively less corrupt while Italy remained the same. A second explanation – a variation on the same theme – is that Italy improved, but that elsewhere in the world the improvement was greater. And, finally, there is the possibility that Italy simply became more corrupt during those years. Unfortunately, there are reasons for thinking that this last explanation may be the correct one.

It is notable that Italy's ascent of Transparency International's table ended in the year that Silvio Berlusconi was elected to office and at the beginning of a ten-year period in which he was to dominate the affairs of his country. His leadership unquestionably changed the atmosphere.

It was not just that, during his premierships, he was constantly on trial or under investigation for an array of suspected or alleged white-collar offences, including the bribing of judges (of which he was acquitted in 2007) and tax fraud (of which he was convicted in 2013). It was also that from time to time Berlusconi said things that were taken to mean that his view of sleaze was relative. On one occasion, commenting on allegations that the defence firm Finmeccanica had bribed its way to a contract in India, Berlusconi declared that: 'When big groups like ENI, ENEL and Finmeccanica negotiate with countries that are not complete and perfect democracies, there are conditions that have to be accepted if they are to sell their products.'

Under Berlusconi's governments, moreover, the law was changed more than once in such a way that it made it more difficult for the courts to indict, or convict, him. Those changes have also made it harder to bring to justice ordinary Italians involved in corruption in the wider sense of the term. In 2002, for example, his government slashed the maximum sentence for false accounting from five years to two and limited the circumstances in which charges could be brought so that businesspeople who cooked the books could be put on trial only if the amount involved was more than 1 per cent of the firm's assets or 5 per cent of its profits. Berlusconi was also prime minister when parliament brought forward the points at which various offences, and particularly white-collar crimes, were 'timed out' by statutes of limitations. Because of the slowness of Italian justice, it has meant that many trials for such offences have been guillotined before a verdict could be reached.

Some of Berlusconi's own trials ground to a halt because of changes to the relevant statutes of limitations introduced by his government. That much is known outside Italy. But what has been less widely publicized is the effect that this tampering with the law has had on society as a whole. Resigning from the prosecution service in 2007, Gherardo Colombo, one of the former Clean Hands prosecutors, said Italy was witnessing a 'renaissance of corruption'. By then, numerous trials for white-collar offences were being held in the full knowledge of all concerned that they would have to be abandoned before they were concluded. The result was to send a message to Italians that they could commit corrupt acts with little fear of the consequences.

Berlusconi justified his changes to the law by saying that he was being unjustly hounded by left-wing prosecutors seeking to achieve through the courts what his political adversaries had repeatedly failed to achieve by means of the ballot box: his removal from the public life of Italy. For over twenty years – in fact, ever since the billionaire media proprietor entered politics and began to voice that claim – the issue of justice has been central to the life of the nation.

Pardon and Justice

' "Se noi riconosciamo," pensavo, "che errare è dell'uomo, non è crudeltà
sovrumana la giustizia?" '
    ' "If we accept," I thought, "that to err is human, then is not just-
ice superhuman cruelty?" '

– Luigi Pirandello, *Il fu Mattia Pascal*
(*The Late Mattia Pascal*), 1904

If Italy had a navel, it would be the Piazza Venezia. On one side
looms the grandiose structure that foreigners know as the Victor
Emanuel monument but the real name of which is the Altare della
Patria or Altar of the Fatherland. To the right of the altar – and
where else but in Italy, you may ask, would a secular monument be
called an altar? – is a road that runs through the Forums to the Colosseum, Italy's most instantly recognizable tourist sight. On the left
is the balcony from which Mussolini ignited the patriotic fervour of
the masses. And standing directly opposite the giant, white marble
altar is a less well-known fragment of Italy's rich past: the palazzo in
which Napoleon's mother, Maria Letizia Ramolino, lived out her
days after her son was sent into exile on St Helena.

'It's all there,' said an Italian fellow journalist as he stared medita-
tively at the square through one of the tall windows of Palazzo
Bonaparte. He was holding a bag of crisps and dipping into it from
time to time as he waited for his expenses to be dealt with in an
office which, in those days, was adjacent to mine. At first, I assumed
he meant all those richly symbolic buildings visible from the
window.

'No. I'm talking about the people,' he said. 'Just look. Everything you need to know about Italy is there before your eyes.'

It was winter and there was scarcely a tourist in sight. The Romans had reoccupied the Piazza Venezia. And it was a riot of confusion, even more frenzied than at the height of summer. There were people crossing the square on foot at every conceivable angle, blithely ignoring the pedestrian crossings. *Motorini** and cars, vans and buses roared past within inches of them, swerving left and right and avoiding each other by inches, too. Some of the vehicles being gunned around the square on that chilly afternoon were *macchinette*, micro-cars with 50cc engines that you can drive in Italy as soon as you turn fourteen (or even if you have lost your licence because of reckless or drunken driving). *Macchinette* can easily be adjusted to go at well over their legal maximum speed of 45kph and are involved in about twice as many accidents as ordinary cars. In the midst of this chaos, a lone policeman stood on a raised plinth attempting to direct the traffic. Every so often a motorist – usually a *motorino* rider† – would pretend not to have noticed his upraised hand and continue into one of the streets leading off the square, prompting a volley of whistles from other policemen standing nearby. Pulled over to the side of the road, the *motorino* rider would soon be engaged in a heated dispute with the cops, pleading his innocence with upturned palms and the desperate expression of one who has been cruelly misunderstood.

What we were gazing down on was precisely the Italy that Mussolini had in mind when, sitting in his office behind that famous balcony, a German asked him if it was difficult to govern the Italians. 'Not at all,' he replied. 'It is simply pointless.'[1]

Delve into any of the lanes near the Piazza Venezia and you will soon pass a pavement café that – although this may not be obvious – was never authorized to be one. The way it would have been done is as follows: you acquire your café; then, after a few months, you

---

* Mopeds. But the term is often taken to include scooters as well.
† Known charmingly in Italian as a *centauro* ('centaur').

put a couple of flower pots outside; if no one objects, you replace them with tubs that have bigger plants or even little trees in them; if that passes unnoticed, you are ready to set out a table and a couple of chairs between the tubs and the door to your café; then another, then another, until you are ready to box in the entire area with a line of shrubs and maybe even some chains strung between posts to protect what is, by law, public property, but which by now looks as if it belongs to the café. At this point – and it may have taken you years to get this far – you are ready to top off the project with an awning and perhaps some transparent plastic or glass walls to protect your customers during the winter. Inch by inch, step by step, you have succeeded in doubling the size – and profitability – of your café.

The Italian way is to do first, and ask permission later, if at all. The principle has been applied to literally millions of home improvements and extensions that no local authority official would dream of approving, unless perhaps given a *bustarella* (literally, a 'little envelope') tightly packed with banknotes. And not just that. It has been applied to the construction of entire houses, even neighbourhoods. In 2007 a small town consisting of fifty buildings housing more than four hundred flats was discovered near Naples. The whole thing was *abusivo* (the term applied to a construction project that lacks official approval). The environmental group Legambiente once calculated that altogether 325,000 buildings in Italy were *abusivi*. '*Fatta la legge trovato l'inganno*,' as the Italians say: no sooner is a law made than a way around it is found.

Look more closely, though, and you will see quite another side of Italy. As mentioned earlier,* all sorts of other things are rigidly disciplined in private life. It is one of the great paradoxes: that Italians will not obey laws, yet they will adhere – and with steely rigidity – to conventions. Just look at the way people sunbathe. In most other countries you arrive at the beach to find people scattered around higgledy-piggledy. But that applies in Italy only to so-called *spiagge*

* See Chapter 13.

libere ('free beaches'). The majority of beaches look like something a North Korean commissar might have dreamt up: row after row of identical loungers with identical sunshades and perhaps an aisle in the middle giving access to the waterfront. Not that anyone can just walk down it and into the sea. Entrance is controlled by the owners of the *stabilimento balneare* (literally, the 'bathing establishment') which has charge of that stretch of the beach. Some *stabilimenti balneari* are run by local authorities, but the majority are private concerns (though usually with a licence issued by the town or city council).

Only when a law happens to lie close to the blurred frontier that separates it from being a convention is there a good chance it will be respected. In 2005, for example, the authorities decided to slap a ban on smoking in public places. No one thought the Italians would pay it the slightest notice. But in the months leading up to the introduction of the ban the idea got around that it was a pretty sensible measure and might even do something to improve people's health. When it came into effect at the start of 2006, from one day to the next, people stopped smoking in restaurants, bars and other establishments. By some semi-miraculous process, a law had turned into a convention and everyone was ready to respect it.

The response to the smoking ban prompted commentators at the time to ask just how anarchic their compatriots really were. My own answer goes back to the many years I lived among another supposedly anarchic people, the Spanish. I well remember the bedlam of the Madrid traffic, and in particular the double-parking. But in those days – as in much of Italy today – the fines were derisory. And, in any case, they were seldom collected. Only if you left your car blocking the entrance to a maternity hospital, say, and then walked off to watch a football match could you expect to run foul of the law. Since then, fines have been increased to the point at which they can make a painful impact on household budgets. What is more, ways have been found to ensure they are collected. The result is that, even on Saturday nights, you can drive around the centre of Madrid without seeing a double-parked vehicle. What has made the difference is quite simply the threat of punishment. Daunted by the prospect of stiff penalties, the anarchic *madrileños* have become law-abiding motorists. In most parts of Italy, on the other hand, no such measures have been imposed and the accent is still to a far greater extent on forgiveness rather than retribution.*

Not far from Piazza Venezia lies Via Arenula. At the bottom, just by the River Tiber, stands an imposing building which a large plaque proclaims to be the 'Ministry of Pardon and Justice'. It is no longer officially known as such, the 'Pardon' having been dropped from the title in 1999. But the thinking that inspired the name of the ministry lives on. To outsiders, the Italian system of criminal justice can often seem as if it was set up with no other purpose than to make sure people are let off.

Once indicted (and that sometimes requires a lengthy pre-trial hearing), defendants get a trial and then an automatic right to two appeals – the first in a local court on the merits of the case and the second in the supreme court, known as the Court of Cassation, on the legal basis of the conviction or acquittal (because the prosecution, too, is entitled to appeal). It is only after this entire three-stage process has been exhausted that a defendant is considered 'definitively convicted'. On average, it takes more than eight years. In a sixth of cases, it takes more than fifteen. And, throughout the period from initial to final conviction, unless the defendant is alleged to belong to a mafia or has been accused of a very serious offence such as murder or rape, he or she will usually remain at liberty.

Prison sentences, when they are eventually confirmed, are comparatively lenient. A study by the think tank Eures of the ten years to the end of 2004 found that the average sentence for murder was less than twelve and a half years, even though the minimum laid down in the penal code was twenty-one years. For the embezzlement of public funds, the average sentence was a year and four months – less than half the ostensible minimum of three years.

* I stress 'most'. Very broadly speaking, rule-breaking diminishes as you head north. There are towns in places such as Tuscany, Emilia-Romagna and Piedmont where the population is as law-abiding as anywhere in Scandinavia.

If the convicted criminal has reached the age of seventy during the many years of waiting for a definitive sentence, it is highly unlikely that he or she will actually go to jail. The same is true of many younger defendants whose offences have been quashed in the meantime by a statute of limitations or by one of several instruments that the authorities deploy from time to time to create space in the prisons.

The most comprehensive of these is the *amnistia*, which extinguishes both the crime and the sentence. Understandably, there was a rash of amnesties after the Second World War to ensure, for instance, that people were no longer going to be put on trial for having tried to subvert Mussolini's dictatorship. But over the next four decades Italian governments granted no fewer than thirteen more amnesties: some general; others confined to a specific category of offence or those carrying a sentence of less than a certain number of years.

Since 1990 there has been a preference for the *indulto* ('pardon'), which quashes the sentence but not the crime. There have been three. But their effects have been – and continue to be – greater than that modest figure might suggest. In many other legal systems, amnesties and pardons apply only to those who have already been jailed. But in their Italian versions they cover any offence committed before the date on which they are promulgated, even if the person who has committed the offence has not yet even been tried, let alone sentenced or jailed. When Silvio Berlusconi was definitively convicted for the first time – of tax fraud in 2013 – he was given a four-year jail sentence. But seven years earlier a pardon had been granted by the then centre-left government that wiped three years off the sentences for offences committed before it was declared. So the former prime minister's jail term was immediately reduced to one year. And since he was over the age of seventy, he was given a choice between house arrest and community service. Other, less famous Italians will continue to benefit from the 2006 measure for years to come.

One of the reasons why Italians are so willing to try their luck at flouting the planning regulations (and dodging tax) has been the existence of yet another form of legal forgiveness. This is the *condono*. Every so often the government of the day will approve a measure that allows Italians to pay a relatively small fine in return for having their debts to the state wiped out or getting official sanction for an illegal conversion or building. Some *condoni* have been applied to both tax dodging and illegal construction. In recent decades, a *condono* has been declared about once every five years.

They are popular with governments because they give the Treasury an instant cash infusion. But the effect is to encourage Italians in their already well-consolidated belief that they can get away without having to pay taxes or seek permission for building projects. It also means that eyesores in protected areas such as beaches, national parks and even archaeological sites remain on the landscape, having been fully legalized. Recent governments have forsworn the *condono* as a means of squaring the public accounts, but it remains to be seen whether future administrations will be as virtuous.

For an example of leniency, it would be hard to better the story of what happened after the media floodlight swivelled away from Italy's biggest-ever corruption scandal. Tangentopoli caused a sensation far beyond Italy's frontiers. Because so many people were involved, the arrests were on a scale never before seen in Italy and perhaps not in any country outside the Communist Bloc. I was living elsewhere in 1992, when the first unhappy suspect was led away in handcuffs, and I well recall the mounting incredulity and excitement of the reporting from Italy as one distinguished captain of industry after the next was slung into jail to cool his heels alongside others who, until the police knocked on their doors, had been arbiters of fortune for their city, region or even country.

More than 5,000 people were placed under investigation, of whom 2,735 were indicted in Milan alone. Another 1,785 cases were sent to other jurisdictions either before or after indictment, and what happened to them has never, so far as I am aware, been researched. The outcome of the proceedings in Milan, however, has been examined in detail.[2] Ten years after the start of the first investigation more than a sixth of the cases were still awaiting an initial verdict, a fact that speaks volumes about the pace of Italian justice. Roughly another one sixth had ended in verdicts of not guilty. But of the remaining two thirds, almost none had resulted in a prison sentence. Some of the defendants had died in the meantime. A large number plea-bargained their way to reduced sentences, which meant they did not have to go to jail. Others opted for a fast-track trial and obtained similar concessions. In quite a few cases – also about one sixth of the total – the charges had to be dropped after being 'timed out' by a statute of limitations. Two years earlier, at a time when many of the trials initiated in the early 1990s were coming to an end, *Corriere della Sera* reported that out of the thousands of men and women who were caught up in the Tangentopoli investigations, only four were in prison.[3]

Indulgence spreads like a fine layer of soothing balm over many other areas of Italian life. Politicians who lose elections seldom vanish to go off to write their memoirs in the way they do in other societies. The principle of 'up or out' so beloved of Americans has no place in Italian politics. A few years or even months later the defeated candidate pops up on a TV chat show, sometimes at the head of a new party he has just founded, and soon resumes his career as if nothing had happened. Public employees caught embezzling or pilfering taxpayers' money may be tried and convicted. But they are not automatically dismissed as a result.

Part of the reason for all this pardon and leniency is straightforward soft-heartedness. Italians may tend to cynicism, but they are also – for the most part – kindly people. In addition, though, there are at least two other factors at work, which may well be connected.

One is upbringing. Disciplinarian parents exist in Italy just as they do in every country (a teacher who once worked at a school in rural Piedmont told me that *padri padroni** were the norm there), but

---

* 'Overbearing, authoritarian fathers'. *Padre padrone* is the title of an autobiographical work by Gavino Ledda, the son of just such a parent. His father, a Sardinian shepherd, removed him from school before he could learn to read and

modern Italian parents, and particularly mothers, are generally extremely indulgent. Every foreigner who has lived in Italy has a favourite story of a child allowed to run amok. My own stems from a dinner with friends at a restaurant in Umbria. The restaurant had a piano, and a little girl of about five decided to play it. Unfortunately, she had no idea how to do so. Throughout the meal, I and about thirty other customers had to listen to intermittent bursts of noise as she returned to the piano to slam her fists up and down on the keyboard. Neither of her parents made a move to stop her. But then nor did any of the restaurant staff. Unsurprisingly, people grow up feeling it is their right to enjoy the maximum possible freedom. And, for the most part, they are prepared to concede the same right to others.

A second factor is obviously Catholicism, with its strong emphasis on the mutually dependent concepts of confession, penitence and absolution. One of the many proverbs about forgiveness in Italian has it that *Peccato confessato, mezzo perdonato* ('A sin confessed is a sin half forgiven'). And it is telling that when the authorities made it possible for terrorists, and later mobsters, to earn favourable treatment in return for collaborating with investigators, the beneficiaries of the scheme should have come to be known as *pentiti*. A recurrent feature of the reporting of crimes in the media* is the journalists' insistence on knowing whether the victims – or the late victims' relatives – forgive the alleged perpetrator. Their responses – whether they do or do not feel ready to offer pardon – often provide the

---

write, and kept him in check with savage beatings. By dint of sheer determination, Ledda provided himself with an education. After graduating from university, he returned to Sardinia as an assistant professor of linguistics at the University of Cagliari. His story, published in 1975, was made into a film of the same title by the Taviani brothers.

* Known by the name of *cronaca nera*. The news in Italian newspapers (apart from sports, business and foreign news) is divided between two sections. One is *politica* (which also includes news about the Vatican and the Italian Church); the other is *cronaca*, which takes in everything else. Reporters who do not cover the police and courts form a subsection known as *cronaca bianca*.

headlines for stories written in the aftermath of grisly crimes such as murder, manslaughter or violent robbery.

The positive side of this is that Italians are generally far more ready to allow for human frailty than is the case among Britons or Americans. The driver who accidentally turns into a one-way street is more likely to be reprimanded than fined, as is the pensioner found travelling without a ticket on a bus or train. The negative side is a widespread resistance in Italian culture to the notion of accepting responsibility for one's actions. Breaking the rules, or the law, and then dodging the consequences are quintessential components of *furbizia*. Avoiding responsibility can even be regarded as, if not a virtue, then a merit: something to be applauded. It is an important reason why so many Italians admired Silvio Berlusconi and continued to vote for him: though repeatedly indicted, he managed time and again to wriggle free of conviction, sometimes because of changes to the law introduced by his own governments.

Perhaps the most extraordinary judicial saga of recent years, though, was that of a very different political figure, Adriano Sofri. Following the student revolts that swept through Europe in 1968, Sofri shot to prominence as the leader of a radical left-wing group Lotta Continua ('Continuous Struggle'). After it became clear that the masses were not going to heed its call to revolution, Lotta Continua fell apart in 1976 and Sofri became a teacher and journalist. Twelve years later he and two other former members of the group were arrested and charged with the murder of a man who has a place in Italy's literature as well as its history: Luigi Calabresi, a senior police officer. It was from the window of Calabresi's office at police headquarters in Milan that a young anarchist, Pino Pinelli, had fallen – or jumped, or been thrown – while being interrogated in 1969. His death inspired Dario Fo, who later won the Nobel Prize for Literature, to write his play *Accidental Death of an Anarchist*. Calabresi was suspected – perhaps understandably, but without any evidence – of having murdered Pinelli. He became a left-wing hate target. A few months later he was shot dead as he left his home in Milan.

Lotta Continua's newspaper unquestionably bore much of the blame for whipping up the lynch-mob atmosphere that engulfed Calabresi. But the case against Sofri was based solely on the evidence of a fourth ex-Lotta Continua militant, who confessed to being the getaway driver for the killing and was given a drastically reduced sentence in return for his collaboration with the police. His account was full of details at odds with the known facts, and in 1992 the Court of Cassation ordered a rehearing of the appeal. The defendants were again acquitted, but fell victim to one of the most pernicious devices in the Italian judicial system. Their fourth trial was held in a court with a bench that included not only professional judges but lay ones. Lay judges are the nearest thing in Italy to jurors. They sit either side of the professional *magistrati*, decked out in sashes in the red, green and white of the Italian flag, usually looking a bit self-conscious. They can outvote the career judges six to two. But, once a verdict has been reached, it is left to one of the professionals to write up the reasons for the decision. And this provides the opportunity for what is known as a *sentenza suicida*: a judge who disagrees with a verdict can explain it in his written judgement in such a blatantly absurd way that it is bound to be overruled on appeal to the Court of Cassation.

Because of the *sentenza suicida* sent to the Court of Cassation in the Sofri cases, the judges of the supreme court had no option but to overturn the acquittal and order yet another hearing, at which the trio were found guilty. Finally, in 1997, at the seventh hearing of the case, the Court of Cassation – the very court that five years earlier had challenged their conviction – handed down a new verdict, this time of guilty.

Sofri spent the next ten years in jail. After he almost died of a ruptured oesophagus, he was transferred to house arrest for convalescence. But it was not until 2012 that he was finally deemed to have served his time.

The *sentenza suicida* was not the only surreal aspect of the Sofri affair. Once he had been definitively convicted, his case became entangled in a logical short-circuit that clearly arises from Catholic doctrine. His supporters, including some on the political right, made impassioned appeals for the president to grant him a pardon. But, just as in Catholicism absolution can be granted only after confession, in Italy a pardon can be granted only if the person who has been convicted asks for one. In doing so, though, he or she makes an implicit admission of guilt. Sofri obstinately insisted that he was innocent. And so he had to go on being punished.

His case illustrates a fundamental point about Italy's endlessly controversial legal system: that for all its benevolence, it can also be frighteningly cruel. And at the root of much of the cruelty is the slowness with which justice is administered. Judges in Italy not only mete out justice; they also manage the judicial machine, an activity for which they have no proper training. No party of left or right has even wanted to discuss this problem, but it is a central reason for the gross inefficiency to be found in the courts.

For a start, trials are not held on consecutive days but at leisurely intervals over a period of months or even years. At the first hearing in, say, November, the judge will discuss with the lawyers for the prosecution, the defence and other parties who may have joined themselves to the case the dates on which they can all be present. Since the lawyers are all engaged in other cases that are being held simultaneously, it is more than likely that the first convenient date will be sometime in December and that no more than a couple of hearings will be possible before the courts break for Christmas. Come the new year, the trial will resume, usually at the rate of a hearing a week or even less. One of the effects of holding trials in this way is that it becomes progressively harder for all concerned – and particularly the lay judges – to keep a mental grip on the intricacies of the evidence. Another is that defendants who are sent to jail to await trial and who are subsequently found to be innocent of the crime of which they have been accused are deprived of their freedom for far longer than necessary.

There are even worse delays in civil justice. And they are an important reason why foreign investors are so reluctant to put money into Italy: they discover that, if they are defrauded, for example, or just not paid for the goods or services they have provided, they may have to wait a decade or more to get their money. A particularly grotesque example involving an Italian came to light in 2010 when a 94-year-old woman living in a village near Rome died after waiting forty years for the settlement of a dispute over her mother's will. Exasperated by the slowness of the courts, she had brought a case against the state. She won and was awarded €8,000 in compensation. But, despite numerous attempts on her behalf, she never succeeded in obtaining more than a fraction of the award in her favour. Some of the cash that she did get came from the sale of photocopiers seized by debt collectors from public buildings.

In 2012 there was a backlog of 3.4 million criminal cases and 5.5 million civil ones.

One of the underlying problems of the Italian legal system is that, insofar as criminal justice is concerned, it has become an uneasy mix of two largely incompatible systems. For most of its history, it was what jurists define as inquisitorial. By far the most important stage in the proceedings was the investigative one, known as *istruzione*: an investigating judge, known as a *giudice istruttore*, helped by the police, would try to establish who was responsible for a crime. Until the 1970s, when changes were introduced, the defendant and his or her lawyers had no right to challenge or contradict the information the judge gathered, let alone present evidence of their own. The *dibattimento* – the trial in open court – was thus little more than a formality and the role of defence lawyers, the *avvocati*, was pretty much confined to making pleas in mitigation. The trial judge could base his decision on evidence recorded during the investigation, even if it was not confirmed by witnesses called to testify in open court. He – or, very exceptionally in those days, she – seldom reached a decision that was at variance with the conclusions of the *giudice istruttore*.

A reform in 1989 was meant to bring about a revolution: the conversion of Italy's inquisitorial system, based on the Napoleonic Code, into an adversarial one such as those in the US and Britain. But, as so often happens in Italy, compromise – the tendency

always to search for the middle ground, even at the cost of imple-
menting a half measure – won the day. Within a few years, the
constitutional court was chipping away at the edifice that had been
constructed and, among other things, restoring to the trial judge
the right to base a verdict on evidence not produced in court.[4]
Unable to contest decisions of the constitutional court, parliament
decided to change the constitution on which they were based. In
2001 the changes were incorporated into a modified code of criminal procedure. But the system remains an awkward hybrid.

Crucial to an understanding of the controversies that have surrounded the courts – and indeed the entire political history of Italy
since the early 1990s – is the role of the prosecutor, known as the
pubblico ministero (PM) or *procuratore*. In the opinion of many Italians, the powers they have inherited from the *giudici istruttori*
continue to stack the odds against the defence. What is more, they
will argue, individual prosecutors have abused the powers at their
disposal so as to win notoriety, particularly when they are hoping
one day to leave behind the law and embark on a career in politics.
As in so many other fields, Italians divide into two camps on this
issue. Critics of the PMs describe themselves as *garantisti* and brand
those on the other side of the argument *giustizialisti*.

Silvio Berlusconi's arrival on the political stage in 1994 gave a
vivid political colouring to a debate that had previously cut across
party lines. The property and media tycoon claimed he had entered
politics to save his country from communism or, rather, the heirs
of the old PCI.* His critics have always believed he went into
parliament to save himself from possible bankruptcy and jail. Tangentopoli had yet to run its course. Many another senior figure
from the business world was in prison, and Berlusconi's political
sponsor, Bettino Craxi, had already fled the country to escape incar-
ceration. The new leader of the Italian right had good reason to fear

---

* Berlusconi himself has never made the distinction, and was still describing his
left-wing opponents as *communisti* almost a quarter of a century after their prede-
cessors had forsaken Marxism.

that he himself could soon be brought to trial: the Milan prosecutors were already looking into claims that he had bribed members of the revenue guard sent to inspect his companies' books and that he had used offshore companies and bogus accounting to illegally fund Craxi's Italian Socialist Party.*

Berlusconi argued that this only proved his claim to be the victim of a witch-hunt mounted by left-wing prosecutors and justified his contention that the entire judicial system needed reforming in such a way as to curb the powers of the PMs. All of a sudden, the cause of the *garantisti* became that of his party, and by extension that of the right. Ever since, many left-wingers have dismissed out of hand criticisms of the Italian judicial system to which they might otherwise have given a fair hearing.

Take, for example, the alleged misuse of wiretapping. That had been a *garantista* cause since the early 1990s, but became ever more important to Berlusconi's supporters as wiretapped conversations were used to indict – or merely embarrass – their leader. The prosecutors and their supporters protest that, in the land of the mafia, wiretapping is an essential weapon in the investigators' armoury. But that argument is hard to sustain in the face of the Max Planck Institute's finding† that the number of warrants issued in Italy is proportionately more than a hundred times the number granted in the United States, which is not exactly free of organized crime. Official figures giving a city-by-city breakdown of the spending on wiretapping in Italy punched another hole in the arguments of the *giustizialisti*. They showed only a limited correlation between the volume of wiretapping and the presence of the mafia. Predictably enough, Palermo was top of the list. But Milan and Varese, just to the north of Italy's business capital, came next. Trento, one of the

---

* He was acquitted of bribing the revenue guards. The other accusations gave rise to two trials. One was cut short by a statute of limitations. The other had to be abandoned after Berlusconi's own government changed the law on false accounting.

† See above, pages 75–6.

most tranquil cities in the country, was eleventh – four places above Catanzaro, the capital of the 'Ndrangheta's homeland of Calabria. It is hard to avoid the suspicion that prosecutors and police alike have become addicted to wiretaps as a substitute for more demanding but less invasive methods of investigation.

What infuriates the *garantisti* more than anything is that the transcripts of wiretapped conversations routinely find their way into the media, doubly violating the rights to privacy of those whose conversations have been recorded. Sometimes, they are people who have not committed any wrongdoing but who just happened to have spoken on the telephone to a suspect. On occasion, the publication takes place quite legally: if, for example, the transcript of a wiretap has been annexed to a prosecutor's request for a search, arrest or other warrant, or to the report that prosecutors must submit at the end of an inquiry in support of their application for an indictment. But quite often wiretaps are leaked while the investigation is still in progress, and in some cases titillating or embarrassing extracts are published that have nothing to do with the substance of the case. Leaks can come from defence lawyers, court administrators, police officers and others. But, though it is impossible to prove, it is widely assumed that many of the juiciest morsels thrown to reporters come from PMs.

Technically, the leaking of evidence is an offence, as is its publication. But it is almost unheard of for a reporter or an editor to be prosecuted, because of the difficulty of proving what happened: journalists are protected in Italy from being forced to reveal their sources, so the identity of the person who leaked the information is well-nigh impossible to establish. The concept of *sub judice* exists in Italy, but it is violated almost daily. This, too, is an example of how the 1989 reform got uncomfortably stuck halfway. In the days when the verdict depended entirely on professional judges who had access to the entire investigative dossier, it was a reasonable assumption that the selective leaking of evidence could do nothing to influence the outcome of a trial. But under the new system, as mentioned earlier, many cases are heard before lay as well as professional judges and the former are clearly susceptible to media influence. Feeding a stream of titbits to reporters, a wily prosecutor can build up a presumption of guilt that can be hard for the defence to demolish in court.

Another hangover from the old, purely inquisitorial system is the liberal use of pre-trial custody. Suspects – and during investigations they are still only that – are sometimes confined for good reason. There can be a real danger that they could flee abroad, tamper with the evidence or intimidate witnesses. But suspects in Italy are sometimes thrown into jail on pretty flimsy grounds and, from the speed with which they are often released after they begin to collaborate with the investigators, it seems more than possible that they were jailed to loosen their tongues. The alleged misuse of pre-trial custody first became an issue of public debate during Tangentopoli, as hundreds of men more accustomed to sitting on plush boardroom chairs than hard prison benches were consigned to Milan's San Vittorio jail. Yet very few, as has been seen, were ultimately given custodial sentences. In fact, it can often seem that Italians accused of wrongdoing are far more likely to go to jail *before* they are convicted than after. According to the Council of Europe's Annual Penal Statistics for 2012, more than 40 per cent of prisoners were still awaiting a final sentence – the second highest proportion in the EU.[5]

Prosecutors cannot, of course, simply order people to jail. That has to be done by a judge. But then the relationship between judges and prosecutors in Italy is one of the most controversial issues of all. The 1989 reform separated their functions, but they remained part of the same institutional body, as indeed was required by the constitution. Together, the judges and prosecutors form what is termed the *magistratura*. Whereas defence lawyers are self-employed, the *magistrati* are employees of the state. They take the same exam to enter the profession and, as they progress through their careers, they can switch from one role to the other: a young prosecutor working in, say, Ferrara can apply to become a judge in Bari and then move on from there to be a prosecutor in Rome. In 2005 the then Berlusconi government introduced a law that held them to separate career paths for five years after they entered the profession. But before the law came into force it was largely reversed by another introduced by the centre-left.

Ordinary Italians continue to regard judges and prosecutors as having similar functions. It is not unusual, in fact, for prosecutors to be referred to, even in the media, not just as *magistrati* but as *giudici*. *Garantisti* complain that the two branches of the *magistratura* share a common *esprit de corps* and that judges are all too ready to grant prosecutors' requests for, among other things, the imprisonment of suspects. Indeed, it would be unnatural if a judge who had spent several years of his or her life as a prosecutor did not intuitively see things from the prosecution's standpoint.

But what of Berlusconi's assertion that the *magistratura* is infested with left-wingers? Some of his followers even talk about a *partito della magistratura*. A subtler version of the same contention is that Italy's judges and prosecutors are like the Turkish military – a body of men and women with a broadly similar political outlook who do not need to belong to a party or group in order to act in concert.

It is probably true to say that the number of left-wingers among Italy's *magistrati* is higher than among their counterparts in other countries. Lawyers in general, and judges in particular, tend to be conservative. For many years, the same was true in Italy. The judiciary bequeathed by Mussolini stood well to the right. Partly as a way of loosening the conservatives' grip on the institutions, the Italian Communist Party during the Cold War adopted what it termed 'a war of position'. The idea was that the proletariat – or rather its allies in the intelligentsia – would infiltrate key areas of power and influence. After 1968 the idea was taken up in a modified form by followers of the New Left, which had gathered strength from the student revolts. There is little doubt that in the years that followed, a number of radical idealists did indeed enter the *magistratura*.

But to argue, as Silvio Berlusconi has done, that the judiciary is saturated with Marxists is nonsense. If that were the case, he would not have got off as many times as he has. And Adriano Sofri would never have been convicted. The overwhelming majority of judges and prosecutors belong to the Associazione Nazionale Magistrati (ANM), which is simply a professional association. Within the ANM there are two *correnti* ('currents'): Magistratura Democratica, which aligns with the left, and Magistratura Indipendente, which leans to the right. But judges and prosecutors alike deeply resent the implication that their political views play any role in the decisions they take in a professional capacity. Most of the defence lawyers I have spoken to have been more critical of the minority of prosecutors who have one eye on a career in politics and who take up cases they know will give them a high profile in the media.

'But if I thought that when I went into court to argue a case I needed to worry about the political affiliations of the judge, then, frankly, I'd give up this job and go off and do something else,' said one *avvocato*.

At the time of writing, Magistratura Indipendente is the stronger of the two factions, its candidates having had more success than those of Magistratura Democratica in the most recent elections to the profession's self-governing body, the Consiglio Superiore della Magistratura. The prosecutor in the Court of Cassation who in 2013 successfully argued for the rejection of Berlusconi's final appeal against his conviction for tax fraud belonged to Magistratura Indipendente.

19.

Questions of Identity

'Italia significa Verdi, Puccini, Tiziano, Antonello da Messina . . . Io non penso che Tiziano sia nato lassù e Antonello da Messina sia nato laggiù: per me sono due italiani.'

'Italy means Verdi, Puccini, Titian [and] Antonello da Messina . . . I don't think of Titian as being born up there and Antonello da Messina as being born down there; for me, they are two Italians.'

– Riccardo Muti, *Corriere della Sera*, 22 March 2011

In 2011 Italy had its 150th birthday. On 17 March, the day in 1861 that King Vittorio Emanuele proclaimed the foundation of the Kingdom of Italy, there was a ceremony in Rome and the air force aerobatics team used vapour trails in the national colours to trace what was claimed to be the world's biggest Tricolore.

Elsewhere, though, the celebrations were mostly limited to exhibitions recalling this or that local aspect of the Risorgimento. By the standards of a relatively young country, it was all fairly muted. To some extent, this was because the governing coalition at the time included the Northern League, which regards Unification as an unmitigated disaster. And by then Italy was immersed in the deep economic crisis that had begun to swamp the euro zone two years earlier. Its modest anniversary celebrations were nevertheless taken by many, inside and outside the country, as further evidence that the work of nation building that started in the 1860s was far from complete.

Italians tend to reinforce that notion. Most seem more eager to

tell foreigners about the differences between them than their similarities. So, unsurprisingly, it is an idea that runs through much of
the foreign writing on Italy: entire books are still being written
around the view that Italy today is little more than a 'geographical
expression'.*

As a geographical term, in fact, the word 'Italia' is not all that useful, since it has been understood in different ways at different times.
For the Romans, it meant only the peninsula. The Po Valley was
regarded as part of Gaul. The idea that the entire area south of the
Alps comprised a natural geographical territory seems only to have
taken shape after the collapse of the Roman Empire and may have
had something to do with the fact that the roads the Romans had
built through the mountains gradually fell into disrepair, limiting
contact between Italy in the modern sense of the term and the rest
of Europe.

As outlined earlier, geography and history combined to divide
the inhabitants of the territory that stretched down from the Alps
to Sicily.† But there is plenty of evidence to suggest that they
regarded the people who invaded them from beyond the Alps or
across the Mediterranean as being more foreign than other Italians.
There were even moments when they felt a certain amount of
mutual solidarity. When, for example, in the fourteenth century
one Cola di Rienzo seized power in Rome and declared a republic,
he convoked an assembly of representatives from all over Italia.
Quite a few of the communes of the day sent delegates to speak on
their behalf.

Occasionally, moreover, the states that coexisted uneasily in what
we now call Italy were able to see a common interest in banding
together to overcome a foreign invader. Most of the city states
of northern Italy combined their forces to defeat the emperor

---

* The contemptuous description applied to Italy in the early nineteenth century
by the then Austrian chancellor, Prince Klemens von Metternich.
† See above, pages 4–11.

Frederick I at the Battle of Legnano* in 1176, and just over three centuries later, in 1495, the Republic of Venice allied with the duchies of Milan and Mantua to drive out the French king Charles VIII at the Battle of Fornovo. By then, an idea of Italy had taken shape in the minds of several Renaissance intellectuals. Machiavelli ended his greatest work, *The Prince*, with an appeal for a leader who could unite the Italians and liberate Italy 'from the barbarians'.

It was not, however, until the late eighteenth century that anything resembling an Italian nationalist ideology began to take shape. Even then, the idea of a united country seemed like an unrealizable dream until well into the nineteenth century. The great Piedmontese statesman Camillo Benso, the Count of Cavour, who was instrumental in bringing about Italian unification, never really believed in the idea and tried to undermine Garibaldi's audacious expedition to Sicily, which brought the Mezzogiorno into the new state. Not that ordinary Italians were themselves much convinced: more than half the population abstained from Italy's first general election in 1870.

But that was then. And this is now. It seems to me that many Italians, and many of those who write about their country, fail to make a crucial distinction: between diversity and disunity. The two concepts are related, but different. The United States, for instance, is a country of immense diversity. But it is scarcely disunited. In the same way, Italy is hugely diverse, geographically, linguistically, ethnically and culturally. But that does not necessarily mean it is disunited.

Italians, who as a nation tend to be quite self-absorbed† and not

---

* The battle has been made a central part of the nationalist mythology created by the Northern League, which depicts it as an example of 'Padanians' uniting to drive out the hated Germanic interloper. This is more than a little inconsistent with the rest of the League's reading of history, according to which the Padanians are ethnically separate from other Italians, being descended from the Lombards, who were, well, Germanic invaders.

† In 2005 *Corriere della Sera* reported the discovery by NASA of an asteroid named Apophis that was on course to collide with the earth later this century. The headline was: '2036, *UN ASTEROIDE CONTRO L'ITALIA*'.

particularly interested in what happens outside their frontiers, seem largely unaware of the considerable diversity – and disunity – to be found in other European countries. Italy does not, for example, have a sizeable minority like the Basques with a language that is not even Indo-European. Italians certainly have a tradition of parochialism: many have a fervent attachment to their town or city and there is even a special word in Italian to describe it, *campanilismo*, which derives from *campanile*, the word for a bell tower, the bell tower of the church being, historically, the focal point of Italian communities. But the effect of *campanilismo* is to detract from the loyalty that might otherwise be felt towards a bigger territorial unit, such as a region, which in turn could form the basis for a movement in support of autonomy, or even independence. Since 1970 Italy has had a fair degree of regional self-government. Yet so far none of its regional administrations has served as a springboard for the promotion of a separatist movement, as has happened in Scotland and Catalonia.

In the 1940s a Sicilian independence movement took shape that had links to the Mafia. But it fizzled out after the Second World War. And while there has long been widespread support for an independent Sardinia, the island's separatist movements remain hopelessly divided. The most important regional grouping in recent years has been the Northern League. But though from time to time its leaders play at being separatists, their real concern is with what they and their supporters perceive as the squandering of northern taxes in southern and central Italy. After the League was ravaged by the financial scandal that engulfed its founder, Umberto Bossi, and his family in 2012, there were signs of an emerging nationalism in the Veneto that aimed, not to invent Bossi's ahistorical Padania, but to restore the old Venetian republic, the Serenissima. It remains to be seen whether it will gain traction.

In several ways, the Italy viewed from outside by foreigners is a more homogeneous country than the one seen from inside by its inhabitants. However different Italians may be in other respects, perhaps the greatest similarity – the attitude they most often share – is a reliance on the family. It is probably most intense in Sicily and least so in the far north. But the difference is one of degree. The point was highlighted in a made-for-television movie[1] based on the life of Felice Maniero, the boss of the Mala del Brenta, an organized crime syndicate active in the Veneto in the 1980s and 1990s. There is a scene in which Maniero arrives to buy a consignment of drugs from the local representative of Cosa Nostra. He introduces the man with him as his cousin. The Sicilian observes wrly that, when it comes to money, even northerners like Maniero will trust only the members of their family. 'You're not really so different from us, are you?' he says.

Because they take it for granted, Italians seldom notice that they are all – or almost all – brought up within a Catholic culture. That does not mean they all go on to become observant Catholics. But even the atheists among them absorb a wide range of common attitudes and assumptions. Compare that with, for example, the deep historic rifts between Catholics and Protestants in Germany and the Low Countries.

Nor do Italians remark on the fact that the vast majority of children in their country have the same education. More than 80 per cent attend state schools. Of the remainder, all but a handful go to schools run by the Catholic Church. And since, on average, the educational standards of the public sector are higher than those in the private sector, Italy does not have to contend with the sort of insidious social division that exists in Britain between the mass of the population and a privately schooled elite.

Language remains divisive, to be sure. But not to anything like the same extent as was once the case. At the time of Unification, it is likely that less than one Italian in ten of the population could speak the literary tongue based on the dialect of Tuscany that was adopted as the country's official language. Even the new state's first monarch, Vittorio Emanuele, had difficulty speaking it fluently. Over the years that followed compulsory military service did much to spread a working knowledge of standard Italian, as did the movement of millions of Italians who left their homes in the south to travel to the north during the years of the 'economic miracle' and subsequently. Internal migration resumed in the late 1960s and it has been calculated that by 1972 more than 9 million people had moved from one region to another. One of the consequences was marriages between men and women from different parts of the country, and in a family in which, say, the wife was from Puglia and the husband from Piedmont, the common language was highly likely to be Italian.

Even so, by the early 1980s less than 30 per cent of the population spoke only, or predominantly, the national language. Since then the figure has risen steadily, largely because of television. A study published by Istat in 2007 found that it had reached 46 per cent. And there were striking differences according to age, which suggested that the proportion of habitual Italian speakers was almost certain to continue rising: among people under the age of twenty-four, it was almost 60 per cent.

Every so often there is a reminder of how many Italians still converse in dialect. Not long ago the judges chose a Miss Italy who came from a rural area of Calabria. In her first encounter with the media after her victory, she demonstrated all too clearly that her Italian left much to be desired. But the amused and slightly disparaging way in which her mistakes were reported made an important point: that the use of dialect is regarded in most parts of Italy today as a sign of lack of education; something of which to be slightly embarrassed. So far, at least, there is no sign that any of the dialects or languages of Italy (with the possible exceptions of Sardu and Venetian) could form the basis for an effective independence movement.

Another variation on the 'no-such-thing-as-Italy' argument has it that, despite internal migration, Italy continues to suffer from a vast disparity in wealth between north and south – and, what is more, one that is widening. History has indeed divided the Mezzogiorno from the rest of the country politically and socially. Historians are still wrangling over whether the south has always – or at least since Roman times – been poorer than the north. But what is certain is that Sicily, Amalfi, Salerno and Naples all enjoyed moments of splendour in the Middle Ages. The world's first medical school was established in Salerno, perhaps as early as the ninth century.* The world's oldest public university is in Naples: it was founded in 1224 by Frederick II and still bears his name today. In later centuries Naples had periods of great affluence and influence, particularly in the setting of Europe-wide trends in fashion and cuisine. For a time, it was the continent's second-largest city after Paris. The first railway line to be built in Italy, in the early nineteenth century, did not run along the Po Valley but through the Mezzogiorno. By the time of Unification, Naples was the most industrialized city in Italy. Most of the evidence nevertheless suggests that the south was still poorer than the rest of the country (though not much poorer than the Papal State, or indeed Tuscany).

What is clear is that Unification did anything but help. The early, Piedmontese-led governments imposed higher taxes and seized Church lands, sparking an insurgency that the authorities dismissed as brigandage. By the mid-1860s there were a hundred thousand Italian troops struggling to keep the peace in the Mezzogiorno. Palermo was bombarded into submission by the navy. In the decade that followed Unification almost ten thousand people were sentenced to death in the south. The northerners not only imposed their laws but wrecked the emerging industries of the Mezzogiorno by lifting the protectionist measures that had shielded them from competition under the Bourbons.† It is quite possible that if the south had remained independent, it would be richer today than it is.

Whether there would have been less inequality among southerners is another matter. Though the prosperity of the Mezzogiorno as

---

* One of its most distinguished teachers was a woman, Trotula, believed to have been the author of the first treatise on gynaecology, published around the year 1100.

† It is therefore ironic that the pejorative term used by northerners in reference to southerners should be *terrone*, which derives from *terra* ('earth') and equates very approximately to 'yokel'.

a whole may at times have rivalled that of the north, there seems always to have been evidence of immense disparities in wealth as far back as Roman times, when the southern countryside was a patchwork of *latifundia*, vast landed estates worked by slaves. Poverty deepened in the rural Mezzogiorno in the eighteenth century when landowners, in a movement that had parallels elsewhere in Europe, grabbed much of the common land. The peasantry never forgot or forgave the expropriations, and the recovery of what they believed was theirs was a constant theme in the rural uprisings that erupted at intervals in the centuries that followed.

The poverty of the rural south was the driving force behind the emigration from mainland Mezzogiorno and Sicily which began in the 1880s. In the years that followed millions of southerners flooded across the Atlantic to begin new lives in the United States, Canada, Brazil, Argentina and elsewhere. Strict immigration laws in the US and depressed economic conditions in much of Latin America contrived to keep Italians at home during the Fascist era. But in the post-war period more than a million departed. This was when many Calabrians, in particular, emigrated to Australia and Canada.

By then, however, the Italian authorities were making genuine efforts to tackle the 'Mezzogiorno question'. There were some clumsy and only partially successful attempts at land reform in the late 1940s. But a fund for public investment in the south, the Cassa per il Mezzogiorno, was founded in 1950 and, as the economy recovered from the devastation of war, private investors became increasingly keen to sink money into an area that offered lower wage costs than the north. That, however, was an indication of the continuing deprivation in the Mezzogiorno. As late as 1973 Naples was hit by an outbreak of cholera, a disease caused by poor sanitation and associated with what in those days was called the Third World. When Italy equipped itself with a comprehensive welfare system, many of the benefits flowed to the south and pensions, notably for disabilities, were often given – or fraudulently obtained – as a way of saving the beneficiaries from destitution rather than in response to genuine disabilities or other qualifying circumstances.

The imbalance between south and north is clearly apparent even today. But geographical disparities are not unique to Italy and – contrary to what many Italians believe – the gap has narrowed since reaching its widest point in the 1950s. Per capita income in Piedmont, Italy's wealthiest region, was 74 per cent above the national average in 1954. In the poorest region, Calabria, it was 48 per cent below it.[2] By 2010 the most prosperous region was the Valle d'Aosta, where average income was 36 per cent above the national mean. The least well-off was Campania, where it was 36 per cent beneath it. In other words, a gap of 122 percentage points had shrunk in the intervening 56 years to one of 72.

Nor was the gap any longer exceptional in the context of Italy's European neighbours. In France and Spain, too, the richest regions were about twice as rich as the poorest. In Britain the disparity was even greater than in Italy. Measuring inequality takes economists on to notoriously slippery terrain, because a lot depends on the size of the territory that is used for comparison: a relatively high regional average income can hide the fact that there are pockets of extreme poverty, while a quite low one can mask the existence of great wealth in specific areas. To address this problem, the OECD computes a composite index of geographical inequality, using what is known as the Gini coefficient. Italy's score is better than the average of the organization's member states. It emerges as more economically homogeneous than Britain, the US, Canada or even Austria.

Statistics, of course, are one thing and sentiments another. If people feel themselves to be different from others, that is more important than any number of averages and coefficients. So how Italian do Italians feel?

In my experience, those least attached to the concept of Italy are to be found at either end of the socio-economic scale. The aristocracy pretty much everywhere but in Piedmont lost out as a result of Unification: from being big fish in small ponds, they suddenly became rather small fish in a much larger pond. The least educated and most disadvantaged Italians, on the other hand, are the least likely to have travelled outside their region and the most likely to speak dialect at home and with their friends. But, among the millions of Italians who make up their country's sizeable and growing middle class, there is plenty of evidence of a strong sense of identification with Italy.

Nationality, in fact, is stressed far more often in public than in other countries. It is not at all uncommon to find yourself reading an article about how *noi italiani* ('we Italians') ought, say, to give more to the developing world and then hear the weather forecaster on television describe how high winds are about to blow through *il nostro paese* ('our country'). During the commercial break that follows, you are quite likely to be assured that this or that range of sofas, brand of crockery or even van rental firm is the one *più amato dagli italiani* ('most beloved of the Italians').

It all betokens a strong sense of ethnicity that is evident in other areas. No one thinks it is strange, for example, that an Argentinian footballer of Italian origin, Mauro Camoranesi, should have lined up as a member of the Italian national side that won the 2006 soccer World Cup. But then Camoranesi was no less than the thirty-fifth foreign national of Italian descent to have played for Italy.

People who in other countries would be considered foreigners sit in the Italian parliament. Nationality under Italian law is determined mainly by what is known as *jus sanguinis* ('right of blood', i.e. descent) and not *jus soli* ('right of soil', i.e. place of birth). Having just one Italian parent makes you an Italian* and qualifies you to pass on your citizenship to the next generation. But since your Italian parent may also owe his or her nationality to a single Italian parent, you can have only one genuinely Italian grandparent and still be an Italian (even if you have never set foot in Italy and do not speak a word of the language). The government keeps a register of overseas Italians, known as the Anagrafe degli Italiani residenti all'Estero (AIRE). There are well over 4 million people on it and, if they fulfil the age requirements for Italian elected representatives,

---

* Only those born after 1947 qualify for descent through the maternal line.

they can run in Italian elections for a seat in the Senate or the Chamber of Deputies. There are four overseas constituencies: one each for Europe, South America, Central and North America, and the rest of the world.

Until a few years ago there was even a beauty contest to choose a Miss Italia nel Mondo. Winners included contestants with such un-Italian first names as Rudialva, Stephanie and Kimberly.

The idea that Italian-ness is something you inherit rather than something you acquire because of where you grew up has inevitably complicated the task of integrating the immigrants who began to arrive in Italy in sizeable numbers in the early 1980s. The application of *jus sanguinis* also means that tens of thousands of second-generation immigrants, who are far more culturally Italian than many of the 'overseas Italians', grow up in a kind of limbo. Since, for example, they have no right to a passport, they cannot travel abroad on school trips. To acquire citizenship, they have to make an application before their nineteenth birthday. If they fail to do so, they lose the right for ever.

There had always been a sprinkling of foreigners in Italy. But in the censuses taken between 1871 and the outbreak of the Second World War they accounted for barely a quarter of 1 per cent of the population.[3] After the war, Italians returning from the colonies brought with them some of the first non-European immigrants, often as servants. The next wave consisted mainly of seasonal workers who, beginning in the late 1960s, arrived to take part in harvesting and, in some cases, stayed on to find other employment: Tunisians in Sicily; sub-Saharan Africans in Campania hired to pick tomatoes, and Eastern Europeans in Trentino employed to bring in the apple crop. The earliest Filipino immigrants, most of whom went into domestic service, also reached Italy at about this time. During the 1970s and 1980s some immigrants from outside the EU – known in those days as *extracomunitari* – began to take factory jobs in the north.

When I came to Italy for my first tour of duty as a foreign correspondent in 1994, I nevertheless found a country that was still largely white. According to the census carried out three years earlier, resident and non-resident foreigners accounted for just 1.1 per cent of the total population. The count and countess who lived in the flat next door had a Sri Lankan manservant. A couple of streets away, there was a bar owned by an Eritrean. And that was about as far as multiculturalism went in our neighbourhood of Rome.

Within a year or so, though, the square nearest to our flat had become a meeting place for women from the Cape Verde islands, who were much in demand as cleaners and nannies. And when the next census was held, the proportion of foreigners was found to have doubled. Since then the figure has soared. By 2014 it was reckoned that nearly 8 per cent of the population had been born in another country.

By far the largest community was made up of Romanians. But since their country had joined the EU seven years earlier, they could no longer be classed as *extracomunitari*.* The next-biggest groups were, in order, from Morocco, Albania, China, Ukraine and the Philippines. What is striking about that list is that not one of those countries on it is in sub-Saharan Africa. Yet the images that Italians and others have come to associate with migration to Italy are those of people, mostly of African origin, crowded into rickety boats that have set off from the other side of the Mediterranean. One explanation for this is that a high percentage of the Africans soon move on to other countries further north. The majority of the immigrants who stay in Italy come in by other means. Some cross a land border into the EU and then take advantage of the open borders within the Schengen area to make their way to Italy. Others arrive on a tourist or business visa and then overstay.

They unquestionably come in response to a demand for labour.

---

* Romania became a member state in 2007. But, under transitional arrangements, its citizens did not acquire an automatic right to work in Italy until 2012. It was at around the time that Romania entered the EU that the term *immigrati* began to replace *extracomunitari*, perhaps because it could be used to encompass the Romanians and preserve their 'otherness'.

But, the overwhelming majority arrived on Italian soil in a way that was either unauthorized or illegal (in 2009 Silvio Berlusconi's government made entering Italy without proper documentation an offence, but irregular immigration has since been decriminalized). That makes it easier for those native Italians who resent the newcomers to find reasons for criticizing their presence. The OECD has estimated that for every twenty legal immigrants in Italy, there could be as many as three illegal ones.

Italians will often tell you – and with vehement conviction – that their country is free of racism. That ought maybe to be the case: Italians themselves have experienced prejudice as immigrants and should therefore be less inclined than most to discriminate against outsiders. In the US, for example, they had to contend with being identified with the mafia and branded as 'Wops'.

But to anyone with eyes to see and ears to hear, it is clear that racism in Italy does exist. It is especially prevalent in two areas: among the supporters of the Northern League and in and around football stadiums. When Cécile Kyenge, a naturalized Italian born in the Democratic Republic of Congo, became her country's first black minister in 2013, she had to put up with a barrage of insults from members of the Northern League. Roberto Calderoli,* by then the deputy speaker of the Senate, said that she reminded him of an orang-utan. Long before that, it was common for black soccer players on visiting – and even sometimes home – teams to be greeted with banana throwing and outbreaks of monkey noises from the terraces where the *ultras* hang out. But the footballing authorities have cracked down with growing severity on fan racism, and the brilliant if erratic performance on the field of Italy's first black striker, Mario Balotelli,† has done much to draw the sting of race hate in Italian soccer.

---

* See above, pages 40–41.

† Balotelli was born in Palermo to parents from Ghana. His parents moved to Lombardy, where he was adopted at the age of three by a Jewish-Italian family, whose name he later took.

What you notice more in Italy than outright racism is gross insensitivity. Take, for example, what happened on a TV game show one evening in 2013. The host, one of Italy's leading showbiz personalities, Paolo Bonolis, put on a black wig to make fun of the Filipinos, mimicking their accent in Italian. At any time, the Philippine community might have taken offence, especially since the sketch began with a playing of their national anthem. But Bonolis did his comic turn for millions of viewers as the Filipinos were struggling to recover from the devastation caused by Typhoon Haiyan, which had ripped through their country just five days earlier, leaving more than six thousand people dead.

'In Britain, I have certainly encountered racism,' said a young African who worked with me in Rome. 'But there the racists know they are racists, and so do you. Here, people will say the most offensive things to me, but without in any way meaning to be racist. It is disconcerting: they just don't know you should not say those kinds of things to a black woman. I often don't know how to react.'

Arguably, this kind of thing is a result of the speed with which Italy has acquired its immigrant population and the relatively short period in which Italians have had to adapt to the sensitivities of foreigners. Cringe-making examples of a lack of racial awareness include gollywog-like figures advertising chocolate, news reports that identify the ethnic origin of suspects only when they are non-Italians and exploitative bosses described as *negrieri* (a trafficker or overseer of *negri*, or 'negroes').

Using data from 2005 to 2007, the World Values Survey gave Italy a mixed report card: it found that racist attitudes in Italy were more prevalent than in some other European countries, but less common than in others. Eleven per cent said they did not want neighbours of a different race, against fewer than 5 per cent in Britain, but almost 23 per cent in France. Bearing in mind that Britain – not to mention France – has had a longer time in which to adjust to immigration, Italy's showing could be regarded as promising. As Italy's immigrants become more integrated into society, it is to be hoped that the prejudice which the early arrivals encountered will diminish.

But that remains to be seen. A comparison with Spain is less encouraging. The Spanish have experienced even more rapid and recent immigration. Yet less than 7 per cent of the respondents there told the World Values Survey's pollsters they did not want neighbours of a different race (although that, of course, leaves open the question of whether the Spanish were really more inclined to welcome outsiders or just more reluctant to admit that they did not).

Other factors argue for caution in assessing whether racism in Italy will be reduced to irrelevance. One is the objective difficulty that immigrants face in becoming part of Italian society. Successive amnesties have given most of the new arrivals the right to stay in Italy. But since citizenship depends primarily on ancestry, it is much more difficult for them to take the next step and become Italian. In practice, it is almost impossible for first-generation immigrants to acquire citizenship unless they marry an Italian. Their children must wait until they are eighteen to apply.

Another doubt stems from the absence of any widespread reckoning with Italy's colonial past. It is not that this is a divisive issue; it could almost be said that it is not an issue of any kind. Until very recently it was as if the Italians had never had anything to do with Ethiopia, Eritrea, Somalia or Libya. The question of whether the plight of the Horn of Africa might have something to do with its conquest and exploitation by Italians in the nineteenth and twentieth centuries was never raised in the media. And, according to a recent study, in the sixty years from 1945 to 2005, only one film was produced and one novel published about Italy's colonial past.[4] The book – Ennio Flaiano's *Tempo di uccidere* – was the basis for the film of the same title. Movies made by foreigners about the period were ignored. *Lion of the Desert*, a critically well-received movie about the Libyan resistance leader Omar Mukhtar, funded by the Libyan government and featuring a number of Hollywood stars, was never released in Italy.

This reluctance to face up to the colonial past may now be changing, if only very slowly. Since the mid-2000s several Italian novelists have shown an interest in the period, as have members of a first generation of immigrant authors.

If attitudes have changed towards Italy's Romani population, however, it has been in the direction of more, not less, intolerance. *Zingari* (Gypsies) have been living in Italy since the fifteenth century. The Sinti, who regard themselves as a subgroup distinct from the Roma, arrived from the north. Other Romani groups migrated from the Balkans and settled in the south and centre of Italy. But in recent years Italy's Romani population has doubled. First came an influx of Roma from the former Yugoslavia. It began modestly in the 1970s, but increased dramatically in the 1990s as wars erupted, tearing the country apart. Finally, large numbers of Roma arrived from Romania, particularly after Romania joined the EU in 2007. Even so, the total number of Roma and Sinti in Italy is reckoned to be around 150,000: about a quarter of one per cent of the total population, one of the lowest proportions in Europe.[5]

Anti-Gypsy prejudice is scarcely confined to Italians, nor are the authorities in Italy the only ones who have had difficulty in framing policies for their Romani minority. But what is unusual is the Italian insistence on regarding all Sinti and Roma as *nomadi* ('nomads'). The term is widely used not only by politicians, officials and journalists but also by those who seek to offer support to the Romani population. The oldest Catholic voluntary association in the field, which has been recognized by the government since 1965, is known as Opera Nomadi.

Leaving aside the fact that it was discrimination and persecution that forced an itinerant lifestyle on the Romani peoples in the first place, and that many of Italy's own Sinti and Roma integrated when they could, the term *nomadi* when applied to the previously settled Roma of the Balkans is more than just misleading. It implies that the newcomers should be put into camps (on the assumption that, as nomads, they will soon wish to move on, and perhaps in the hope that they will want to move on to somewhere outside Italy).

Segregation has been at the core of official Italian policy since the 1980s, when local authorities began establishing camps in response to a spate of regional laws that called for them as a way of respecting the Romani people's 'nomadic' culture. In 2007 the particularly savage murder of an Italian woman on the outskirts of Rome sparked an explosion of anger. Police arrested an immigrant Romani man and the then centre-left government – already under pressure from the right to do something about growing numbers of informal encampments in and around the main cities – panicked. It rushed out a decree that enabled the authorities to deport from Italy any EU citizens held to be a threat to security. More than six thousand people were subsequently evicted from camps in Rome.

The Berlusconi government, which came into office the following year, took matters a big step further by declaring 'a state of emergency in relation to the encampments of the nomad community in the territories of the regions of Campania, Lazio and Lombardy'. Two more regions, Piedmont and Veneto, were added later.

In the capital, the authorities used what the media termed the 'Roma emergency' to enforce the closure of all unauthorized encampments and move their occupants to fenced Roma-only camps away from residential areas. As several human rights organizations have complained, this is not only discriminatory on grounds of race but makes it virtually impossible for the Roma to find and keep regular jobs that would allow them to integrate with the rest of Italian society. In 2013 the Court of Cassation ruled that the law which imposed a state of emergency was indeed discriminatory, and overturned it. But the judges' ruling seems to have made precious little impact on official policy.

The 'Roma emergency' fed into a wider controversy over the link between immigration and crime. Berlusconi and his allies stressed the connection in all their electoral campaigns during the 2000s. Official figures did indeed show a disproportionately high level of arrests among foreigners. But the crime rate among immigrants who had regularized their situation was no greater than in the rest of the population. As might be expected, the problem was largely confined to those who were still illegal and did not have the right to take up regular work.

Only very recently have politicians begun to acknowledge publicly the vital role that immigrants play in a society with one of the world's lowest birth rates and fastest-ageing populations. Without their contribution, the imbalance between the number of Italians contributing to the welfare system and the number drawing pensions and benefits from it would soon become unsustainable. Contrary to popular opinion, moreover, immigrants do not take jobs from the native workforce. For the most part, they do work that native Italians are reluctant to do, or which they are not qualified for: the skilled jobs in the construction industry done by Albanians are one example. A Bank of Italy study found that the effect of immigration has been to push Italians into more qualified work, increasing their earnings.[6]

This is not the only area in which Italians, like many others, have a skewed perception of immigrants and immigration. In 2012 a think tank commissioned a poll in which people were asked, among other things, to estimate the number of foreigners in their midst. The average response was between 1 and 2 million, which was less than half the real figure. Respondents also overestimated the number of illegal immigrants and grossly underestimated the contribution made by immigrants to national output. Though at the time foreigners accounted for about 8 per cent of the population, they were producing more than 12 per cent of Italy's GDP.[7]

Epilogue

'E benché fino a qui si sia mostro qualche spiraculo in qualcuno, da potere iudicare che fussi ordinato da Dio per sua redenzione, tamen si è visto da poi come, nel più alto corso delle azioni sua, è stato dalla fortuna reprobato. In modo che, rimasa senza vita, espetta qual possa esser quello che sani le sue ferrite . . .'

'Although lately some spark may have been shown by one, which made us think he was ordained by God for our redemption, nevertheless it was afterwards seen, at the height of his career, that fortune rejected him; so that Italy, left as without life, waits for him who shall yet heal her wounds . . .'

– Niccolò Machiavelli, *Il principe*, 1513 (trans. W. K. Marriott)

Few countries are as comprehensively associated with happiness as Italy. Just the mention of its name brings to mind sunny days, blue skies, glittering seas; delicious, comforting food; good-looking, well-dressed people; undulating hills topped with cypress trees and museums crammed with much of the best of Western art. So it may come as a surprise to discover that a lot of evidence suggests that the Italians themselves are unhappy. A slew of polls inspired by economists' growing interest in non-economic measures of well-being have found high levels of dissatisfaction among them.

Surveys in 2002 and 2004 of the fifteen countries then making up the European Union suggested that Italy was the unhappiest of them all. Judged by the broader criterion of 'life satisfaction', it was fourth from the bottom.[1] Subsequent attempts to gauge life satisfaction in 2007 and 2011 produced similar results: Italy scored lower than any of the other EU-15 countries in the first survey and was third from last in the second (though several of the states, mostly ex-communist, which joined the Union after 2004 produced even lower ratings).[2]

Italians certainly had one good reason for feeling miserable: they were becoming poorer. The decade in which Silvio Berlusconi dominated Italy's public life was disastrous for the economy. Towards the end of the period, there was a moment when the only two countries with a worse economic performance were Haiti, which had been hit by a devastating earthquake, and Robert Mugabe's Zimbabwe. By 2011, when Berlusconi left office, Italy's real GDP per head, the conventional measure of average prosperity, was lower than it had been in 2000, the year before he took power.[3]

In other ways, too, the country had slipped back. There were signs, for example, that despite the spread of digital technology in the 2000s, bureaucracy was getting worse, not better. One study concluded that the time spent by Italians queuing for public services had increased over the ten years to 2012. In post offices, the average waiting time had increased by 39 per cent.[4]

The problems were not all of Berlusconi's making. Like other countries in southern Europe, Italy had adopted the euro without fully appreciating that it meant competing on a level playing field with the other members of the single-currency zone, including Germany. In the past, Italy had been able to restore its competitiveness and keep its exports booming by means of devaluation. After it joined the euro zone that was no longer possible. Unlike Spain and Portugal, moreover, Italy was saddled with an extraordinarily high level of public debt. For the most part, this was the result of the Italians having given themselves a modern welfare state without building an economy strong enough to afford one. But it was also the price of a fair amount of waste and corruption.

The economy was thus in pretty bad shape when it was hit by the shock waves from the euro crisis in 2009. As unemployment climbed, bankruptcies mounted and Italy's elderly ruling class showed no sign of surrendering power, the reaction of many of the brightest young people was to flee. Between 2003 and 2014 the number of Italians who emigrated more than doubled. In the last of those years, more than half were men and women under the age of thirty-five.[5] Whereas, back in the 1950s and 1960s, the Italians who left for other parts of Europe were mostly unskilled or semi-skilled, the most recent wave of emigrants has been made up largely of graduates seeking opportunities in the labour markets of Britain, America, Canada, Germany, Scandinavia and elsewhere.

Italy's most renowned corporate trouble-shooter, Guido Rossi, once said that his country's worst maladies were 'the rejection of rules and an aversion to change'.[6] It is hard to disagree. But these are not necessarily immutable characteristics. In recent years, for example, Italians have been coerced into being more respectful of the rules of the road. In 2003 Berlusconi's then transport minister introduced a system whereby drivers are allotted a certain number of points, which are deducted if they are caught breaking the law; if they lose enough of their points, they lose their licence, too. This and other measures have succeeded in bringing about a drastic reduction in road deaths. By 2012 the number of fatalities had almost halved.[7] There are also reasons for cautious optimism about Italians' willingness to change. As mentioned earlier, while this book was being written, a 39-year old prime minister was appointed to govern the country, and he selected a Cabinet in which half the ministers were women.

Not the least of the tasks facing Matteo Renzi and others of his generation will be to give Italy a new dream – a new source of inspiration for, and confidence in, the future. Italy is certainly not the only country to have found itself bereft of a dream. For years after the loss of its empire my own country, Britain, drifted aimlessly until, for better or for worse (that debate continues), Margaret Thatcher gave it the free-market ethos that has permeated its economy and society ever since.

Italy under Mussolini also had an imperial dream, which was swept away during the Second World War. It was replaced by several new ideas. One was anti-fascism, which extended to the nation as a whole the aura of the Partisan movement. Another was Atlanticism: Italy became one of America's most steadfast allies in Europe during the Cold War; perhaps even more so than Britain. After 1957, when Italy joined the European Economic Community (EEC) as a founder member, this Atlanticism fused with a growing Europeanism. As recently as 2010 polls were showing that Italians' trust in the EU institutions was even greater than that of Germans.

To some extent, Italian Europeanism, like Italian Atlanticism, was self-interested. Just as it had made a lot of sense to do the bidding of the US, a country that had extended to Italy the benefits of the Marshall Plan, so it was natural to be enthusiastic about a union of neighbouring states that offered Italy a vast new market for its products, not to mention generous subsidies for its poorer regions. Entry into the EEC was followed two years later by a burst of economic growth that lasted until 1963. The average annual increase in GDP during those years was 6.3 per cent.[8]

But there was, I think, another and nobler reason for Italians' enthusiasm for the European project. It is often said that the French and the Germans threw themselves into the task of building a new Europe because it held the promise of an end to the wars that had devastated their countries three times in less than a century. But it is seldom remarked that Italians had a similar motive, having also been the victims of military conflict with other Europeans, and over a much longer period of their troubled history.

Recent years have seen dark shadows cast across all the ideas that sustained Italy through the Cold War. Anti-fascism was the first to go – killed off in 1994 by the election of Berlusconi's first government, which included the political heirs of neo-fascism. Italy's special relationship with the United States has yet to recover from the setback it suffered after 2001, as many Italians recoiled in dismay from the policies adopted by President George W. Bush and his decision to invade Iraq. Italy's Europeanism, too, has suffered greatly from the crisis in the euro zone: between May 2007 and November 2012 the proportion of Italians who said they tended not to trust the EU institutions almost doubled, from 28 per cent to 53 per cent.[9]

By the beginning of 2012 Italy's morale had reached perhaps its lowest point since the Second World War. The year before, the country had seemed to be heading towards default on its huge debts, as investors' confidence in the Berlusconi government's ability to manage the economy sank and the interest rates on Italy's government bonds soared. When, on 13 January, the *Costa Concordia* – an Italian liner skippered by an Italian captain – crashed into the rocks off the Tuscan island of Giglio and capsized with the loss of thirty-two lives, it seemed to many like a metaphor for the failure of an entire society.

There are two ways of looking at what lies ahead. The view of many Italians, and particularly those of middle age or above, is that their country is doomed to relative decline: that the boom years of the 1950s, 1960s and 1980s were little better than a mirage; that Italians will never be able to hold their own in a German-dominated euro zone; and while their country may not become poorer in absolute terms, it will continue to lose ground to its neighbours in Europe.

'We are an old country,' a distinguished political commentator once said to me over lunch. 'The best we can hope for is to manage the decline.'

A similar view was put forward by another renowned journalist and author in a recent work with the despairing title *Poco o niente. Eravamo poveri. Torneremo poveri* (*Little or Nothing: We Used to be Poor [and] We Shall go Back to being Poor*).[10]

The more optimistic approach was expressed more than five hundred years ago by Machiavelli in the same passage that contains the quote that opens this final chapter: 'In order to discover the virtue of an Italian spirit, it was necessary that Italy should be reduced to the extremity that she is now in.'

In 2014 the country's self-esteem was given a much-needed boost when an Italian film, *La grande bellezza*, won the Oscar for the best film in a language other than English. Paolo Sorrentino's movie focuses on one Jep Gambardella, who has sacrificed his career as a novelist to become the kingpin of Rome's decadent, vulgar social life. At times, his mind reaches back to an incident in his youth in which – the last frame before the final credits suggests – he was unable to give physical expression to his first real love; a metaphor for his literary impotence.

The movie was given the thumbs-down by most of Italy's leading critics when it was first shown. It was seen as a tawdry remake of Fellini's masterpiece, *La dolce vita*. I, too, disliked the film, but only until about two thirds of the way through. In the days that followed, its enigmatic plot and the memorable images that Sorrentino had created reverberated in my brain in the way a great creative work should.

La grande bellezza is open to more than one interpretation. For some, it is a movie about Rome and its seemingly unstoppable decline. In fact, the Oscar was awarded just days after Renzi's government acted to save the Italian capital from bankruptcy; a few days later, arsenic and asbestos were detected in parts of the water supply network. For others, *La grande bellezza* is an existentialist work: a rumination on the purpose, or perhaps purposelessness, of life. But it also caught the spirit of what could be a turning point for Italy – if the Italians are able to make it one.

As the film progresses, Jep, who at one point is dispatched by his editor to the scene of the wreck of the *Costa Concordia*, suggests he might finally write another book. Then, on the advice of an ancient, saintly nun who tells him that 'roots are important', he goes back to the scene of his first, apparently unconsummated passion.

The movie ends with a monologue of its hero's thoughts voiced over images of the aged nun and of Jep standing amid the rocks by the shore:

This is how it always ends, with death. But first there was life, hidden beneath the blah blah blah. It's all settled beneath the chitter-chatter and the noise: silence and sentiment; emotion and fear; the haggard, inconstant flashes of beauty, and then the wretched squalor and miserable humanity; all buried under the cover of the embarrassment of being in the world. Beyond, there is what lies beyond. I don't deal with what lies beyond.

And then Jep begins to smile as he continues: 'Therefore, let this novel begin. After all, it's just a trick. Yes, it's just a trick.'

Notes

Chapter 1

1 Luigi Barzini. *The Italians*. Touchstone. 1964.

Chapter 2

1 Einhard. *The Life of Charlemagne*. Trans. Samuel Epes Turner. Harper & Bros. 1880.
2 *Annales regni Francorum*. Trans. Richard E. Sullivan in *The Coronation of Charlemagne*. D. C. Heath. 1959.
3 Einhard. *Op. cit.*

Chapter 3

1 Robert D. Putnam with Robert Leonardi and Raffaella Y. Nanetti. *Making Democracy Work: Civic Traditions in Modern Italy*. Princeton University Press. 1993.
2 Example taken from J. J. Kinder and V. M. Savini. *Using Italian: A Guide to Contemporary Usage*. Cambridge University Press. 2004.
3 Paolo Conti. '*De Rita: non siamo crudeli. Ma ci sentiamo superiori*'. *Corriere della Sera*. 12 January 2010.
4 Marco Managò. *Italiani in fila*. Serarcangeli. 2009.
5 Quoted in Indro Montanelli. *L'Italia dei notabili (1861–1900)*. Rizzoli. 1973.

Chapter 4

1 Enrico Borghetto and Francesco Visconti. *The Evolution of Italian Law. A study on post-enactment policy change between the First and Second Republic.* Paper prepared for the XXVIth SISP Annual Meeting, 13–15 September 2012.

2 'I am the way, the truth, and the life': John 14:6.

Chapter 5

1 Simona Ravizza. *'Copiare a scuola è sbagliato. Come spiegarlo ai figli?'* *Corriere della Sera.* 25 May 2013.

2 The relevant table does not indicate the year to which the figures apply. But other statistics in the report suggest it is 1999.

Chapter 6

1 Sandro Veronesi. *La forza del passato. Bampiani.* 2000. Trans. Alastair McEwen. *The Force of the Past.* Fourth Estate. 2003.

2 *'Berlusconi: "Mio padre mi ha insegnato ad avere il sole in tasca"'*. *Il Giornale.* 19 March 2008.

3 A video of the song made for the 2008 general election campaign can be watched at https://www.youtube.com/watch?v=WXf-YbsShoY

4 http://www.silvioberlusconifansclub.org/main.asp?IDL=5

5 *'Fisco: Berlusconi, se tasse a 50–60% evasione giustificata.'* Ansa. 2 April, 2008.

6 http://www.forbes.com/sites/briansolomon/2011/11/10/the-rise-and-fall-of-silvio-berlusconis-fortune/

7 Nando Pagnoncelli. *'Europee, la crescita di Grillo. Forza Italia ancora sotto il 20%'.* *Corriere della Sera.* 3 May 2014.

8 John Hooper. 'Italy's web guru tastes power as new political movement goes viral'. *Guardian*. 3 January 2013.

Chapter 7

1 http://www.mcdonalds.it/azienda/storia/cifre
2 http://outfront.blogs.cnn.com/2013/03/20/outfront-extra-why-are-there-no-starbucks-in-italy/
3 *La cucina italiana: Storia di una cultura*. Laterza. 1999. Trans. Aine O'Healy. *Italian Cuisine: A Cultural History*. Columbia University Press. 2003.

Chapter 8

1 *La vita quotidiana nel 2005*. Istat. 6 April 2007.
2 Survey conducted by JupiterResearch, quoted in Michael Fitzpatrick. 'This is Social Networking, Italian style.' *Guardian*. 6 November 2008.
3 http://unstats.un.org/unsd/EconStatKB/Attachment540.aspx

Chapter 9

1 Clara Petacci. Ed. Mauro Suttora. *Mussolini segreto*. Rizzoli. 2009.
2 C. Falconi. *La Chiesa e le organizzazioni cattoliche in Italia (1945–1955)*. Turin. 1956. Quoted in Paul Ginsborg, *A History of Contemporary Italy: Society and Politics 1943–1988*. Penguin Books. 1990.
3 http://www.cdo.org/Portals/0/Pubblicazioni/CDO-BROCHURE_ITA_WEB.pdf
4 Giambattista Anastasio. '*Il sistema di potere del movimento nella prime regione d'Italia*'. *Il Giorno*. 22 April 2012.

Chapter 10

1 http://www.psicolab.net/public/pdfart/11286.pdf
2 Norman Douglas. *Old Calabria*. Secker. 1915.
3 Romana Frattini and Paolo Rossi. '*Report sulle donne nell'università italiana*'. *Meno di Zero*. III, 8–9 Jan–Jun 2012.

Chapter 11

1 Marcantonio Caltabiano. '*L'età al primo rapporto sessuale*'. 2013. http://www.neodemos.it/index.php?file=onenews&form_id_notizia=681
2 *The Global Face of Sex*, 2012.
3 Marcantonio Caltabiano and Letizia Mencarini. '*Le prime fasi della vita sessuale e di coppia*'. Paper delivered to the Decima Conferenza Nazionale di Statistica. Rome. 15–16 December 2010.
4 *Sexual Wellbeing Global Survey, 2007–08*.
5 Tobias Smollett. *Travels through France and Italy*. Letter XXVII.
6 International Social Survey Programme. 'Family and Changing Gender Roles II'. 1994.
7 *Price Runner Safe Sex League Table*. 2009.
8 '*Il 37% delle italiane fedeli al coito interrotto*'. *Corriere della Sera*. 10 October 2006.
9 *The Global Face of Sex*, 2012.
10 *Mamma*, composed in 1941 by Cesare Andrea Bixio with Italian lyrics by Bruno Cherubini.
11 *Mama*, lyrics by Harold Barlow and Phil Brito. 1946.
12 Marina D'Amelia. *La Mamma*. Le Edizioni del Mulino. 2005.
13 Eric Hobsbawm and Terence Ranger, eds. *The Invention of Tradition*. Cambridge University Press. 1983.
14 Fabrizio Blini. *Mamma mia!* Baldini Castoldi Dalai. 2007.
15 Raeleen D'Agostino. 'Global Psyche: Forever Mamma's Boy'. *Psychology Today*, US Edition. March/April 2008, Volume 41, No. 2. The full

interview is to be found at http://www.roberto-vincenzi.com/inter vista_mammismo.htm

16 Tim Parks. *An Italian Education*. Secker & Warburg. 1996.

17 Commissione Affari Sociali. Camera dei Deputati. *'Indagine conoscitiva su aspetti sociali e sanitari della prostituzione'*. 1999.

18 Istat. *'La popolazione omosessuale nella società italiana'*. 17 May 2012.

Chapter 12

1 Francis X. Rocca. 'Italy's Family Ties: Rome's austerity package threatens the country's traditional social structure'. *Wall Street Journal*. 15 July 2011.

2 Marco Manacorda and Enrico Moretti. 'Why Do Most Italian Young Men Live with Their Parents? Intergenerational Transfers and Household Structure'. Discussion paper no. 5116. Centre for Economic Policy Research. London. June 2005.

3 Alessandro Rosina, Letizia Mencarini, Rosella Rettaroli. *'Inizio dell'età adulta'*. 2005.

4 Martin Ljunge. 'Was Banfield right? Family ties and civic virtues'. University of Copenhagen. 2011.

Chapter 14

1 John Foot. *Calcio: A History of Italian Football*. Fourth Estate. London. 2006.

2 Gianni Brera. *'Quel calcio lineare e sovrano'*. *La Repubblica*. 3 February 1987.

3 Paddy Agnew. *Forza Italia: A Journey in Search of Italy and Its Football*. Ebury Press. 2006.

Chapter 15

1 Adrian Michaels. 'Barbarian at the gate'. *Financial Times*. 15 March 2008.

2 Francesco Viviano. *'Io e mio padre Provenzano. Così faccio i conti con la mafia'*. *La Repubblica*. 1 December 2008.

Chapter 16

1 Roberto Saviano. *Gomorra: Viaggio nell'impero economico e nel sogno di dominio della camorra*. Mondadori. 2006. Trans. Virginia Jewiss as *Gomorrah: Italy's Other Mafia*. Macmillan. 2007.

2 http://www.investimentioc.it/files/PON-Presentazione_Linea%201_Gli%20investimenti_delle_mafie.pdf

3 Leonardo Sciascia. *Il giorno della civetta*. Einaudi. 1961. Trans. Archibald Colquhoun and Arthur Oliver as *The Day of the Owl*. Jonathan Cape. 1963.

4 George Armstrong. 'Mafiosi Widen Their Horizons – by Order'. *Guardian*. 1 April 1974.

5 Nicola Gratteri and Antonio Nicaso. *Fratelli di Sangue*. Pellegrini Editore. 2006.

6 Diego Gambetta. *The Sicilian Mafia: The Business of Private Protection*. Harvard University Press. 1996.

Chapter 17

1 Giuseppe Prezzolini. *Codice della vita italiana*. La Voce. 1921.

2 http://ec.europa.eu/anti_fraud/documents/anti-fraud-policy/research-and-studies/identifying_reducing_corruption_in_public_procurement_en.pdf#page=7&zoom=auto,0,480

3 Pino Nicotri. *Tangenti in confessionale: Come preti rispondono a corrotti e corruttori*. Marsilio Editori. 1993.

4 See Giovanni Cerruti. '*Il Belpaese dei felici e raccomandati*'. *La Repubblica*. 1 July 2008.

5 Its findings were summarized in Filippo Ceccarelli. '*Siamo tutti raccomandati*'. *La Repubblica*. 16 November 2007.

Chapter 18

1 The same remark in slightly different form is ascribed to Giolitti. But whereas I have never been able to find a source for Giolitti's supposed quip, Mussolini's appears in Emil Ludwig. *Mussolinis Gespräche mit Emil Ludwig*. 1932. Translated into English by Paul Eden and Paul Cedar as *Talks with Mussolini*. AMS Press, Inc. 1933.

2 www.terrelibere.org/doc/storia-di-tangentopoli

3 Luigi Ferrarella. 'Mani pulite, 2565 imputati'. *Corriere della Sera*. 17 February 2000.

4 See William T. Pizzi and Mariangela Montagna. 'The Battle to Establish an Adversarial Trial System in Italy'. *Michigan Journal of International Law*, Volume 25: 429, 2004.

5 M. F. Aebi and N. Delgrande. SPACE – Council of Europe Annual Penal Statistics: Prison Populations. Survey 2012. Strasbourg. Council of Europe.

Chapter 19

1 *Faccia d'angelo* (*Angel Face*). Broadcast by Sky Cinema 1, 12 & 19 March 2012, and by La7 on 15 December 2013.

2 Paul Ginsborg. *A History of Contemporary Italy: Society and Politics 1943–1988*. Penguin Books. 1990.

3 Asher Colombo and Giuseppe Sciortino. 'Italian Immigration: The Origins, Nature and Evolution of Italy's Migratory Systems'. *Journal of Modern Italian Studies*. 9 (1), 2004.

4 Paolo Jedlowski and Renate Siebert. 'Memoria coloniale e razzismo'. In *Un paese normale? Saggi sull'Italia contemporanea*. Andrea Mammone, Nicola Tranfaglia, Giuseppe A. Veltri (eds.). Dalai Editore. 2011.

5 Nando Sigona. 'Rom e Sinti come "problema": discorso pubblico, politiche e prassi'. In Mammone, et al. Ibid.

6 Francesco D'Amuri and Giovanni Peri. 'Immigration, Jobs and Employment Protection: Evidence from Europe before and during the Great Recession'. Banca d'Italia working papers: 886. October 2012.

7 Rapporto Unioncamere 2011. The figure was put at exactly 12 per cent in Unioncamere's 2012 report (http://www.starnet.unioncamere.it/Rapporto-Unioncamere-2012_5A33).

Epilogue

1 Aqib Aslam and Luisa Corrado. 'No Man is an Island: The Inter-personal Determinants of Regional Well-Being in Europe'. Cambridge Working Papers in Economics. April 2007.

2 Eurofound (2013). 'Third European Quality of Life Survey – Quality of Life in Europe: Subjective Well-being'. Publications Office of the European Union. Luxembourg.

3 http://www.economywatch.com/economic-statistics/Italy/GDP_Per_Capita_Constant_Prices_National_Currency/

4 'Burocrazia, se cambiare diventa un'impresa'. Avvenire. 18 October 2013.

5 Censis. 47° Rapporto sulla situazione sociale del Paese/2013.

6 'Face Value: The Troubleshooter'. The Economist. 9 December 2006.

7 http://assicurazione-auto.supermoney.eu/news/2013/06/meno-morti-sulle-strade-italiane-i-nuovi-dati-istat-0020382.html

8 Ginsborg. Op. cit.

9 Ian Traynor. 'Crisis for Europe as Trust Hits Record Low'. Guardian. 24 April 2013. http://www.theguardian.com/world/2013/apr/24/trust-eu-falls-record-low

10 Giampaolo Pansa. Poco o niente. Eravamo poveri. Torneremo poveri. Rizzoli. 2011.

Index

Index